October

OCTOBER

THE STORY OF THE RUSSIAN REVOLUTION

CHINA MIÉVILLE

First published by Verso 2017
© China Miéville 2017
Illustrations supplied by Press Association Images, with the exception of
the pictures of Maria Spiridonova, Baku, and the *Aurora*, which came from
Alamy, and the picture of the Red Guard, supplied by the author.

1 3 5 7 9 10 8 6 4 2

Verso

UK: 6 Meard Street, London W1F 0EG
US: 20 Jay Street, Suite 1010, Brooklyn, NY 11201
versobooks.com

Verso is the imprint of New Left Books

ISBN-13: 978-1-78478-277-1
ISBN-13: 978-1-78663-450-4 (EXPORT)
ISBN-13: 978-1-78478-279-5 (US EBK)
ISBN-13: 978-1-78478-280-1 (UK EBK)

British Library Cataloguing in Publication Data
A catalogue record for this book is available from the British Library

Library of Congress Cataloging-in-Publication Data

Names: Miéville, China, author.
Title: October : the story of the Russian Revolution / China Mieville.
Description: London ; Brooklyn, NY : Verso, 2017.
Identifiers: LCCN 2016051217 | ISBN 9781784782771 (hardback)
Subjects: LCSH: Soviet Union – History – Revolution, 1917–1921. | BISAC:
 HISTORY / Europe / Russia & the Former Soviet Union. | HISTORY /
 Revolutionary.
Classification: LCC DK265 .M475 2017 | DDC 947.084/1 – dc23
LC record available at https://lccn.loc.gov/2016051217

Typeset in Fournier by MJ & N Gavan, Truro, Cornwall
Printed and bound by CPI Group (UK) Ltd, Croydon, CR0 4YY

To Gurru

'..................................
..................................'

Nikolai Chernyshevsky,

What Is to Be Done?

Contents

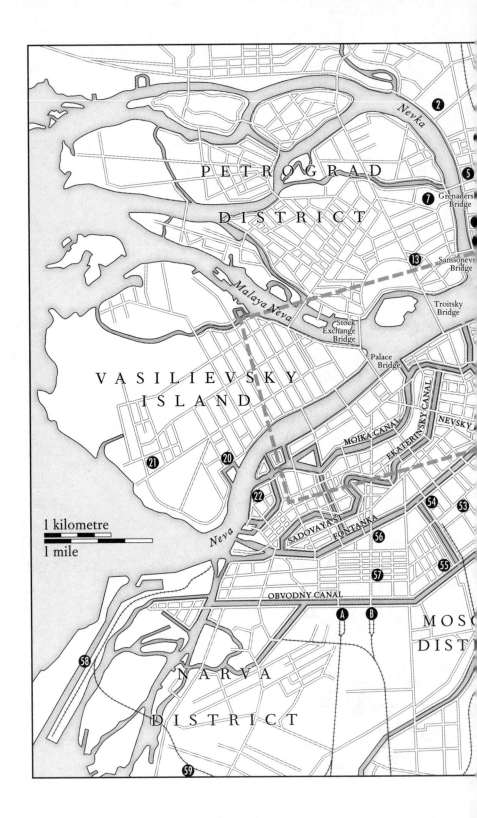

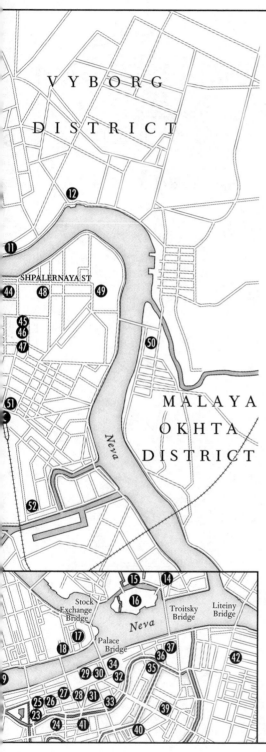

PETROGRAD, 1917

1 Russki Reno factory
2 Novy Lessner factory
3 Moskovsky Regiment
4 Meeting place of Sixth Congress
5 Erikson factory
6 First Machine Gun Regiment
7 Grenadier Regiment
8 Bolshevik HQ, Vyborg district
9 Trud printing press
10 Mikhailovsky Artillery School
11 Crosses Prison
12 Metallist factory
13 Cirque Moderne
14 Kshesinskaya Mansion
15 Kronwerk Arsenal
16 Peter and Paul Fortress
17 Stock exchange
18 Petersburg University
19 *Aurora*
20 Finliandsky Regiment
21 180th Infantry Regiment
22 Franco-Russian shipyard
23 Second Baltic Fleet Detachment
24 Keksgolmsky Regiment
25 Central telegraph office
26 Petrograd telegraph agency
27 Post office
28 War Ministry
29 Admiralty
30 Palace Square
31 St Isaac's Cathedral
32 General Staff headquarters
33 Petrograd telephone station
34 Winter Palace
35 Pravda editorial offices and printing plant
36 Pavlovsky Regiment
37 War Memorial Field
38 Kazan Cathedral
39 City Duma
40 State Bank
41 Mariinsky Palace
42 Priboi publishing house
43 Litovsky Regiment
44 Fourteenth Cossack Regiment
45 Preobrazhensky Regiment
46 Sixth Engineer Battalion
47 Volynsky Regiment
48 Tauride Palace
49 Smolny
50 First Reserve Infantry Regiment
51 Znamensky Square
52 First and Fourth Cossack Regiments
53 Semenovsky Regiment
54 Petrograd electric station
55 Egersky Regiment
56 Petrogradsky Regiment
57 Izmailovsky Guards Regiment
58 Harbour Canal
59 Putilov factory
A Baltic Station
B Warsaw Station
C Nikolaevsky Station
D Finland Station

EUROPEAN RUSSIA, 1917

0   200   400   600 kilometres

0   100   200   300   400 miles

SWEDEN

FINLAND

Gulf of Bothnia

White Sea

Arkhangelsk

ARKHANGELSK

North Dvina

Lake Onega

OLONETS

VOLOGDA

Helsingfors

Lake Ladoga

Gulf of Finland

Revel

ESTLAND

Petrograd

PETROGRAD

NOVGOROD

LIFLAND

KURLAND   Riga

PSKOV

YAROSLAVL

KOSTRAMA

VYATKA

Volga

KOVNO

VITEBSK

TVER

Nizhniy Novgorod

VLADIMIR

NIZHEGOROD

KAZAN

Vilna

VILNA

Smolensk

SMOLENSK

Moscow

MOSCOW

RYAZAN

SIMBIRSK

Minsk

MOGILEV

KALUGA

Tula

PENZA

GRODNO

Brest-Litovsk

MINSK

CHERNIGOV

TULA

TAMBOV

SARATOV

SAMARA

Samara

Orel

OREL

Kursk

KURSK

VOLYNSK

Kiev

POLTAVA

Dnieper

Kharkov

VORONEZH

Don

Saratov

URAL

KIEV

KHARKOV

PODOLSK

ROMANIA

BESSARABIA

Ekaterinoslav

YEKATERINOSLAV

DON

Tsaritsyn

Volga

ASTRAKHAN

KHERSON

Odessa

TAVRIDA

Rostov

Astrakhan

Krasnodar

STAVROPOL

Caspian Sea

Danube

Sebastopol

KUBAN

BULGARIA

Black Sea

TEREK

Constantinople

TIFLIS

Tiflis

OTTOMAN EMPIRE

Trebizond

Introduction

Midway through the First World War, as Europe shuddered and bled, an American publisher released Alexander Kornilov's acclaimed *Modern Russian History*. Kornilov, a liberal Russian intellectual and politician, concluded his narrative in 1890, but for this 1917 English-language edition, his translator, Alexander Kaun, brought the story up to date. Kaun's final paragraph opens with minatory words: 'One need not be a prophet to foretell that the present order of things will have to disappear.'

That order disappeared, spectacularly, as those words appeared. In the course of that violent and incomparable year, Russia was rocked and wracked by not one but two insurrections, two confused, liberatory upheavals, two reconfigurings. The first, in February, dispensed breakneck with a half-millennium of autocratic rule. The second, in October, was vastly more far-reaching, contested, ultimately tragic and ultimately inspiring.

The months from February to October were a continuous jostling process, a torquing of history. What happened and the meaning of what happened remain overwhelmingly controversial. February and, above all, October have long been prisms through which the politics of freedom are viewed.

It has become a ritual of historical writing to disavow any chimerical 'objectivity', a disinterest to which no writer can or should want to cleave. I duly perform that caveat here: though not, I hope, dogmatic or uncritical, I am partisan. In the story that follows, I have my villains and my heroes. But, while I do not pretend to be neutral, I have striven to be fair, and I hope readers of various political hues will find value in this telling.

There are already many works on the Russian Revolution, and a good number of them are excellent. Though carefully researched – no event or spoken word described here is not recorded in the histories – this book does not attempt to be exhaustive, scholarly or specialist. It is, rather, a short introduction for those curious about an astonishing story, eager to be caught up in the revolution's rhythms. Because here it is precisely as a *story* that I have tried to tell it. The year 1917 was an epic, a concatenation of adventures, hopes, betrayals, unlikely coincidences, war and intrigue; of bravery and cowardice and foolishness, farce, derring-do, tragedy; of epochal ambitions and change, of glaring lights, steel, shadows; of tracks and trains.

There is something in the Russia-ness of Russia that often seems to intoxicate. Again and again, discussions of the country's history, particularly those of non-Russians but sometimes those of Russians themselves, veer into romanticised essentialism, evocations of some supposed irreducible, ineffable Russian Spirit, with a black box at its heart. Not only uniquely sad but uniquely inscrutable, evasive of explanation: *mnogostradalnaya*, much-suffering Russia; Little Mother Russia. The Russia where, as Virginia Woolf puts it in her most dreamlike book, *Orlando*, 'the sunsets are longer, the dawns less sudden and sentences are often left unfinished from doubt as how to best end them'.

This cannot stand. That there are Russian specifics to the story is hardly in doubt; that they explain the revolution, let alone explain it away, is. The story must honour those specificities without losing sight of the general: the world-historic causes and ramifications of the upheaval.

The poet Osip Mandelstam, in a poem that goes by various names, a celebrated first-anniversary commemoration of the start of 1917, speaks of 'liberty's dim light'. The word he uses, *sumerki*, usually portends twilight, but it may also refer to the darkness before dawn. Does he honour, his translator Boris Dralyuk wonders, 'liberty's fading light, or its first faint glimmer?'

Perhaps the glow at the horizon is neither of longer sunsets nor less sudden dawns, but is rather a protracted, constitutive ambiguity. Such crepuscularity we have all known, and will all know again. Such strange light is not only Russia's.

This was Russia's revolution, certainly, but it belonged and belongs to others, too. It could be ours. If its sentences are still unfinished, it is up to us to finish them.

A Note on Dates

For the student of the Russian Revolution, time is literally out of joint. Until 1918, Russia used the Julian calendar, running thirteen days behind the modern Gregorian. As the story of actors immersed in their moment, this book follows the Julian, the one they used at the time. In some of the literature one might read that the Winter Palace was stormed on 5 November 1917. But those doing the storming did so on the 26th of their October, and it is their October that is a clarion, more than a mere month. Whatever the Gregorian calendar might claim, this book is written in October's shadow.

1

The Prehistory of 1917

A man stands on a windswept island, staring up at the sky. He is powerfully built and enormously tall, and his fine clothes whip about him in the May squalls. He ignores the chop of the Neva river that surrounds him, the scrub and greenery of a sprawling littoral marshland. His rifle dangling from his hand, he gazes up in awe. Overhead, a great eagle soars.

Transfixed, Peter the Great, all-powerful ruler of Russia, watches the bird for a long time. It watches him back.

At last the man turns abruptly and plunges his bayonet into the wet earth. He forces the blade through the dirt and roots, hacking out first one, then two long strips of turf. He peels them from the ground and drags them, filthying himself, to just below where the eagle hovers. There he lays the strips down cruciform. 'Let there be a city here!' he bellows. Thus in 1703, on Zayachy Island in the Gulf of Finland, in land wrestled from the Swedish Empire in the Great Northern War, the tsar ordains the creation of a great city named for his own patron saint – St Petersburg.

This never happened. Peter was not there.

The story is a tenacious myth of what Dostoevsky called 'the most abstract and premeditated city in the whole world'. But although Peter is not present on that founding day, St Petersburg goes on to be built according to his dream, against odds and sense, in a mosquito-ridden Baltic estuary floodplain, assaulted by fierce winds and punishing winters.

First the tsar directs the building of the Peter and Paul Fortress, a sprawling, star-shaped complex to fill that little island, ready for a Swedish counterattack that never comes. And then around its walls Peter orders a great port raised, in accord with the latest designs. This will be his 'window to Europe'.

He is a visionary, of a brutal kind. He is a moderniser, contemptuous of Russia's churchy 'Slavic backwardness'. The ancient city of Moscow is picturesque, unplanned, a tangle of quasi-Byzantine streets: Peter directs that his new city be plotted by rational design, in straight lines and elegant curves of epic scale, its vistas wide, canals criss-crossing its avenues, its many palaces grand and palladian, its restrained baroque a determined break from traditions and onion domes. On this new ground, Peter intends to construct a new Russia.

He hires foreign architects, dictates that European fashions be worn, insists on building in stone. He populates his city by fiat, ordering merchants and nobles to relocate to the nascent metropolis. In the early years, wolves prowl the unfinished streets at night.

It is forced labour that lays those streets down, that drains the wetlands and raises columns in the quag. Tens of thousands of conscript serfs and convicts, forced under guard to struggle across the vastness of Peter's lands. They come and dig foundations in the muck, and die in vast numbers. One hundred thousand corpses lie beneath the city. St Petersburg will be known as 'the city built on bones'.

In 1712, in a decisive move against a Muscovite past he scorns, Tsar Peter makes St Petersburg Russia's capital. For the next two centuries and more, it is here that politics will move most quickly. Moscow and Riga and Ekaterinburg and all the countless other towns and cities and all the sprawling regions of the empire are vital, their stories cannot be neglected, but St Petersburg will be the crucible of the revolutions. The story of 1917 – born out of a long prehistory – is above all the story of its streets.

★

Russia, a confluence of European and easterly Slavic traditions, is long gestated among debris. According to a key protagonist of 1917, Leon Trotsky, it is thrown up by 'the western barbarians settled in the ruins of Roman culture'. For centuries a succession of kings – tsars – trade and war with nomads of the Eastern steppes, with the Tatars, with Byzantium. In the sixteenth century, Tsar Ivan IV, whom history calls the Terrible, slaughters his way into territories east and north until he becomes 'Tsar of All Russias', head of a colossal and multifarious empire. He consolidates the Muscovite state under ferocious autocracy. That ferocity notwithstanding, rebellions erupt, as they always do. Some, like the Pugachev uprising of Cossack peasants in the eighteenth century, are challenges from below, bloody insurgencies bloodily subdued.

After Ivan come motley others, a dynastic jostling, until nobles and clergy of the Orthodox Church elect Michael I tsar in 1613, founding the Romanov dynasty that will continue to 1917. That century the status of the *muzhik*, the Russian peasant, becomes entrenched in a rigid system of feudal serfdom. Serfs are tied to particular lands, whose owners wield extensive power over 'their' peasants. Serfs can be transferred to other estates, their personal property – and their family – retained by the original landowner.

The institution is bleak and tenacious. Serfdom endures in Russia well into the 1800s, lifetimes after Europe dispenses with it. Stories of grotesque abuse of peasants by landlords abound. 'Modernisers' see serfdom as a scandalous brake on progress: their 'Slavophile' opponents decry it as a Western invention. On the fact that it must go, both groups agree.

At last, in 1861, Alexander II, the 'Tsar Liberator', emancipates the serfs from their obligations to the landlord, their status as property. For all that reformers have long agonised over the serfs' atrocious lot, it is not their softening hearts that drives this. It is anxiety at waves of peasant riots and rebellions, and it is the exigencies of development.

The country's agriculture and its industry are stunted. The Crimean War of 1853–55 against England and France has exposed the old order: Russia stands humiliated. It seems clear that modernisation – liberalisation – is a necessity. And so are born Alexander's 'Great Reforms', an overhaul of the army and schools and justice system, the relaxation of censorship, the granting of powers to local assemblies. Above all, the abolition of serfdom.

The emancipation is carefully limited. The serfs-turned-peasants do not receive all the land they formerly worked, and that which they do is saddled with grotesque 'redemption' debts. The average plot is too small for subsistence – famines recur – and it shrinks in size as the population grows. Peasants remain legally constrained, tied now to the village community – the commune, the *mir* – but poverty drives them to seasonal labour in construction, mining, industry and commerce legal and illegal. Thus they become imbricated with the country's small but growing working class.

It is not only tsars who dream of kingdoms. Like all exhausted peoples, Russian peasants imagine utopias of rest. Belovode of the White Waters; Oponia at the edge of the world; the underground Land of Chud; the Golden Islands; Darya; Ignat; Nutland; the submerged city of Kitezh, immortal below the waters of Lake Svetloyar. Sometimes bemused explorers strike out physically for one or other of these magic territories, but peasants mostly try to reach them in other ways: in the late nineteenth century comes a wave of countryside revolt.

Informed by dissidents, writers like Alexander Herzen, Michael Bakunin, the trenchant Nikolai Chernyshevsky, this is the tradition of the *narodniki*, activists for the *narod*, the people. The narodniks in groups such as Zemlya i Volya, Land and Liberty, are mostly members of a new layer of self-identified, quasi-messianic purveyors of culture, of the Enlightenment – an intelligentsia that includes a growing proportion of commoners.

'The man of the future in Russia', says Alexander Herzen at the start of the 1850s, 'is the peasant.' Development being slow, with no meaningful liberal movement in sight, the narodniks look beyond the cities to rural revolution. In the Russian peasant commune, the *mir*, they see a glimmer, a foundation for an agrarian socialism.

Dreaming their own better places, thousands of young radicals 'go to the people', to learn from, work with, raise the consciousnesses of a suspicious peasantry.

A chastening and bitter joke: they are arrested en masse, often at the request of those very peasants.

The conclusion that one activist, Andrei Zhelyabov, draws? 'History is too slow.' Some among the narodniks turn to more violent methods, so as to hasten it.

In 1878, Vera Zasulich, a radical young student of minor noble background, draws a revolver from her pocket and seriously wounds Fyodor Trepov, chief of the St Petersburg police, a man loathed by intellectuals and activists for ordering the flogging of a discourteous prisoner. In a sensational rebuke to the regime, Zasulich's jury acquits her. She flees to Switzerland.

The next year, from a split in Zemlya i Volya, a new group, Narodnaya Volya – People's Will – is born. It is more militant. Its cells believe in the necessity of revolutionary violence, and they are ready to act on their conviction. In 1881, after several failed attempts, they take their most coveted prize.

The first Sunday in March, Tsar Alexander II travels to St Petersburg's grand riding academy. From the crowd the young Narodnaya Volya activist Nikolai Ryasov hurls a handkerchief-wrapped bomb at the bulletproof carriage. An explosion scorches the air. Amid the screams of wounded onlookers, the vehicle shudders to a halt. Alexander staggers out into the chaos. As he sways, Ryasov's comrade Ignacy Hryniewiecki comes forward. He throws a second bomb. 'It's too early to thank God!' he shouts.

There is another almighty blast. 'Through the snow, debris and blood', one of the tsar's entourage will recall, 'you could see fragments of clothing, epaulets, sabres and bloody chunks of human flesh.' The 'Tsar Liberator' is ripped apart.

For the radicals, this is a pyrrhic victory. The new tsar, Alexander III, more conservative and no less authoritarian than his father, unleashes ferocious repression. He decimates People's Will with a wave of executions. He reorganises the political police, the fierce and notorious Okhrana. In this climate of reaction comes a slew of the murderous organised riots known as pogroms against the Jews, a cruelly oppressed minority in Russia. They face heavy legal restrictions; are allowed residence only in the region known as the Pale of Settlement, in Ukraine, Poland, Russia's west and elsewhere (though exemptions mean there are Jewish populations beyond that stretch); and they have long been the traditional scapegoats at times of national crisis (and indeed whenever). Now, many who are eager to blame them for something blame them for the death of the tsar.

The embattled narodniks plan more attacks. In March 1887, St Petersburg police break up a plot against the new tsar's life. They hang five student ringleaders, including the son of a school inspector in the Volga region, a bright, committed young man called Alexander Ulyanov.

In 1901, seven years after the brutal and bullying Alexander III dies – of natural causes – and his dutiful son Nicholas II takes the throne, several narodnik groups merge, under a non-Marxist agrarian socialist programme (though some of its members consider themselves Marxists) focusing on those particularities of Russia's development, and its peasantry. They anoint themselves the Socialist Revolutionary Party, henceforth better known as the SRs. They still hold with violent resistance: for a while yet, the SRs' military wing, its 'Combat Organisation', does not flinch from a campaign of what even its advocates call 'terrorism', the assassination of government figures.

Given such commitment, there is irony to come. One of the party's leaders, the extraordinary Evno Azef, leader of the Combat Organisation itself for some years, will within a decade be unmasked as a faithful Okhrana agent, in a hammer blow to the organisation. And a few years later, in the pivotal moments of the revolutionary year of 1917 itself, two more, Catherine Breshko-Breshkovskaya and its main theoretician Victor Chernov, will be high-profile and anxious partisans of order.

★

In the final years of the nineteenth century, the state pours resources into its infrastructure and industry, including an immense programme of railway building. Great crews drag iron rails across the country, hammering them down, stitching the limits of the empire together. The Trans-Siberian Railway. 'Since the Great Wall of China the world has seen no one material undertaking of equal magnitude,' breathes Sir Henry Norman, a British observer. For Nicholas, the building of this transit route between Europe and East Asia is a 'sacred duty'.

Russia's urban population soars. Foreign capital flows in. Huge industries arise around St Petersburg, Moscow, the Donbass region in Ukraine. As thousands of new workers struggle to eke out livings in cavernous plants under desperate conditions, subject to the contemptuous paternalism of their bosses, the labour movement takes unsteady steps forward. In 1882, the young Grigory Plekhanov, later to be Russia's leading socialist theorist, joins the legendary Vera Zasulich herself, the failed assassin of Trepov, to found Osvobozhdenie truda, Liberation of Labour – the first Russian Marxist group.

In its wake come more reading circles, cells of agitators, gatherings of the variously like-minded, aghast at a world of ruthless, exploitative capital and the subordination of need to profit. The future for which the Marxists yearn, communism, is as absurd to their detractors as any peasant's Belovode. It is rarely distinctly outlined, but they know it beckons beyond private property and its violence, beyond exploitation and alienation, to a world where technology reduces labour, the better for humanity to flourish. 'The true realm of freedom', in Marx's words: 'the development of human powers as an end in itself'. This is what they want.

The Marxists are a gaggle of émigrés, reprobates, scholars and workers, in a close weave of family, friendship and intellectual connections, political endeavour and polemic. They tangle in a fractious snarl. Everyone knows everyone.

In 1895, a Union of Struggle for the Liberation of the Working Class is formed in Moscow, Kiev, Ekaterinoslav, Ivanovo-Vosnessensk and St Petersburg. In the capital, the founders of the

Union are two fervent young activists: Yuli Tsederbaum and his friend Vladimir Ulyanov, brother of Alexander Ulyanov, the narodnik student executed eight years before. *Noms de politique* are the norm: Tsederbaum, the younger of the two, a scrawny figure peering through pince-nez over a thin beard, calls himself Martov. Vladimir Ulyanov, a striking, prematurely balding man with distinctive narrow eyes, is known as Lenin.

Martov is twenty-two, a Russian Jew born in Constantinople. He is, in the words of one leftist sparring partner, 'a rather charming type of bohemian … by predilection a haunter of cafés, indifferent to comfort, perpetually arguing and a bit of an eccentric'. Weak and bronchial, mercurial, talkative but a hopeless orator, not much better as an organiser, affecting, in these early days, a worker's get-up, Martov is every inch the absent-minded intellectual. But he is a celebrated mind. And while certainly not above the sorts of sectarian machination typical of political hothouses, he is renowned, even among his adversaries, for integrity and sincerity. He is widely respected. Even loved.

As for Lenin, all who meet him are mesmerised. As often as not, it seems, they feel driven to write about him: libraries' worth of such books exist. He is a man easily mythologised, idolised, demonised. To his enemies he is a cold, mass-murdering monster; to his worshippers, a godlike genius; to his comrades and friends, a shy, quick-laughing lover of children and cats. Capable of occasional verbal ogees and lumbering metaphors, he is a plain rather than a sparkling wordsmith. Yet he compels, even transfixes, in print and speech, by his sheer intensity and focus. Throughout his life, opponents and friends will excoriate him for the brutality of his takedowns, his flint and ruthlessness. All agree that his is a prodigious force of will. To an extent unusual even among that ilk who live and die for politics, Lenin's blood and marrow are nothing else.

What particularly distinguishes him is his sense of the political moment, of fracture and traction. To his comrade Lunacharsky, he 'raise[s] opportunism to the level of genius, by which I mean the kind of opportunism which can seize on the precise moment and which always knows how to exploit it for the unvarying objective of the revolution'.

Not that Lenin never makes mistakes. He has, however, an acutely developed sense of when and where to push, how, and how hard.

In 1898, a year after Lenin is banished to Siberia for his activities, the Marxists organise into the Rossiskaya Sotsial-Demokraticheskaya Rabochaya Partiya, the Russian Social-Democratic Workers Party (RSDWP). For several years, despite such periods of exile, Martov and Lenin remain close collaborators and friends. With characters so different, exasperations are inevitable, but they complement and like each other, a pair of Marxist *Wunderkinder*.

From Marx, whatever their divisions over other points, the RSDWP thinkers take a vision of history as necessarily proceeding through historical stages. Such 'stageist' conceptions can differ wildly in terms of detail, degree and rigidity – Marx himself opposed extrapolating his 'historical sketch' of capitalism into a theory of an inevitable path for all societies, as 'both honouring and shaming me too much'. Still, it is uncontroversial among most Marxists at the end of the nineteenth century that socialism, the initial phase beyond capitalism and en route to communism, can only emerge from bourgeois capitalism, with its particular political freedoms and its working class positioned to take control. It follows that autocratic Russia, with its huge rural masses and small working class (substantially made up of semi-peasants), with its private estates and omnipotent tsar, is not yet ripe for socialism. There is, as Plekhanov puts it, not yet enough proletarian yeast in Russia's peasant dough to make a socialist cake.

Serfdom is a living memory. And a few miles beyond the cities, peasants still dwell in medieval squalor. In winter, farm animals share their homes and fight for space by the stove. A stench of sweat, tobacco and lamp fumes. Whatever improvements are slowly coming, many villagers still walk barefoot through muddy, unpaved streets, and latrines are open pits. Agricultural decisions about common land are reached by no more rigorous a system than competing shouts in chaotic village meetings. Transgressors of traditional mores are subjected to what is called 'rough music', cacophonous intervention, public shaming, a sometimes murderous violence.

But there is worse.

According to the ecstatic rant of Marx and Engels in the *Communist Manifesto*, it is the bourgeoisie which 'historically, has played the most revolutionary part … put an end to all feudal, patriarchal, idyllic relations … pitilessly torn asunder the motley feudal ties' – and thus, through the concentration of the working class at the point of productive power, created 'its own grave-diggers'. But in Russia, the bourgeoisie are neither pitiless nor revolutionary. They tear asunder nothing. As the RSDWP manifesto has it: 'The further east one goes in Europe, the more base, weak and cowardly does the bourgeoisie appear, and the more gigantic are the cultural and political tasks that fall to the lot of the proletariat.'

The author of these words, Peter Struve, will soon lurch to the right. In Russia, such so-called 'Legal' Marxists often find in their Marxism a roundabout way to be liberals, their focus shifting from workers' concerns to the necessity of the capitalist 'modernisation' that Russia's cowardly bourgeoisie cannot bring forth. An obverse or complementary left heresy is 'Economism', according to which workers must focus on trade union activity, leaving politics to those struggling liberals. Pilloried by those more orthodox for downplaying socialist struggle, and indeed quite ineffectual in their quietist solutions, such 'Legal' and 'Economist' heretics nonetheless focus on key questions. They have come up against a conundrum of left catechism: how does a movement go about being socialist in an unripe country with a weak and marginal capitalism, a vast and 'backward' peasantry, and a monarchy that has not had the decency to undergo its bourgeois revolution?

★

The tail end of the nineteenth century sees a flurry of imperial machinations, allegiance and counterallegiance underlying a steady hunger for expansion. Internally, the colonial drive means upholding the language and culture of dominant Russian elites at the expense of minorities. Nationalists and the left recruit prolifically from subordinated peoples and nations: Lithuanians, Poles, Finns, Georgians, Armenians, Jews. The socialist movement in the empire is always multi-ethnic, disproportionately comprising those of minority groups and nations.

Ruling over the whole patchwork since 1894 is Nicholas Romanov. As a youth, Nicholas II submitted stoically to his father's bullying. As tsar he is distinguished by courtesy, dedication to duty, and little else. 'His face', one official hesitantly reports, 'is expressionless.' Absence defines him: absence of expression, imagination, intelligence, insight, drive, determination, *élan*. Description after bemused description turns on the 'otherworldliness' of a man adrift in history. He is a well-educated vacuity stuffed with the prejudices of his milieu – including pro-pogromist antisemitism, aimed particularly at revolutionary *zhidy*, 'yids'. Averse to change of any kind at all, he is wholeheartedly wedded to autocracy. Uttering the word 'intelligentsia', he makes the same disgusted face as when he says 'syphilis'.

His wife, Alexandra Fedorovna, a granddaughter of Queen Victoria, is deeply unpopular. In part this is jingoism – she is German, after all, at a time of mounting tensions – but it is also due to her frantic intrigues and patent contempt for the masses. The French ambassador Maurice Paléologue sketches her concisely: 'Moral disquiet, constant sadness, vague longing, alternation between excitement and exhaustion, constant thought given to the invisible and supernatural, credulousness, superstition.'

The Romanovs have four daughters, and a son, Alexis, who is stricken with haemophilia. They are a close, loving family, and, given the tsar and tsarina's obdurate myopia, they are utterly doomed.

★

From 1890 to 1914, the working-class movement grows in size and confidence. The state pursues ham-fisted strategies against it; in the cities, it attempts to contain burgeoning popular discontent with 'police unions', workers' societies organised and overseen by the authorities themselves. But to have any traction at all, these must channel real concerns, and their organisers must be what the Marxist historian Michael Pokrovsky calls 'clumsy imitations of the revolutionary agitators'. The demands they issue are mere echoes of workers' calls – but in echoes, words can still be made out, with unintended consequences.

In 1902, a police-union strike takes over the whole city of Odessa. Similar mass protests spread throughout south Russia the following year, and not all under the aegis of the authorities' puppet bodies. A strike spreads from the Baku oilfields through the Caucasus. Sparks of revolt flare in Kiev, Odessa again, and elsewhere. By now the strikers' demands are political as well as economic.

During this slow acceleration, in 1903, fifty-one of the great and good of Russian Marxism relocate a crucial meeting from a vermin-flecked Brussels flour warehouse to London. There, in backrooms and cafés or overlooked by the fishing trophies of an angling club, over three disputatious weeks, the RSDWP holds its Second Congress.

It is in the twenty-second session of that gathering that a chasm opens between the delegates, a split remarkable not only for its depth, but also for the seeming triviality of its catalyst. The question is whether a party member should be one who 'recognises the party's programme and supports it by material means and by regular personal association *under the direction of* one of the party organisations', or 'by *personal participation in* one of the party organisations'. Martov demands the former. Lenin stakes all on the latter.

Relations between the two have been cooling for some time. Now after an intense, vigorous debate, Martov wins, twenty-eight to twenty-three. But various fits of huff and dudgeon ensue on other issues, and by the time the party leadership is to be decided, walk-outs by the Jewish socialist group the Bund and by the Economist

Marxists mean Martov has lost eight of his original supporters. Lenin manages to push through his choices for the Central Committee. Minority in Russian is *menshinstvo*, majority *bolshinstvo*. From these words the two great wings of Russian Marxism take their names: Martov's Mensheviks and Lenin's Bolsheviks.

At bottom this schism is about far more than membership conditions. Already during the conference Lenin was referring to his supporters as 'hard' and his opponents as 'soft', and the distinction will generally remain glossed in such terms: the Bolsheviks considered hard leftists, the Mensheviks more moderate – though this is not to deny the substantial range and evolution of opinions on each side. What fundamentally underlies the membership dispute – in winding, mediated fashion, and far from clearly, even to Lenin – are divergent approaches to political consciousness, to campaigning, to working-class composition and agency, ultimately to history and to Russian capitalism itself. This will emerge more plainly fourteen years later, when issues of the centrality of the organised working class will come to the fore.

For now, a Martovian counterattack comes quickly: the London decisions are rescinded, and Lenin resigns from the board of the party journal *Iskra* in late 1903. On the ground, however, in so far as they even know about it, many RSDWP activists consider the split absurd. Some simply ignore it. 'I don't know,' one factory worker writes to Lenin, 'is this issue really so important?' Years pass while Mensheviks and Bolsheviks veer towards and away from semi-unity. The bulk of party members consider themselves simply 'Social Democrats', right up to 1917. Even then, Lenin will take some time to convince himself that there is no going back.

Russia eyes the east, pushing into Asia, grasping at Turkestan and Pamir, as far as Korea: continuing work on the Trans-Siberian Railway, with China's collaboration, puts it on a collision course with a similarly expansionist Japan. 'We need', says Prime Minister von Plehve, 'a little victorious war to stem the tide of revolution.'

What better foil in a jingoist epic than a 'lesser race' such as the Japanese, whom Tsar Nicholas calls 'monkeys'?

The 1904 Russo-Japanese War begins.

The regime, in the depths of self-delusion, expects an easy victory. Its forces, however, are incompetently led and inadequately equipped and trained, and they are catastrophically routed at Liaoyang in August 1904, Port Arthur in January 1905, Mukden in February 1905, Tsushima in May 1905. By the autumn of 1904, even the timorous liberal opposition is raising its voice. After the Liaoyang defeat the journal *Osvobozhdenie*, which six months before trumpeted 'Long live the army!', denounces the expansionism behind the war. Through regional self-government assemblies known as *zemstvo*s, liberals organise a 'banquet campaign', large lavish suppers that culminate in pointed toasts to reform. Political activism through passive–aggressive dinner parties. The following year, opposition to the regime's trajectory reaches such a pitch that even Nicholas feels forced to make grudging concessions. But the wave of revolt stretches way beyond the liberals, into the peasantry and the restive working class.

In St Petersburg, one 'police socialist' union, the Assembly of Russian Factory and Workshop Workers, is led by an unusual former prison chaplain named Georgy Gapon. This fierce-faced man is, in the words of Nadezhda Krupskaya, the Bolshevik militant to whom Lenin is married, 'by nature not a revolutionary, but a sly priest … ready to accept any compromises'. Father Gapon nevertheless heads a social ministry, inflected by Tolstoy's quasi-mystical concern for the poor. His theology – devout, ethical, quietist and reformist all at once – is confused but sincere.

In late 1904, four workers at the city's colossal Putilov metallurgy and machine-building plant – which employs more than 12,000 people – get the sack. At sympathy meetings organised by their workmates, an appalled Gapon finds leaflets calling for the tsar's overthrow. He rips them to pieces: that is well beyond his mission. But to the workers' petition calling for the men's reinstatement he adds demands for a wage increase, improved sanitation, an eight-hour day. Radicals to his left add further calls, resonating far beyond sectional interests: for the freedom of assembly and of the press, the separation of church and state, an end to the Russo-Japanese War, a Constituent Assembly.

On 3 January 1905, a city-wide strike is declared. Very soon, between 100,000 and 150,000 people are out.

Sunday 9 January: protestors gather in the freezing pre-dawn darkness. A numerous group from the working-class Vyborg district sets out for the monarch's sumptuous residence, the Winter Palace, whose windows survey the confluence of the two Nevas, the cathedral in the Peter and Paul Fortress, the rostral columns at the tip of Vasilievsky Island, at the heart of the city.

Deep water, frozen solid. From its north bank, the marchers descend onto the Neva ice. Tens of thousands of workers with their families, shivering in threadbare clothes, begin to trudge. They hold icons and crosses. They chant and sing hymns. At their head, Father Gapon in his robes, bearing an entreaty to the tsar. 'Lord', it beseeches, in exquisite combination of the lickspittle and the radical. It begs 'little Father' Nicholas to grant 'truth and protection' from the 'capitalist exploiters'.

Opposition like this could easily be placated. But these authorities are cruel as well as stupid. Thousands of troops are lined up and expectant on the ice.

It is mid-morning as the marchers approach. Cossacks draw their sabres and gallop at them. The crowd scatters in confusion. The tsar's forces face them down. The people do not disperse. The troops raise their guns and begin to fire. The Cossacks flail *nagaikas*, their vicious whips. Gore melts the frost. The desperate people scream and slip and fall.

When the carnage comes to an end, as many as 1,500 people lie dead in the drifts. This is Bloody Sunday.

The impact is incalculable. It unleashes a sea change in popular attitudes. That evening, Gapon, his world view shattered, 'red hot', Krupskaya will recall, 'from the breath of the revolution', fulminates to a crowd of survivors: 'We have no Tsar!'

★

That day accelerates revolution. Information travels the sprawl and spread of the railway lines, racing across its territories in the company of the trains, and it brings fury with it.

Strikes rage across the empire. They are embraced by groups new to such actions – clerks, hotel maids, cab drivers. More confrontations follow, and more deaths – 500 in Lodz, ninety in Warsaw. In May, a mutiny over spoiled meat shakes the battleship *Knaz-Potemkin*. Further revolts come in November, in Kronstadt and Sebastopol.

The regime is frantic. It experiments with combinations of concession and repression. And the revolution provokes not only bloody official crackdowns, but the traditional ultra-right sadism quasi-sanctioned by the state.

Only two years previously, the Bessarabian city of Kishinev suffered the first pogrom of the twentieth century. For thirty-six hours, marauding bands, untroubled by the police and blessed by Orthodox bishops, practised butchery. Jewish adults and children were tortured, raped, mutilated, killed. The tongue of a toddler was cut out. Murderers emptied out the disembowelled bodies of their victims and stuffed them with feathers. Forty-one people died, almost 500 were wounded, and, a journalist observed, most Gentile citizens expressed 'neither regret nor remorse'.

Amid the anguish, many claimed that the Kishinev Jews had not resisted hard enough. This supposed 'shame of passivity' provoked soul-searching among Jewish radicals. So now, in April 1905, when the Ukrainian Jews of Zhitomir get word of an impending attack, the response is defiant: 'We will show that Zhitomir is not Kishinev.' And when, indeed, they fight back against the murderers, limiting damage and death, the Zhitomir defenders inspire the Jewish Bund to declare that 'the times of Kishinev have gone forever'.

Almost instantly, this proves horrifyingly wrong.

Prominent in the Zhitomir attack were the Black Hundreds, an umbrella name for various cells of proto-fascist ultra-reactionaries, which sprang up out of authoritarian outrage at the 1905 revolution. They are apt to sprinkle a few populist calls, such as for land redistribution, atop fervour for an autocratic tsar – Nicholas II is an honorary member – and murderous spite against non-Russians, most particularly Jews. They have street-fighting thugs, and plenty of friends in high places, parliamentary deputies like Alexander Dubrovin and Vladimir Purishkevich. Dubrovin is leader of the Union of the Russian People (URP), an advocate of extreme racist violence, a doctor who gave up medicine to fight the creep of liberalism. Purishkevich is the URP's deputy chair. Flamboyant, fearless and eccentric to the point of derangement, characterised by the author Sholem Aleichem as an 'atrocious villain' and 'high-strutting cockerel', he is a devout believer in God-sanctioned autocracy. Indeed, some Black Hundreds – such as the sect known as the Ioannity – spice their race-hate with ecstatic religiosity, directing the enthusiasms of Orthodoxy against 'Christ-killers', fever dreams of blood-drinking Jews, icons and eschatology and mysticism in the service of depravity.

In October the Black Hundreds commit mass murder in the cosmopolitan city of Odessa, butchering more than 400 Jews. In the Siberian city of Tomsk, they stop up all entrances to a building where a meeting is taking place, set it alight and gleefully burn their scores of victims alive. They throw petrol on the flames. A teenage boy, Naum Gabo, escapes with minutes to spare to witness the depredation. Years later, an elderly man, by then a leading sculptor of his generation, he will write, 'I do not know if I can convey in words the horror that oppressed me and seized my soul.'

This is the Black Hundreds' carnival, but they will continue with the work for years.

And while reaction is on its violent march, the tsar still flounders, groping for compromise. In August 1905 he announces a consultative parliament, a Duma. But its complex franchise favours the rich: the masses remain unappeased. The Treaty of Portsmouth ends the Russo-Japanese War, and is merciful to Russia, given the circumstances. Nevertheless, the state's authority has been crushed abroad and at home, among all classes.

Insurgency has strange triggers. In Moscow, October 1905, a matter of punctuation sparks the final act of the revolutionary year.

Moscow printworkers are remunerated per letter. Now, in the Sytin publishing house, they demand payment for punctuation, too. An arcane orthographic revolt that prompts a wave of sympathy strikes. Bakers and railway workers join in, some bankers as well. Dancers with the Imperial Ballet refuse to perform. Factories and shops close, trams stand still, lawyers refuse cases, jurors to hear them. Rolling stock is motionless on the railways, the iron nerves of the country frozen. A million troops are stranded in Manchuria. The strikers demand pensions and decent pay and free elections, an amnesty for political prisoners, and, again, a representative body: a Constituent Assembly.

On 13 October, at Menshevik instigation, about forty workers' representatives, SRs, Mensheviks and Bolsheviks meet in the St Petersburg Technological Institute. Workers vote them in, one for every 500 workers. They name their gathering with the Russian word for 'council' – the *Soviet*.

In the three months before mass arrests put an end to it, the Petersburg Soviet spreads its influence, draws personnel from a wider pool, begins to assert extensive authority. It sets strike dates, controls telegraphs, considers public petitions, issues appeals. Its leader is the well-known young revolutionary Lev Bronstein, known to history as Leon Trotsky.

Trotsky is hard to love but impossible not to admire. He is at once charismatic and abrasive, brilliant and persuasive and divisive and difficult. He can be compelling and he can be cold, even brutal. Lev Davidovich Bronstein was the fifth of eight children born in a village in modern-day Ukraine to a comfortably off, non-observant Jewish family. A revolutionary by the age of seventeen, a brief narodnik flirtation took him to Marxism, and in and out of prison. The name Trotsky was borrowed from a jailer in Odessa in 1902. Once considered 'Lenin's cudgel', he sided with the Mensheviks at the contentious 1903 congress, though he soon broke with them. During these, his 'non-factional' years, he and Lenin repeatedly exchange ill-tempered polemics on various issues.

The Marxists, almost all of the view that the country is not ready for socialism, are broadly agreed that a Russian Revolution can only be, must be, a democratic and capitalist one – but, crucially, that it could be a catalyst for *socialist* revolution in more developed Europe. For the most part, the Mensheviks are holding out for active bourgeois leadership in Russia, as befits a liberal revolution: until 1905's debacle, therefore, they opposed taking part in any government thrown up by a revolution. The Bolsheviks, by contrast, contend that in the context of pusillanimous liberalism, the working class itself must lead the revolution, in alliance not with those liberals but with the peasantry, taking power, in what Lenin has called a 'revolutionary–democratic dictatorship of the proletariat and the peasantry'.

Trotsky, for his part, already famed as an outstanding and provocative thinker, will soon develop a very distinct take, move in different directions on such questions, formulating theories that will come to define his contested legacy. At present he is deeply engaged in the workings of the Soviet, as participant and witness in this distinct, embattled kind of governance.

In the countryside, the 1905 revolution is chiefly manifest at first in illegal and ad hoc local activities, like felling state- or landlord-owned timber, and strikes among agricultural workers. But in late July, peasant delegates and revolutionaries meet near Moscow and declare themselves the Constitutional Assembly of the All-Russian Peasants' Union. They demand the abolition of private property in land and its reconstitution as 'common property'.

On 17 October, the tsar, still reeling from the upheavals, reluctantly issues his 'October Manifesto', appointing the shrewd conservative Count Witte as premier. In a fillip to Russian liberalism, Nicholas concedes the principles of legislative powers for the Duma and limited suffrage for urban male workers. The same month sees the founding congress of the Constitutional Democratic Party, known as the Kadets.

A liberal party, the Kadets stand for civil rights, universal male suffrage, a degree of autonomy for national minorities, and moderate land and labour reform. The party's roots include a certain strain of radical(ish) liberalism, though that wanes swiftly as the revolution retreats. By the end of 1906, their ambiguous republicanism will have mutated into support for a constitutional monarchy. The Kadets' 100,000 members are mainly middle-class professionals: the party chair, Pavel Milyukov, is a pre-eminent historian. Another new party, about a fifth the size of the Kadets, the Octobrists, forms in supportive response to the tsar's October Manifesto, attracts conservative liberals, and mostly comprises of landowners, cautious businesspeople and the moneyed. They support some moderate reforms, but oppose universal suffrage as a threat to the monarchy and themselves.

Dissent has its momentum: a second, more radical peasant congress meets in early November. In the central provinces of Tambov, Kursk and Voronezh, in the Volga, in Samara and Simbirsk and Saratov, around Kiev and in Chernigov and Podolia, peasant crowds attack, sack, often burn manor houses, and loot their estates. Revolutionary ideas spread like electricity along roads and along those conductive railway tracks. Soviets are formed in Moscow, Saratov, Samara, Kostroma, Odessa, Baku, Krasnoyarsk. In December, the Novorossiysk Soviet deposes the governor, and, briefly, runs the city.

In Moscow on 7 December the general strike becomes an urban insurrection, backed by the SRs and Bolsheviks – in the latter case out of agonised solidarity, rather than any great faith in the likelihood of its success. For days the ring of the outer city is in revolutionary hands. Workers throw up barricades across the streets and Moscow is wracked by guerrilla fighting.

At last news that loyalist Semyonov Guards are coming from St Petersburg buoys the counterrevolutionary volunteers. They bombard the insurgent textile workers in the Presnya district with artillery. In these, the uprising's death throes, 250 radicals are killed. The revolution dies with them.

January 1906, in the chilling words of Victor Serge, is 'a month of firing squads'. A wave of orchestrated pogroms shakes the country. The American Jewish Committee collates evidence of a staggering upswell of racist violence, taking perhaps 4,000 lives.

Resistance does continue, including assassinations. In February 1906, at the railway station in the town of Borisoglebsk, a twenty-year-old Socialist Revolutionary named Maria Spiridonova guns down the local security chief, a man notorious for his savage repression of the peasants. She receives a death sentence, commuted to hard labour in Siberia. At each stop on the journey to the penal colony, Spiridonova emerges to address crowds of sympathisers. Even the liberal press, no fan of the SRs, publishes her letters. She tells of her torture at her captors' hands. Her mistreatment becomes a cause célèbre.

But the state's punitive expeditions spread out from the cities to reassert its authority, and the resilience of the radicals ebbs. By the time the revolt is finally put down, 15,000 have died – the great majority revolutionaries – and 79,000 are in prison or exiled. Pyotr Stolypin, governor of Saratov, earns infamy for his recourse to the gallows. The hangman's noose becomes known as 'Stolypin's necktie'.

'Better', one workers' slogan has it, 'to fall a pile of bones than live like slaves.'

The rubble of the 1905 defeat and the subsequent repression put paid to any naivety about the regime's goodwill, any residual faith in the tsar, and, for radicals, any hope of collaboration with 'census society', as the propertied classes and liberal intelligentsia are known. For most of that layer, the October Manifesto proves sufficient to justify capitulating, and the workers learn that they are alone.

What that knowledge stokes among the most 'conscious', the

small, growing group of worker–intellectuals, autodidacts and activists, is an implacable class pride. A trenchant sense of culture, discipline and consciousness, of outright irreconcilability with the bourgeoisie. From now on from below come escalating calls not only for economic improvements, but also for dignity. One indignant grassroots soldiers' song is clear in these priorities:

> Sure we'd like some tea
> But give us with our tea
> Some polite respect
> And please have officers
> Not slap us in the face.

Soldiers and workers demand to be 'respectfully' addressed, in the courteous second-person plural, *vy*, rather than as *ty*, the singular, which is deployed from a position of authority.

In this fraught and protean political culture, the pride and shame of the oppressed are inextricable. On the one hand, there is the furious scolding one Putilov worker gives his son, when the young man 'allows himself' to be beaten by military officers for speaking positively of the Bolsheviks. 'A worker should not endure a blow from a bourgeois,' he shouts. '"You hit me? – There, take one back."' On the other hand there is the disgust one activist, Shapovalov, feels at his own impulse to cower, to avoid meeting his boss's gaze. 'It was as if two men were living inside of me: one who for the sake of the struggle for a better future for the workers was not afraid of sitting in the [jail of the] Peter and Paul Fortress and in Siberian exile: and another who had not fully liberated himself from the feeling of dependence and even fear.'

In reaction to such 'slavish feelings', he nurses a furious honour. 'I came to hate capitalism and my boss … even more intensely.'

In March 1906, the grudgingly promised Duma meets. By now, though, the tsar's government feels strong enough to clip the parliament's already weak wings. Together, the Kadets, the Social Democrats – as the Marxists are known – and the narodnik Socialist Revolutionaries have a majority: the resulting programme of agrarian reform is anathema to the regime. Which, on 21 July 1906, therefore dissolves the Duma.

Radical attacks on government officials continue, but now the tide is with reaction. Peasants are tried under military law, to allow the death penalty. The tsar replaces the able Witte with the ruthless Stolypin, he of the 'neckties', sower of more bones. In June 1907, Stolypin peremptorily dissolves the follow-up Second Duma, arrests the Social Democratic deputies, restricts the vote, favouring property owners and nobility, and slashes non-Russian representation. It is on this rump franchise that the Third Duma is elected in 1907, and the fourth in 1912.

To modernise agriculture, the regime wants to break up the *mir*, the commune, and create a layer of smallholders. Stolypin gives peasants the right to buy individual plots. Progress is slow: still, by 1914 – three years after the assassination of Stolypin himself – some 40 percent of peasant households will have abandoned the *mir*. Only a few, though, will ever make it as small farmers. The poorest are instead forced to sell their tiny holdings, becoming agricultural labourers or migrating to the cities. Stolypin cracks brutally down on the peasant movement, leading the SRs to refocus somewhat toward work in cities.

These are hardly, though, a fertile arena. Around 1907–08, a new landscape of repression emerges. Strike rates are slashed. Revolutionaries are forced into miserable, defeated exile. By 1910, membership of the RSDWP collapses from 100,000 to a few thousand. Lenin, in Geneva and then Paris, clings to a pitiful optimism, managing to interpret any scrap – an economic dip here, an uptick in radical publications there – as a 'turning point'. But even he grows despondent. 'Our second period of emigration', says Krupskaya, 'was ever so much harder than the first.'

The Bolsheviks are riddled with informers. Their numbers plummet. They are destitute. The émigré insurrectionists have to seek any work to survive. 'One comrade', Krupskaya will recall, 'tried to become a French polisher.' The 'tried' is poignant. Among the left diaspora, despair, mental illness and suicide are not uncommon. In Paris in 1910, Prigara, a starving, deranged veteran of the Moscow barricades, visits Lenin and Krupskaya. His eyes are glassy, his voice loud. He 'begins talking excitedly and incoherently about chariots filled with sheaves of corn and beautiful girls standing in the chariots'. As if he can see one of those peasant Arcadias, as if he can almost touch Nutland, Darya, Opona.

But he is closer to drowned Kitezh. Prigara escapes the protection of his comrades, ties stones to his feet and neck and walks into the Seine.

The twentieth century opens on a great, sluggard, contradictory power. The Russian empire stretches from the Arctic to the Black Sea, from Poland to the Pacific. A population of 126 million Slavs, Turks, Kirghiz, Tatars, Turcomen, countless others, gathered in wildly various polities under the tsar. Cities full of cutting-edge industries imported from Europe punctuate a vastness where four-fifths of the people are peasants tied to the soil, in near-feudal abjection. In the works of visionary artists like Velimir Khlebnikov, the self-styled King of Time, Natalia Goncharova, Vladimir Mayakovsky, Olga Rozanova, a strange modernist beauty illuminates a dominion where the great majority cannot read. Jews, Muslims, animists, Buddhists and freethinkers abound as, in the empire's heart, the Orthodox Church propagates its lugubrious and ornate moralism – against which chafe dissenting sects, minorities, sexual dissidents in the cities' queer hinterlands, radicals.

In his books *1905* and *Results and Prospects*, written shortly after the failed revolution, and throughout his life thereafter, Trotsky develops a particular conception of history as 'a drawing together of the different stages of the journey, a combining of separate steps, an amalgam of archaic with more contemporary forms'. Capitalism is an international system, and in the interrelations of cultures and polities, history does not clean up after itself.

'A backward country assimilates the material and intellectual conquest of the advanced countries,' Trotsky will come to write. 'Though compelled to follow after the advanced countries, a backward country does not take things in the same order.' It is driven to

> the adoption of whatever is ready in advance of any specified date, skipping a whole series of intermediate stages ... [though it] ... not infrequently debases the achievements borrowed from outside in the process of adapting them to its own more primitive culture ... From the universal law of unevenness thus derives another law which ... we may call the law of *combined development*.

This theory of 'uneven and combined development' suggests the possibility of a 'leap', a skipping of those 'stages' – perhaps autocratic order might be sundered without the mediation of bourgeois rule. Reconfiguring a term from Marx and Engels, Trotsky invokes 'Permanent Revolution'. He is not the only leftist to use the term – he draws on an unorthodox Belarussian Marxist, Alexander Helphand ('Parvus') and others are developing similar concepts – but he will become the most celebrated one so to do, and he develops it in particular important ways.

In a 'backward' country like Russia, Trotsky says, where the bourgeoisie is weak, it will not execute a bourgeois revolution, which leaves the working class to do the job. But how can that working class self-stall its demands? Its triumph will be driven by its interests, eroding capitalist property and going beyond 'bourgeois' gains. By now, he is not the only Marxist to hold that if the working class is at the helm of this 'permanent' revolution it must continue beyond capitalism, but far from seeing that as a potential or likely disaster like many others, he is the most enthusiastic about the prospect. Still, for Trotsky as for most of the Russian Marxists, the international dimension is key. 'Without the direct state support of the European proletariat', he writes immediately after 1905, 'the working class of Russia cannot remain in power and convert its temporary domination into a lasting socialistic dictatorship.'

In these bleak post-1905 days, some Mensheviks have shifted on the possible necessity of the party entering government, 'against its will' and without optimism about its prospects, if no appropriate historical agent arises. They continue to hold that the working class should ally with the liberal bourgeoisie they still see as key, and hunt for suitable bourgeois radicals who, even if 'subjectively' anti-revolutionary, Martynov says, contribute 'objectively, without wishing to do so', to the revolution. To their left, the Bolsheviks advocate instead a 'democratic dictatorship of workers and peasants'. Both sides see that 'progressive' bourgeois–democratic revolution as desirable, an aspiration at the limits of the possible and sustainable. To most, Trotsky's 'permanent revolution' is a scandalous eccentricity.

It is May 1912 in Irkutsk, Siberia. The workers in a vast, British-funded goldfield, housed in serf-like conditions in unsanitary barracks, have gone out on strike. They want increased pay, the dismissal of hated supervisors and – again that copula of economic and political demands – the eight-hour day. Troops are deployed. The company gives orders. The troops open fire. The death toll is 270 strikers, in what becomes known as the Lena Massacre.

Huge and angry sympathy strikes shake Moscow and St Petersburg. Industrial action picks up again. In 1914, there is a general strike in the capital, one serious enough to raise concerns about mobilisation for the war that everyone knows is coming, spawned by the predatory tussles of the great powers.

Some in the regime understand that it cannot sustain a conflict, or survive the inevitable fallout. In February 1914, in a prescient memo, the conservative statesman Pyotr Durnovo warns the tsar that if the war goes badly, there will be revolution. He is ignored. Pro- and anti-German factions vie within the elites, but Russia's easterly interests, its alliance with and economic ties to France, necessarily range it against Germany. With some reluctance, after an exchange of urgent, polite telegrams between 'Nicky' and 'Willy' – Nicholas II and Germany's Wilhelm II – wherein they discourage each other's military momentum, shortly after European hostilities start, on 15 July 1914, Nicholas takes Russia into the war.

What comes then is the usual wave of patriotism and pieties, rallying the credulous, the desperate and the politically bankrupt. 'Everyone', reports the poet Zinaida Gippius, 'has gone out of their minds.' Demonstrators attack German shops. In St Petersburg, a crowd clamber onto the roof of the German embassy and throw down its pair of enormous equine sculptures. They land twisted and wrenched, with macabre bronze injuries. Russians cursed with German names rush to alter them. In August 1914, the name of St Petersburg itself is changed to the more Slavonic Petrograd: in semiotic rebellion against this idiocy, the local Bolsheviks continue to style themselves the 'Petersburg Committee'.

To the north-east of the city centre, in Petrograd's great domed Tauride Palace, on 26 July 1914, the Duma deputies vote in favour of war credits, the state's borrowing to fund the carnage. Liberals now pledge themselves again to the sclerotic regime the modernisation of which is their notional *raison d'être*. 'We demand nothing', simpers Milyukov, 'and impose no conditions.'

It is not only the right who line up for war. The peasant–populist Trudoviks, a moderate left party associated with the SRs, enjoin peasants and workers, in the words of their mouthpiece, a flamboyant lawyer named Alexander Kerensky, to 'defend our country and then set it free'. The celebrated anarchist Prince Kropotkin himself supports the fighting. The SRs are split: though many activists, including Chernov, oppose the slaughter, a large number of the party's leading intelligentsia support the country's war effort – including the near-legendary SR figurehead Babushka, the 'Grandmother of the Revolution', Catherine Breskho-Breshkovskaya. Nor is the Marxist left immune. Grotesquely, the venerable Plekhanov tells Angelica Balabanoff of the

Italian Socialist Party: 'If I were not old and sick I would join the army. To bayonet your German comrades would give me great pleasure.'

All across Europe, Marxist parties in the organisation of socialist and labour groupings known as the Second Socialist International break with previous pledges and rally to their governments' war efforts. The moves shock and devastate the few stalwart internationalists. On hearing of the pro-war vote of the powerful German Social Democratic Party, Lenin clings desperately, for the short while that he can, to the belief that such reports are a forgery. The great Polish-German revolutionary Rosa Luxemburg considers suicide.

Within the Duma, only the Bolsheviks and Mensheviks walk out against the war. For this show of principle, many deputies will find themselves exiled to Siberia. When Plekhanov visits Lausanne to argue for the military defence of Russia, a pale, raging, familiar figure comes to confront him. Lenin will not call him comrade, will not shake his hand. Lenin damns his old collaborator with remorseless cold invective.

Russia mobilises more quickly than the Germans expect, invading East Prussia in August 1914, aiding France's early battles. But the country's armed forces, albeit somewhat modernised since 1904, are still in a parlous state. And the Russian high command is totally unprepared for modern war. Its commitment to nineteenth-century methods in an era of rapid-firing war machines leads to appalling carnage. As supply problems, incompetent leadership, corporal punishment and the infernal nature of the fighting take their toll, the war effort is undermined by waves of surrenders, disobedience and desertions.

The German offensive comes in the spring of 1915. Under the barrage Russia loses significant amounts of territory, almost a million soldiers are captured, and more than 1,400,000 killed. The scale of the cataclysm is giddying. Ultimately the war will cost Russia between 2 and 3 million lives – perhaps more.

In September, the tiny Swiss village of Zimmerwald hosts a conference of European anti-war socialists. A pitiful thirty-eight delegates, including Bolsheviks and internationalist Mensheviks and SRs.

Even as they meet, right-wing Mensheviks and SRs in Paris collaborate on the first issue of the pro-war *Prizyv*. 'A revolution is brewing in Russia', the hard-right SR Ilya Fondaminsky writes in its pages, but it 'will be national rather than international, democratic rather than social, and pro-war rather than pacifist'. Right SR intellectuals gravitate away from a narodnik vision of revolution for agrarian socialism, between liberalism and collectivism, towards a jingoistic version of the bourgeois revolution foreseen by their right-Menshevik collaborators.

United in their opposition to such 'social patriotism' of their erstwhile (and in some cases current) comrades, in Zimmerwald the delegates are divided on how sharply to break with them. Eight delegates, including Lenin and his close collaborator and aide-de-camp, the energetic, choleric Grigory Zinoviev, want to leave the corrupted Second International. The Zimmerwald majority, including Mensheviks, will not acquiesce.

Most delegates oppose Lenin's calls for the revolutionary mobilisation of the proletariat against the war as an attempt to split the International – which it is. Moreover, some present consider that given popular patriotism, Lenin's call will endanger anyone who makes it. Instead, the meeting reaches a compromise, and produces a statement of general anti-war sentiments. This, for the sake of unity, Lenin and his supporters sign up to, without enthusiasm or satisfaction.

In a short book of 1916, *Imperialism: The Highest Stage of Capitalism*, Lenin describes the epoch as one of monopoly capitalism entangled with the state, of capital's parasitism on its colonies. Seeing war as systemic, he opposes any concession to anti-war moderation. Lenin is against moralist pacifism, let alone 'defencism', according to which while expansionism is opposed, the 'defence' of a home state is deemed legitimate. Instead, famously, he argues for 'revolutionary defeatism' – a socialist advocacy of the defeat of one's 'own' side in an imperialist war.

Even the radical Trotsky is alienated by the formulation. He cannot, he says, 'agree with your opinion … that Russia's defeat would be a "lesser evil"'. He considers this a 'connivance' with patriotism, supporting the 'enemy'.

One reason his call provokes such consternation is that Lenin is often not clear about whether it is for the defeat of one's state at the hands of *another power*, or, along with *all* imperialist powers, at the hands of the workers. Although the second possibility – international insurrection – is clearly his preference, as well as the telos of his argument, at times he seems to insinuate that the first would suffice. There is an element of performance in the ambiguity. By hammering home this 'defeatism', his intention is to bolster the growing sense that the Bolsheviks, more than any other current, oppose the war utterly and without remission.

The war mobilisation drains Russia's land and industry of workers. Ammunition, equipment, food run short. Inflation soars, with a brutal impact on workers and the urban middle class. The public mood begins to turn. As soon as the summer of 1915, strikes and food riots shake Kostroma, Ivanovo-Vosnessensk, Moscow. The liberal opposition organises into a *soi-disant* 'Progressive Bloc', calling for rights for minorities, an amnesty for political prisoners, certain trade union rights, and so forth. The bloc is furious at incompetence from above, and absolutely opposed to power from below.

The strike wave ebbs, flows and continues, and with it extremes of social desperation. Amid the chaos of the flights of internal refugees, of invaded towns and captured and killed soldiers, thousands of *besprizorniki* – abandoned, lost or orphaned children – make their way to the cities and gang together in makeshift new families, living in the cracks, by theft, begging, prostitution, whatever they can. Their numbers will explode in later years. An underground of profiteering stirs, of despair, decadence, drunkenness, bohemian 'cocainomania'. Febrile symptoms of collapse. Moscow is in thrall to a new tango craze, and it undergoes dark mutations: mimes of murder, jaunty references to carnage. One professional dance duo are notorious for their 'Tango of Death', performed in traditional evening wear, the man's face and head painted to become a skull.

A decade before the war, as the tsar and tsarina sought help for their desperately unwell son, they had made the acquaintance of an unkempt, ill-educated, egocentric Siberian ragamuffin, a self-styled holy man who seemed able, by whatever combination of charm, folk knowledge and luck, to alleviate young Alexis's suffering. Thus Rasputin, the so-called mad monk who is neither mad nor a monk, established himself at the heart of the court – where he remains.

He is a man of rude but substantial charisma. Possibly a member of the Khlysty, one of Russia's many outlawed sects, he certainly emanates a vatic intensity reminiscent of its practices. He represents himself both as the voice of old, simple, royalist Russia, and as a seer, a prophet, a healer. Nicholas tolerates him; Alexandra adores him.

Rumours swirl about Rasputin's excesses. He is certainly a drunkard and braggart, and whether or not the many stories of his sexual conquests are true, he enjoys astonishing licence among the nobility, treating his wealthy patrons, especially women, with eroticised discourtesy. He relishes power, and during the war, his power grows. With Alexandra's support, Rasputin influences governmental patronage according to his whims.

In court circles, even those previously tolerant grow resentful of this upstart *muzhik*. Hawkers of smut do brisk business in pornographic caricatures of the extravagantly bearded ersatz *starets* (holy man), up to no good with the tsarina. The tsar brooks no criticism of 'our friend', as the tsarina calls Rasputin. She relays his advice to her husband, encouraging him to make military decisions based on Rasputin's 'visions'. She gives him Rasputin's comb to brush through his hair before meeting ministers, so that Rasputin's wisdom may guide him. He obeys. She sends him crumbs from Rasputin's bread. He eats them.

Nicholas is already taxing the patience of modernisers by turning his back on the liberals' milquetoast reform programme. Now, in August 1915, he insists on taking overall command of the army. Though the real decisions are made by the capable General Michael Alexeev, the tsar's absence leaves considerable power in the hands of the loathed tsarina – which also means those of Rasputin.

With Nicholas's complicity, Alexandra begins what the ultra-right-wing deputy Vladimir Purishkevich calls 'ministerial leapfrog'. The Romanovian method becomes one of appointing adventurer after incompetent after nonentity to grand offices of state. The liberals and the sharper-witted right grow ever more apoplectic.

As hatred for Rasputin grows in high society, respect for Nicholas plummets.

It is in this context that Milyukov makes a historic Duma intervention in the Tauride Palace. Breaching all rules of etiquette and discretion, he denigrates, by name, both the tsarina and Boris Stürmer, her latest appointee as prime minister, in a litany of governmental failure. Milyukov punctuates his speech with the repeated question: 'Is this stupidity or is it treason?'

His words reverberate throughout Russia. He has said nothing that is not known, but he has *said* it.

It is news to no one by now that 'the present order of things will have to disappear'. In January 1917, General Alexander Krymov, on leave from the front, meets with Duma deputies in the home of the colourful conservative politician Michael Rodzianko – an Octobrist, a committed monarchist but the implacable enemy of Rasputin – to discuss their discontent. The army, he tells them, would accept, even welcome, a regime change, the replacement of the tsar.

Nicholas receives word after desperate word that he must alter course to survive. The British ambassador transgresses protocol to warn him he is on the brink of 'revolution and disaster'.

Nothing seems to stir behind those placid tsarry eyes.

★

By December 1916, a month before the dawn of the revolutionary year, various disgusted aristocratic conspiracies for national renewal are underway: on the 16th, one of them reaches fruition. With collaborators from the highest tiers of the court, including that redoubtable racist Purishkevich, one Prince Felix Yusupov entices Rasputin to visit his palace by the river, ostensibly to meet his wife. While 'Yankee Doodle' plays repeatedly on a gramophone, Rasputin lounges in his smartest clothes in a dim, arched room, eating the cyanide-laced chocolates and drinking the poisoned Madeira his host has provided.

The toxins have no discernible effect. The conspirators consult in frantic whispers. Yusupov is panicking. He comes back in to join his guest, and, as if seeking the most preposterous imaginable circumstance for murder, he invites Rasputin to examine an antique Italian crucifix, crafted in rock crystal and silver, that he has propped up on a commode. As Rasputin bends reverentially to look, crossing himself, Yusupov draws a pistol and shoots.

A legendarily protracted death scene plays out. Rasputin lurches upright, reaching out to grab at the terrified assassin. Yusupov scrambles away, yelling for his accomplice Purishkevich. When the two men return Rasputin has vanished. Mindless with agitation, they rush outside, and find him lurching through the thick snow in the Petersburg night, croaking Yusupov's name.

'I will tell the Empress!' Rasputin gasps, staggering towards the street. Purishkevich seizes Yusupov's weapon and fires several times. The towering figure sways and falls. Purishkevich runs through the snowdrifts to the prone and twitching man and kicks him in the head. Now Yusupov joins in, beating madly at the body with a truncheon, the snow muffling the thuds. Yusupov screams his own name, in echo of his victim's dying fury.

Hearts hammering, they wrap Rasputin's body in chains and drive him through the darkness to the Malaya Moika canal. They shuffle with their burden to the edge, and let the black water take him down.

But they miss one of his boots, and leave it on the bridge, where the police will find it. When, three days later, the authorities pull

Rasputin's contorted body out of the water, word spreads that the underside of the newly formed ice is scratched where, with the frenzied strength of the godly, Rasputin struggled to emerge.

People flock to the spot where the so-called mad monk died. They bottle the water, as if it were an elixir.

The tsarina is overcome with pious grief. The right are delighted, hoping Alexandra will now repair to an asylum, and that Nicholas will magically gain a resolve he has never had. But Rasputin, colourful as he was, was only ever a morbid symptom. His murder is not a palace coup. It is not a coup at all.

What will end the Russian regime is not the gruesome death of that pantomime figure too outlandish to be invented; nor is it the epochal tetchiness of Russian liberals; nor the outrage of monarchists at an inadequate monarch.

What will end it comes up from below.

2

February: Joyful Tears

The pitch-black early hours in the third year of war: a viciously cold winter. In Petrograd, as in countless Russian cities, people gathered in the streets before dawn, trying to keep warm, desperate for bread there was no certainty they would receive. Rationing was in place, but fuel shortages meant bakers could not meet demand even if they had the ingredients. The hungry waited for hours, forming lines that became inching, shuffling, mumbling mass meetings, crucibles for dissent. Very often their wait was in vain: crowds of the furious and famished then roamed the streets, hurling stones through shop windows, hammering on doors, looking for food.

People talked politics in Yiddish, Polish, Latvian, Finnish, German (still), and in many other languages as well as in Russian: this was a cosmopolitan city. Around its wealthy heart it was a city of workers, swollen by the war to around 400,000, an unusual proportion of them relatively educated. And it was a city of soldiers, of whom 160,000 were stationed there in reserve, their morale poor and getting worse.

In January, the tsar's government had ordered General Sergei Khabalov, the commander of the military district, to suppress any disorder in Petrograd. He had readied 12,000 troops, police and Cossacks for this purpose. He had machine guns stationed at strategic locations, in case of riots. The agents of the Okhrana ramped up their spying, including within a demoralised left, many of its leaders in exile.

Repression notwithstanding, on 9 January, the twelfth anniversary of Bloody Sunday, 150,000 Petrograd workers came out and marched in what was, for many, the first strike since the revolt they commemorated. In a portent to which they did not pay adequate attention, police reported that watching soldiers cheered the workers' red banners. After that day, Petrograd's working class struck and struck again.

Every moment of political confrontation throws up its myths and kitsch. But it is not sentimentality to insist that the workers' culture that had grown since 1905 was becoming stronger. Patchily, unevenly, these were strikes inflected by economic rage, by opposition to the war, and also, for an activist minority, by that striving for class honour.

Though most pronounced there, strikes were not restricted to the capital. More than 30,000 workers downed tools in Moscow, a less radical city than Petrograd, more dominated by the liberal middle classes, its working class more dispersed. The strikes continued, sporadic, into February, putting activists in constant danger of arrest. In Petrograd on 26 January, eleven labour representatives on the official Central War Industries Committee – created by industrialists in response to the government's utter lack of coordination – were jailed for 'revolutionary activity'.

Krupskaya and Lenin mouldered in their Swiss exile. In a speech to a young audience in the Zurich People's House, Lenin remained bullish that revolution in Russia could be a detonator, 'the prologue to the coming European revolution'; that despite its 'present gravelike stillness', the continent was 'pregnant with revolution'. 'We of the older generation', he added melancholically, 'may not live to see the decisive battles of this coming' – European, socialist – 'revolution'.

By 14 February, more than 100,000 workers from sixty factories were still on strike in Petrograd. In the eighteenth-century splendour of the Tauride Palace, the 'consultative' Fourth Duma opened, and immediately attacked the tsar's government over the food shortages. Hundreds of students, fired up with radical ideas, defied the police to march down Nevsky Prospect, the spectacular and fashionable shopping street cutting through the city's heart. The young demonstrators yelled revolutionary songs into the cold air.

Four days later, workers in the Putilov metalworks began a sitdown strike, demanding a 50 per cent raise in their paltry wages. After three days they were sacked. But the punishment did not deter their companions: instead, protest spread through the great plant.

On the 22nd the tsar left the capital for Mogilev, a drab town 200 miles to the east that housed the Stavka, the supreme headquarters of the armed forces. That was the day the Putilov bosses decided to show their strength: they declared a lockout. Closing the factory doors, they put 30,000 militant workers onto the streets – on what happened to be the eve of a recent innovation of the left, International Women's Day.

Celebrations and events across the empire marked 23 February, demanding rights for women and applauding their contributions. In the factories of Petrograd, radicals gave speeches on the situation of women, the iniquity of the war, the impossible cost of living. But even they did not expect what happened next.

As the meetings ended, women began to pour from the factories onto the streets, shouting for bread. They marched through the city's most militant districts – Vyborg, Liteiny, Rozhdestvenskii – hollering to people gathered in the courtyards of the blocks, filling the wide streets in huge and growing numbers, rushing to the factories and calling on the men to join them. An Okhrana spy reported:

At about 1 p.m., the working men of the Vyborg district, walking out in crowds into the streets and shouting 'Give us bread!', started ... to become disorderly ... taking with them on the way their comrades who were at work, and stopping tramcars ... The strikers, who were resolutely chased by police and troops ... were dispersed in one place but quickly gathered in others.

All in all, the police muttered, they were 'exceptionally stubborn'.

'Are we going to put up with this in silence much longer, now and then venting our smouldering rage on small shop owners?' demanded a leaflet issued by one tiny revolutionary group, the Interborough Committee, the Mezhraiontsy. 'After all, they're not to blame for the people's suffering, they are being ruined themselves. The government is to blame!'

Abruptly, without anyone having planned it, almost 90,000 women and men were roaring on the streets of Petrograd. And now they were not shouting only for bread, but for an end to the war. An end to the reviled monarchy.

The night did not bring calm. The next day came a wave of dissent. Close to half the city's workforce poured onto the streets. They marched under red banners, chanting the new slogan: 'To Nevsky!'

The geography of Peter's capital was carefully plotted. The south of Vasilievsky island, the Neva's left bank, as far as its branch, the Fontanka, were sumptuous; this was the quarter of the Mariinsky theatre, the spectacular Kazan and Isaac Cathedrals, the palaces of the nobility and the substantial apartment blocks of professionals, Nevsky Prospect itself. Ringing them were districts more recently thrown up by migration: remoter parts of Vasilievsky, Vyborg and Okhta on the Neva's right bank; on its left, the Alexander Nevsky, Moscow and Narva neighbourhoods. Here the workers, many fresh from the countryside's black earth, lived in their own blocks, in tottering brick barracks, in squalid wooden hovels between the blaring factories.

Such segregation meant that, to make their protests heard, the urban poor had to invade the city centre. They had done so in 1905. Now they tried again.

The Petrograd police blocked the bridges. But the gods of weather showed solidarity in the form of this brutal winter. The streets were lined with thick snowpiles, and the great Neva itself remained frozen. The demonstrators descended in their thousands from the embankments onto the ice. They walked across the face of the waters.

In a telegram home, the British ambassador George Buchanan offhandedly dismissed the disorder as 'nothing serious'. Almost no one had, as yet, any sense of what had begun.

Climbing up from the river on the smarter side of town, the demonstrators pushed on through palatial streets towards the heartland. The police watched nervously. The mood grew brittle.

Jeering, hesitant at first, in ones and twos then growing in confidence and numbers, some in the crowd began to hurl sticks and stones and jags of the ice over which they had come at the detested policemen, 'Pharaohs' in the city's slang.

Towards the army's rank and file, in contrast, the demonstrators were conciliatory. They gathered in great crowds by barracks and army hospitals. There they struck up conversations with curious and friendly soldiers.

The bulk of Petrograd's soldiers were conscripts, recruits in training, or bored, bitter, ill-disciplined, demoralised reservists. Among them, too, were injured and sick personnel evacuated from the front.

A. F. Ilyin-Genevsky was already a convinced Bolshevik when he was gassed and shell shock shattered his memory for a time. From his hospital bed he saw the political awakening of the wounded, 'the rapid revolutionising of the army' under such desperate tutelage. 'After all the bloody horrors of war, people who found themselves in the peaceful quiet of the hospitals involuntarily began to think over the cause of all this bloodshed and sacrifice.' And he saw such reflections devolve into 'hate and rage'. No wonder the war-wounded in particular were notorious for their hostility to military life.

And what of the 12,000 'reliable' troops, on whom the city's rulers pinned their hopes?

What of the implacable Cossacks? Slavic-speakers from, particularly, the Don region of Ukraine and Russia itself, Cossack communities had not known serfdom, and boasted a long if rough tradition of militaristic, self-governing democracy. By the nineteenth century they had become projected as a myth: they were depicted as and often believed themselves uniquely proud, honoured and honourable, a quasi-ethnic, quasi-estate-based cavalry, a people-class. Living symbols of Russia, and traditional agents of tsarist repression: their whips and sabres had spattered a lot of blood on the snow, twelve years before.

But Cossacks were never a monolithic group. They, too, were differentiated by class. And many of them had grown sick of the war, and of how they were being used.

On Nevsky Prospect, a crowd of strikers came to a stand-off with mounted Cossacks, their lances glinting in the sun. A fearful hesitation. For a long moment something was poised in the icy air. Abruptly the officers wheeled and rode away, leaving the demonstrators cheering in astonished delight.

On Znamenskaya Square, other strikers hailed other Cossack cavalrymen, and this time the riders smiled back at the demonstrators they ostentatiously did not disperse. When the crowd clapped them, the police agitatedly reported, the Cossacks bowed in their saddles.

Over the hours, in the Tauride Palace, representatives to the national Duma continued to speechify against the regime. What they demanded was relevance: that the tsar must establish a ministry responsible to the Duma itself. For the left, Alexander Kerensky, the well-known Trudovik with a substantial reputation thanks to his writings on the Lena Goldfields massacre, held forth against the government in such swingeing and grandiloquent terms that the tsarina, hearing of it, wrote furiously to her husband, wishing Kerensky hanged.

Evening came and the air grew even colder. The heaving streets rang with revolutionary songs. Seeing workers from the Promet factory marching behind a woman, a Cossack officer jeered that they were following a *baba*, a hag. Arishina Kruglova, the Bolshevik in question, yelled back that she was an independent woman worker, a wife and sister of soldiers at the front. At her riposte, the troops who faced her lowered their guns.

Two thousand five hundred Vyborg mill-workers took a narrow

44

route down Sampsonievsky Prospect, stopping short, horrified, when they met a Cossack formation. The officers grimaced, grabbed their reins and spurred their horses, and with weapons aloft they shouted for their men to follow. This time, to the crowd's rising terror, the Cossacks began to obey.

But they followed the command with absolute precision. Like dressage riders, their mounts high-stepping elegantly through the slush, they advanced in slow, neat single file. The troops winked at the dumbfounded crowd as they came, dispersing no one at all.

There is an old Scottish term for a particular technique of industrial resistance, a go-slow or a sabotage by surplus obedience, making the letter of the rules undermine their spirit: the ca'canny. That chill evening, the Cossacks did not disobey orders – they conducted a ca'canny cavalry charge.

Their furious officers ordered them to block the street. Once more the men respectfully complied. With their legendary equestrian skills, they lined up their horses into a living blockade breathing out mist. Again, in their very obedience was dissent. Ordered to be still, still they remained. They did not move as the boldest marchers crept closer. The Cossacks did not move as the strikers approached, their eyes widening as at last they understood the unspoken invitation in the preternatural immobility of mounts and men, as they ducked below the bellies of the motionless horses to continue their march.

Rarely have skills imparted by reaction been so exquisitely deployed against it.

Next day, the 25th, 240,000 people were out on strike, demanding bread, an end to the war, the abdication of the tsar. Tramcars did not run, newspapers did not publish. Shops stayed closed: there was no shortage of sympathetic business owners exhausted with the incompetence of the regime. Now, smarter clothes were visible in the crowds, among workers' smocks.

The mood on both sides was growing hard. The Alexander III monument is a massive and ugly bronze, a thickset horse with head bowed as if in shame at the despot it carries. That day, from its shadow, mounted police opened fire on the approaching crowd. But this time, stunning the protestors as much as their adversaries, watching Cossacks fired too – back at the police.

In Znamenskaya Square, the police lashed viciously at the strikers. Demonstrators scrambled away from their whistling knouts. They staggered, they ran to where Cossack troops waited on their motionless horses nearby, watching in uneasy neutrality. The crowds begged for help.

A hesitation. The Cossacks rode in.

There was a moment of wavering confrontation. Then a gasp and a spurt of blood and the crowd were shouting in delight, tossing a cavalryman on their shoulders. He had drawn his sabre, and he had put a police lieutenant to death.

Others died that day, too. In Gostiny Dvor, troops shot and killed three demonstrators, and wounded ten. Crowds launched themselves at police stations across the city, unleashing a hail of stones, smashing their way in and arming themselves with whatever weapons they could find. More and more police officers began to flee the rising onslaught, stripping off their uniforms to escape.

There was unease, an uncoiling in governmental corridors: an understanding, at last, that something serious was underway.

The regime's first reflexes were always repressive. As evening came down in swirls of snow, the tsar sent orders down the wires to General Khabalov. 'I command you to suppress from tomorrow all disorders on the streets of the capital, which are impermissible at a time when the fatherland is carrying on a difficult war with Germany.' As if he might have considered them permissible at any other time. That day, when troops had opened fire it had been in panic, anger, revenge or unsanctioned brutality: henceforth, if crowds would not disperse, such attacks would be policy. And the war itself, that glorious national war, was brandished as a further threat: those not back at work within three days, Khabalov announced to the city, would be sent to join the carnage of the front.

That night, police snatch squads went hunting. They arrested around 100 suspected ringleaders, including five members of the Bolsheviks' Petersburg Committee. But the revolutionaries had not started the insurrection. Even now, they struggled to keep pace with it. Their arrest would certainly not stop it.

'The city is calm.' On Sunday 26 February, the tsarina cabled her husband with strained optimism. But as the day's light came up over the wide stretch of the river, glinting on the ice between the embankments, the workers were already crossing it again, returning. This time, however, they arrived in streets thick with police.

This time, when demonstrators implored the soldiers not to shoot, their appeals would not always be heard.

It was a bloody day. The coughing of machine guns and rifles' reports echoed over the skyline, mingled with the screams of stampeding crowds. People scattered and scurried, past the cathedrals and the palaces, away from the onslaughts. That Sunday, repeatedly, troops obeyed their officers' orders to fire – though, too, the attacks were undermined by weapon 'malfunctions', hesitations, deliberate misaimings. And for every such incident of stealth solidarity, rumours sprang up of scores more.

Not everything went the regime's way. Early afternoon, workers flocked to the barracks of the Pavlovsky regiment. Desperately they begged for help, shouting to the men within that their regiment's training squad was shooting at demonstrators. The soldiers did not come out in response, not immediately. Respect for orders made them hesitate. But they withdrew into a long mass meeting. Men shouting over each other, over the noises of shots and confrontations in the city, flustered and horrified speakers debating what they should do. At six o'clock, the Pavlovsky's fourth company headed at last for the Nevsky Prospect, intent on recalling their comrades in disgrace. They were met by a detachment of mounted police, but their blood was up and they were ashamed of their earlier hesitation.

They did not back down but fired. A man was killed. On returning to their base, the soldiers' ringleaders were arrested and taken across the water, behind the long low walls of the fortress, to the notorious prison of Peter and Paul below the thornlike spire.

Forty people died that Sunday. The slaughter devastated the demonstrators' morale. Even in the militant Vyborg district on the north side, the local Bolsheviks considered winding down the strike. For its part, the autocracy broke off its half-hearted negotiations with the Duma's President Rodzianko, and dissolved the parliament it held in such contempt.

Rodzianko telegraphed the tsar.

'The situation is serious.' His warning sped along the wires by the railway lines, across the wide hard countryside to Mogilev. 'There is anarchy in the capital. The government is paralysed. It is necessary immediately to entrust a person who enjoys the confidence of the country with the formation of a new government. Any delay is equivalent to death. I pray God that in this hour responsibility will not fall upon the sovereign.'

Nicholas did not reply.

The next morning, Rodzianko tried again. 'The situation is growing worse. Measures must be adopted immediately, because tomorrow will be too late. The last hour has come when the fate of the fatherland and the dynasty is being decided.'

At the High Command headquarters, Count Vladimir Frederiks, Nicholas's imperial household minister, waited politely as his master read the message unspooling from the machine. 'That fat Rodzianko has written me some nonsense,' the tsar said at last, 'to which I will not even reply.'

In the capital, the previous day's murder weighed heavy on some of those who had been ordered to commit it. Like that of the Pavlovsky, the Volinsky regiment's training detachment had shot demonstrators, and had spent the night gathered in their barracks in a long session of self-recrimination. Now its men confronted their captain,

Lashkevitch, and declared expiatory mutiny. They would not, they told him, shoot again.

Peremptorily, Lashkevitch read out the tsar's command to restore order. Once, perhaps, that might have persuaded them to submit. Now it was a provocation. There was a scuffle, shouts, alarm. Someone in the crowd of soldiers raised a weapon. Or perhaps, it has even been suggested, Lashkevitch raised his own gun in a panic and turned it on himself. Wherever it came from, a sudden shot sounded. The soldiers stared as the captain fell.

Something died with him. A hesitation.

The Volinsky soldiers roused the Litovsky and Preobrazhensky regiments from their barracks nearby. Officers from the Moscow regiment struggled to assert command. They were overpowered. The soldiers headed out into the city for the Vyborg district. This time it was they who sought to fraternise with the workers.

Under the gun-grey skies, the streets of Petrograd began to rage.

A dumbfounded General Khabalov tried to mobilise six loyal companies. Some officers and soldiers, individually and in make-shift groups, stayed loyal, and even put up armed resistance to the escalating insurrection. But at a mass level, out of conviction or cowardice, exhaustion or equivocation, for whatever reason at all, the troops refused to rally. Those soldiers who would not join with and fight alongside the workers, under leaders thrown up in the rough meritocracy of the moment, simply disappeared. In eye-witness descriptions, the same phrase recurs many times: even the supposedly loyal units 'melted away'.

Crowds of workers and soldiers ransacked government buildings and broke into police arsenals, took the weapons they found and went after the police, killing them where they could. They burned the stations down, sending their records up in smoke with them, firing at any 'Pharaoh' they saw, including the police snipers who had scrambled to the rooftops and sometimes leaned over to take aim. The rebels searched churches for caches of weapons, soldiers and workers rummaging together in uneasy reverential silence. They stormed prisons and tore open doors and freed the bewildered inmates. They set light to the district court and stood watching the bonfire, as if in some new winter festival. In the absence of any counterforce, the overthrowers exuberantly, chaotically overthrew.

Their clamour spread beyond Petrograd. In Moscow, in particular, officials had tried and failed to suppress news of the growing disturbances. Word of what was occurring reached the second city. Moscow workers began to walk out, some heading home, some for the city centre, seeking news and direction.

On the afternoon of the 27th, the tsar was pursuing his military pottering at Stavka, unperturbed. His tranquillity was not unique: the war minister, Bieliaev, cabled him to report, with surreal complacency, that a few minor disturbances were occurring in a few military units in Petrograd, and that they were being dealt with. That all would soon be calm.

In the boulevards of the insurgent city, revolutionary socialists jostled alongside angry liberals and all shades in between, and they were not calm. What they shared was a certainty that change, a revolution, was necessary, and ineluctable. They were in a new city, in eruption, on Red Monday. The old law was dying, the new not yet decided.

Under the darkening sky, accompanied by breaking glass and in the guttering light of fires, groups of men and women drifted aimlessly together and apart, workers, freed criminals, radical agitators, soldiers, freelance hooligans, spies and drunkards. Armed with what they had found. Here, a figure in a greatcoat waving an officer's sabre and an empty revolver. There, a young teenager with a kitchen knife. A student with machine-gun bullets slung around his waist, a rifle in each hand. A man wielded a pole for cleaning tramlines as if it were a pike.

Crowds of thousands surged down Shpalernaya Street, flocking to the spread stone wings of the Tauride Palace, seat of the Duma: ineffectual, divided and blindsided though the body was, huge numbers of citizens looked to it as an alternative government. All the more lamentable, then, that the Duma itself was unwilling, even now, to rebel against the tsar – even against his orders that it dissolve itself.

As directed, with the loyalty of cowardice or the cowardice of loyalty, the Duma members wound their official meeting down. The letter of the tsar's command duly obeyed, they left the assembly hall. They shuffled a little way through the high corridors of the building – and into another chamber, where they reconvened as, technically, a new, private gathering. Struggling for resolve, this remaindered Duma committed to staying in Petrograd and attempting to assert some control. Its members authorised a council to elect a Provisional Committee from among representatives of all the Duma parties except for the extreme right, and except for the Bolsheviks.

Before they chose this group, Rodzianko, accompanied this time by Nicholas's own brother Grand Duke Michael, made yet another effort to breach the tsar's bovine placidity. Only a shift to constitutional monarchy, Rodzianko was now certain, might placate the country, and Michael had agreed, in principle, to take power on this model.

Once again they strove to impress upon the tsar the apocalyptic seriousness of the situation. To the surprise, it must be assumed, of no one, Nicholas riposted with icy politeness that he was perfectly capable of managing his affairs.

There is something almost Herculean about the tsar's ability to refuse reality while his capital went up in flames, his police fled, his soldiers rebelled, and his officials, his own brother, implored him to do something, anything. Shortly thereafter it was the turn of his distraught premier to wire him, begging to be relieved of office. Nicholas stiffly informed Prince Golitzin that there would be no changes to the cabinet, and reiterated his demand for 'vigorous measures' to suppress disturbances.

The tsar paddled on, dignified and proper, eyes on the horizon, the current hauling him towards a cataract.

★

The twelve-, swiftly thirteen-person Provisional Committee of the Duma – to give it its preposterous full name, the Provisional Committee of the Members of the State Duma for the Restoration of Order in the Capital and the Establishment of Relations with Public Organisations and Institutions – was inaugurated by 5 p.m., dominated by the politics of the Kadets and the Progressive Bloc. It mandated itself, vaguely but urgently, to restore order in Petrograd and establish relations with public organisations and institutions. It understood, though, the limits of its own scope and voice at that moment of mass uprising. To make itself heard by the demonstrators, it reached out to two deputies from the left beyond the Progressive Bloc: N. S. Chkheidze, the leader of the Mensheviks; and that excitable Trudovik lawyer, who had earned the tsarina's fury, Alexander Kerensky.

It was 7 p.m. The Kadet deputy Ichas convened a meeting of 150 colleagues to create commissions, above all to handle the military question. Very soon the Reserve First Infantry Regiment, 12,000 soldiers and 200 officers in full formation, marched through the city's upheaval to the Tauride Palace. There they pledged loyalty to the Duma – or rather, to its Provisional Committee. With one of the inspired flashes of which he was, in those days, still capable, Kerensky relayed orders to several military units to take control of strategic locations – Okhrana headquarters, the gendarmerie, those crucial railway stations.

From the streets, meanwhile, as this continued, had arisen another kind of control. Some of the insurgents recalled those councils of 1905, those soviets. Activists and streetcorner agitators had already begun to call for their return, in leaflets, in boisterous voices from the crowds.

So it was that at the very moment when the Duma was planning its Committee, elsewhere in the cavernous Tauride Palace another very different group gathered.

Among those recently sprung from prison by the crowds were Gvozdev and Bogdanov, Mensheviks on the Central War Industries Committee. Immediately on their release they had fought their way through the chaos of Petrograd to join and caucus with their colleagues at the Palace, socialist Duma deputies of the SRs and the Mensheviks, representatives of the trade union and cooperative movements, Kerensky himself.

That day, running south over the wide Liteiny Bridge above the Neva's ice, Gvozdev saw another figure hurtling towards him. In the middle of the bridge, between its decorative mermaids, he came face to face with Zalezhskii, a leading Bolshevik who had also just escaped jail, and was heading in the opposite direction from the city centre towards the Vyborg district. The Menshevik made straight for the corridors of power; the Bolshevik for the workers' districts. So goes the story, whether or not this bridgetop meeting occurred.

At Tauride, the improvised assembly of Gvozdev, Bogdanov and their colleagues declared itself a Temporary Executive Committee of the Soviet of Workers' Deputies. Immediately they sent word to the city's plants and regiments that a soviet session would be held that same evening. In rushed, haphazard gatherings – there was certainly no time for more careful representative arrangements – factories chose representatives to join these deliberations. Within hours, the usual frock-coated Russian gentry, the intellectuals of the Duma and its associates, were joined by these less typical visitors. The corridors of the Tauride Palace nestling in its gardens began to fill with shabby, exhausted soldiers and workers.

That evening, the conclave of socialist intellectuals and hastily delegated workers and soldiers gathered in Room 12 on the left side of the palace. The former chair of the Soviet of 1905, Khrustalev-Nosar, was there; Steklov, close to the Menshevik left; Ehrlich, a leader of the Jewish Bund; and the dogged local Bolshevik leader, the metalworker Shlyapnikov. Workers and soldiers talked over each other in excitement, chosen according to those ad hoc mechanisms while most workers were preoccupied with revolt, without time or inclination to vote for delegates. When Shlyapnikov took a moment to telephone Bolshevik activists, urging them to come and join him, they paid him no attention. They, too, were more concerned to focus on the masses in the streets than on what might be afoot in those rooms. And besides, they were rather suspicious of this nascent organ, the brainchild of the socialists to their right.

At 9 p.m., the socialist lawyer Sokolov called the unruly meeting to order. Perhaps 250 people were in the room: only fifty or so, Sokolov ruled, were qualified to vote: the rest would remain as observers. He made his decisions as much on personal acquaintance as according to any formal structure.

The gathering was repeatedly interrupted by banging doors, newcomers bursting in, excited reports from soldiers that this or that company had come over to the insurrection, roars and applause. Rank-and-file soldiers' representatives came together in the room with those of the workers.

Thus the Soviet of Workers' and Soldiers' Deputies was born, at the suggestion of its own, pre-emptive, Temporary Executive Committee.

Beyond the palace walls, in streets emptied of the detested tsarist police, workers were still plundering weapons from the regime's stores to defend the factories, to impose their own rough order, gathering together, self-organising in armed groups, mostly young, mostly angry, radical, often politically incoherent. Among the urgent tasks of that night, its first, the Soviet set out to coordinate them by organising a workers' militia to establish and maintain order. It inaugurated a food commission to regulate supply. Soon it would authorise certain newspapers to reappear. And unlike the Duma or its Provisional Committee, the Soviet could make such declarations and moves with a degree of connection – however hedged and mediated that chaotic night – to the streets, the workers, the soldiers.

It needed a presidium. The meeting moved to vote in the Menshevik Chkheidze as chair, and as vice-chairs Skobolev and Kerensky. Like Chkheidze, Kerensky was a token socialist who had been approached to be part of the Duma's committee earlier that evening: unlike Chkheidze, following the Soviet elections, and after giving, for him, an unusually perfunctory speech, he left the room.

In Kerensky's absence, the Soviet established an executive committee between the presidium and the full Soviet. This committee would come to be responsible for much of the Soviet's management and many of its decisions. From that point on, it was at that level that the key debates occurred and decisions were made.

Chkheidze, Skobolev and Kerensky of the presidium itself were automatically given executive committee places, along with the four members of its secretariat. Eight others were elected. With six members in total, the Mensheviks were the strongest single party. However, for a brief moment that evening, two-thirds of the executive committee's fifteen places were taken, if not by the radical left, then by those on the internationalist, anti-war wing of the socialist movement, Bolsheviks and others – but, sapped by infighting and uncertainty about the nature of the Soviet, their relationship to it, and its relationship to political power and a new regime, they did nothing with this short-lived majority.

The very next day, in fact, they would lose it, in response to a mishandled manoeuvre by the Bolshevik Shlyapnikov himself. Disgruntled by the small number of Bolsheviks on the executive committee, he moved to add to it members from each socialist party. His proposal was accepted – but along with his comrades and Iurenev of the Mezhraiontsy came those from the Popular Socialists, Trudoviks, SRs, Bund and Mensheviks. Thus expanded, the committee included many more right, or moderate, socialists.

For now, as the Soviet continued bickering and bargaining, Kerensky hightailed his way back through the great palace to its opposite, right wing. He headed to where the other new group of which he was a member, the Duma's Provisional Committee, was meeting.

Late that night, the beleaguered General Khabalov, with no more than 2,000 troops still with him, dodged through a shadowy and dangerous Petrograd to seek refuge within the courtyard and surrounds of the tsar's Winter Palace. On his arrival, the tsar's brother ejected him, humiliatingly, forcing him and his men to scurry to the Admiralty building across the street. There they would hunker down for the night.

At Mogilev, a hazy awareness was at last spreading that all was not as it should be. Nicholas ordered General Ivanov to return to the capital, to restore order with a shock troop of Cavaliers of St George, recipients of the country's highest military honour. Still, neither the tsar nor any advisor took steps to relocate troops from the fronts nearest Petrograd. Ivanov himself prepared for his new mission with absurd, inappropriate languor, sending his adjutant shopping for gifts for friends at home.

The uprising's ripples were still spreading across the country.

Closest, and most crucial, was Kronstadt. Kronstadt was Petrograd's protective naval base, a fortified town of 50,000 – naval crews, soldiers and young sailors, a few merchants and workers – encircled by forbidding batteries and forts on the tiny island of Kotlin in the Gulf of Finland. Its officers were notoriously sadistic and brutal. Only seven years before, several hundred sailors had been executed during an attempted revolt. That memory was raw.

Now the sailors got word of the uprising. They were close enough to see the smoke from fires and hear shooting across the water. They swiftly decided that they, too, would have a revolution.

Late evening on 27 February, and in Petrograd's enormous Marinsky Palace, on the south side of St Isaac's Square, the tsar's council of ministers met for the last time. The city was now firmly in the hands of the revolution: they recognised this fait accompli, ending their inglorious tenure, submitting their resignations to the tsar. A meaningless formality.

Kerensky, a fine speaker with the moral authority of the left, an energetic and ambitious man still only in his mid-thirties, was making himself invaluable to the Duma Provisional Committee. He took a leading role in establishing a kind of military order, announcing that a revolutionary staff had been established at the State Duma, and setting out to drive frantically through Petrograd, declaring to groups of exhilarated insurgent soldiers that the Duma was with them.

The die was cast. Faced with anarchy, fearful of where it might lead, the Duma Committee felt compelled – notwithstanding the hesitance and tenacious loyalty to the regime of many of its members – to assume power. It declared that it would 'take into its hands the restoration of state and public order and the creation of a government corresponding to the desires of the population'.

Rodzianko was one of several of its members to feel deeply uneasy about this turn. But the situation was clearly summarised by V. V. Shulgin, a smart and unsentimental conservative deputy. 'If we don't take power,' he said, 'others will, those who have already elected some scoundrels in the factories.'

He referred, of course, to the neighbouring committee a few doors down, also taking on the tasks of organisation, of power: the Soviet. The tumultuous coexistence of these two conflictual, overlapping, imbricated politics, philosophies and social forces had begun.

The hallways of the Tauride Palace, usually a place of pristine bureaucracy disturbed by nothing more untidy or chaotic than a dropped memorandum, had by now become a military camp. In the main Circular Hall lay the corpse of a soldier. Hundreds of his living comrades camped in the palace corridors, squatting at makeshift stoves, drinking tea, smoking and rubbing their eyes, ready to face down the counterrevolution everybody feared was coming. The corridors stank of sweat, dirt, and gunpowder. Offices had become messy storerooms for food and arms. One large meeting room was full of looted sacks of barley. Slung across them a dead pig lay bleeding.

Rodzianko, always a fastidious man, his colleague Stankevich would recall, squeezed past a knot of dishevelled soldiers, 'preserving a majestic dignity but with an expression of deep suffering frozen on his pale face'. He edged by the rubbish propped against walls and piled at the junctions of corridors. In his memoirs, Shulgin was explicit with his own feelings about this situation. The masses who had overthrown the regime and who now had the temerity to share his palatial workplace were 'stupid, animal, even devilish'.

'Machine guns!' he fantasised. 'That's what I wanted. I felt that only the tongues of machine guns could talk to the mob.'

Such were sentiments that underlay the future relationship between Shulgin's Duma Committee and the Soviet – of which these rough corridor-squatters were the constituency. This would be a foundation of what would, misleadingly, come to be known as *dvoevlastie* – Dual Power.

Almost as quickly as the Duma deputies, the Soviet created its own military commission, issuing orders to the city's ad hoc brigades, preparing them for the anticipated battle against the tsar's forces. But at 2 a.m. on the 28th, Rodzianko and the Octobrist Colonel Engelhardt, of the Duma Committee's Military Commission, crossed the corridors to announce to the Soviet their intention to place the functions of its Military Commission under their own.

Many on the Soviet side were angry at the presumption, and profoundly uneasy about handing over power to these representatives of the bourgeoisie. It was during this tense standoff that Kerensky reappeared.

He, of course, was a man of both camps, and he was in his element. In he came, tense but confident, holding the attention of the room with a fervid speech begging the Soviet to acquiesce to this coalition, reassuring them, guaranteeing them supervision of the Duma's commission by representatives of the revolution.

And his argument found fertile ground. The truth was that most on the nascent Soviet commission had an analysis and sense that history was not yet theirs. That in this context there were, must be, limitations to and necessary brakes on their own role, their own power. As yet inchoate, this would be the start of a strange strain of self-limiting politics.

In the early hours of 28 February, the Soviet Committee distributed a leaflet.

The Provisional Committee of the State Duma with the help of the Military Commission is organising the army and appointing chiefs of all military units. Not wishing to disturb the struggle against the old power, the Executive Committee of the Petrograd Soviet does not recommend that the soldiers reject the existence of this organisation and subordination to its measures and appointments of chiefs.

'Not wishing to disturb the struggle against the old power': here was the hesitancy of those whose socialism taught that a strategic alliance with the bourgeoisie was necessary; that, however messily events proceeded, there were stages yet to come; that it was the bourgeoisie who must first take power, and precluded too vigorous a socialist mobilisation in this, their own unready country.

Decorously glossing this historical anxiety with the convoluted double negative of 'not recommending rejection', the Soviet Military Commission was thus swallowed into the Duma's. So it was the Duma Committee, with this new, grassroots-linked authority, that issued the orders to mutinying soldiers to return to their garrison and recognise their officers.

In those dark hours, in a fug of cigarettes, the exhausted men of the Duma Committee continued dealing with the exigencies of rule, torqued by history into machinating against the tsar and his system, forced to be a revolutionary government. Urgently, they appointed commissars to various vacant ministries.

The Committee had heard of the tsar's orders to Ivanov. They must prevent his counterrevolutionary forces reaching the capital. Nor could Nicholas himself be allowed to reach Tsarskoe Selo, the town in Petersburg's suburbs where the Romanovs had a residence and to where Nicholas had already set out to join his wife and family.

By 3:20 a.m., the Military Commission had rushed to take control of the Petrograd stations, and the train lines along which passed people and goods, weapons and fuel and food, information and rumour and politics. Those tracks were sinews of power.

★

The 28th was a day, Trotsky said, 'of raptures, embraces, joyful tears'. The sun rose on a changed city.

Not that the fighting was all done. Staccato bursts of gunfire continued to sound. It was on this last, lost day for the old regime's defenders that some of the ugliest violence occurred.

In the General Staff building, in the Admiralty, in the huge and splendid Winter Palace itself, guarded by its bevy of blank-eyed rooftop statues, holdouts remained. In the Astoria Hotel, senior officers and their families dug in, protected by trusted men. When jubilant crowds gathered in the streets outside, rumours spread of snipers in the hotel. Confusion. A phase-shift of delight to rage. Shouts that someone was shooting down from the windows. Was it true? Too late: true or not, revolutionary soldiers were smashing the glass and walls with their own volleys. Their comrades broke into the hotel's gilded vestibule, firing, and loyalist soldiers fired back.

A long and spectacular battle, a storm of ricochets, flying plaster chips, gold splinters and cordite, bullets pounding the walls, blood exploding across brocade and stiff-creased jackets. When the smoke and blare ebbed at last, several dozen officers were dead.

The Military Commission occupied the central telephone station and took the post office and central telegraph office. Bublikov, a member of the Duma, took fifty soldiers to the Ministry of Transport and placed everyone there under arrest, including the former minister, Kriger-Voinovskii, unless they pledged allegiance to the Duma Committee. That done, he tapped the iron network, sending a telegram to all the railway stations in Russia. In spurts of electricity, a clicking code following the paths of trains, he informed them that the revolution had taken place. And urged railway workers to come onside with 'redoubled energy'.

In fact, the Duma Committee had nothing like the power at its disposal that Bublikov implied. His message was a speech act, a performance, and it had a powerful effect. Though it would take several days to reach the furthest reaches of the vast territory, with the news of the revolution spread the revolution itself.

Groupuscules and gatherings formulated plans. Latvians and Finns and Poles and others, in their diasporas and in their homelands, debated political forms. Moscow, close by, second only to Petrograd in political and cultural sway, was most immediately and crucially affected. There, having been late to commence, the revolution seemed eager to catch up. From a more-or-less standing start the previous day, now a general strike rocked the city. Workers seized weapons from police stations and arrested the officers. Crowds sacked jails and set the prisoners free.

'To call it mass hypnosis is not quite right,' said Eduard Dune, in 1917 a Moscow teenager just engaging with radical politics, 'but the mood of the crowd was transmitted from one to another like conduction, like a spontaneous burst of laughter, joy, or anger.' Most there, he thought, 'that morning had been praying for the good health of the imperial family. Now they were shouting, "Down with the tsar!" and not disguising their joyful contempt.'

On the Yauza Bridge, police gamely tried to block a huge mass of demonstrators. A metalworker called Astakhov shouted for them to withdraw, and a hot-headed officer replied with lethal fire. Moscow's February had claimed its first, one of its vanishingly few, martyrs.

The enraged horde stormed the blockade, routed the police, hurled the murderer into the waters of the Yauza, and continued to the city centre. Muscovites gathered there to celebrate the new order. 'The old regime in Moscow in truth fell all by itself,' reported the Kadet businessman Buryshkin, 'and no one defended it or even tried to.'

There was class differentiation in the very liberation. Hawkers ran out of red calico for ribbons that night. 'Well-dressed people wore ribbons almost the size of table napkins,' said Dune, 'and people said to them: "Why are you being so stingy? Share it out among us. We've got equality and fraternity now."'

In Petrograd, the Duma Committee ordered the arrest of ex-ministers and senior officials. That 'order' was implicitly a plea, in fact, directed at the revolutionary crowds. And those crowds often had no need to hunt: fearful of the emerging order, representatives of the old rule tended to believe that the newly self-appointed leaders were more likely to keep them alive than was the rough street justice. Tsarist ministers such as the loathed Protopopov, previously minister of the interior, made their own way to the Tauride Palace, in a hurry to hand themselves in. Police officers queued outside its walls, begging to be taken into custody.

And as the Duma Committee took tentative power early on the 28th, as the city lurched, more and more factories and military units assembled and voted representatives to the Petrograd Soviet – a body by then formulating its own plans and powers.

The new delegates overwhelmingly represented moderate socialist groups – fewer than 10 per cent of votes went to the Bolsheviks, the most revolutionary, maximalist wing of the SRs, or to the small militant group, the Mezhraiontsy.

The extraordinary Mezhraiontsy, the Interborough or Interdistrict Group, was a recent radical formation. Dismayed by the hardening split in Russian Marxism, its founders Konstantin Yurenev, Bolsheviks Elena Adamovich and A. M. Novosyolov, the Menshevik Nikolai Egorov and others fostered collaboration. They built goodwill and membership among workers and intellectuals including Yuri Larin, Moisei Uritsky, David Ryazanov, Anatoly Lunacharsky and Trotsky himself.

Lunacharsky was an unorthodox, erudite and sparkling critic, writer and orator. A gentle man, admired for his sensitivity as well as his brilliance, he had long been opposed to traces of stageism and mechanistic orthodoxy, for which he criticised Plekhanov and the Mensheviks. He argued instead for an ethical, aesthetic Marxism, even advocated 'God-building', an atheistic religion of godlessness, of humanity itself. For this and other theoretical sins Lenin had previously attacked him, but by 1917 he and his comrades were all but an external faction of the Bolsheviks.

To the Mezhraiontsy, unity had fast become secondary to the key issue of the war: they gave no quarter to 'defencism'. With many quick and independent thinkers among their ranks, they were 'the only organisation', Yurenev would proudly recall, 'publishing leaflets in the opening skirmishes of the revolution'. As early as the 27th, their agitators encouraged workers to elect representatives to a soviet – about which they were considerably more enthusiastic than were the Bolsheviks at this point.

The rough-and-ready representative mechanisms of that Soviet meant that soldiers would rapidly be overrepresented. For those soldiers, still giddy with freedom, the Soviet was their organisation: Kerensky's interventions notwithstanding, many did not trust the Duma Committee, speaking as it did for the officers against whom they had mutinied.

The Duma Committee itself, that semi-reluctant power, was split as to what it wanted. It included those still aspiring to a constitutional monarchy; those for whom history had removed that possibility, whether it had been once preferable or not; and those who considered a republic not only necessary but desirable.

It was not a day of raptures and joyful tears in Kronstadt. In that tiny island town, it was the 28th that was the day of the revolution.

Soldiers of the Third Kronstadt Fortress Infantry marched out of a barracks in Pavel Street, their band playing the Marseillaise. Their comrades from the Torpedo and Mining Training Detachment followed them, shooting an officer dead as they advanced. Then came the First Baltic Fleet Depot. Then the garrison. Sailors joined the throng. The crews of the training ships in the iron-hard harbour came out in mutiny. 'Do not find it possible to take measures for pacification with personnel from the garrison', Commander Kurosh tersely reported to his superiors, 'because there is not one unit I can rely on.'

Men demonstrated in the streets and in the main Anchor Square; they ranged through their sprawling base and barracks, bayonets in hands, following the paths of those executed mutineers. A few respected officers they protected: others they dragged to the square, hurled into a ditch, and shot dead in the dirt. Perhaps fifty in all were put to death. Many more fled or were thrown in Kronstadt's jail.

The sailors did not know that they lagged a day behind the mainland, that they were joining a revolution already made. They expected a loyalist assault, and their savagery was revenge, yes, but also exigency and urgency in the face of that dreaded battle in a war – a class war. No officer could re-establish discipline now.

'This is not a mutiny, comrade admiral,' shouted one sailor. 'This is a revolution.'

In September of 1916, Governor-General Viren had reported to his superiors that 'one tremor from Petrograd would be enough and Kronstadt ... would rise against me, the officers, the government and anyone else. The fortress is a powder magazine in which a wick is burning down'. Less than half a year later, in the small hours between February and March, Viren was hauled out of his villa in nothing but a white shirt.

He drew himself up and bellowed a familiar order: 'Attention!' This time the men just laughed.

They marched him to Anchor Square, shivering in his underclothes in the sea winds. They told him to face the great monument to Admiral Makarov, engraved with his motto: 'Remember war'. Viren refused. When the Kronstadt soldiers bayonetted him he made them meet his eyes.

The tsar spent the last day of February wandering a frozen Russia by rail. He meandered in luxury, his train a wheeled palace. Gilded baroque interiors, kitchen carriage, filigreed bedroom, study sumptuous with brown leather, Karelian birchwood, cherry-red carpet, swaying through hard and frosted landscapes until darkness descended. A night arrival at Malaya Vishera Station, barely 100 miles from Petersburg. But Bublikov's telegram had done its work: the stations along the line were occupied by revolutionary troops.

The railway authorities had orders from the Provisional Committee to divert the train, to try to draw the tsar back by rail, send him if they could to Petrograd where those who had overthrown his regime awaited him. The iron road could turn him. Cautious at the confused (dis)information about the situation they received on their arrival, Nicholas and his party hastily changed plans. With a rushed clattering of points, the royal train set swiftly out again, no longer for Tsarskoe Selo, but for the headquarters of the northern front, the ancient medieval town of Pskov. From there, Nicholas thought, perhaps he might find a route to somewhere more congenial, and perhaps even some loyal military support.

The man dethroned in all but final formality rattled too late into the dark.

3

March: 'In So Far As'

I n deep night, as the month turned, having cabled with Rodzianko about the situation in the city, General Alexeev sent a telegram to General Ivanov. He ordered him not to advance on the city as planned, because 'complete peace was restored in Petrograd'.

This was quite untrue. But he and the Duma Committee said what they must to forestall the doomed counterinsurgency. Thus the Romanovian counterrevolution was recalled.

At the Tauride Palace, at 11 a.m. on 1 March, the Soviet Executive Committee met again in a tense session to debate the problem of power. Some on its right argued for coalition with the Duma Committee, since, as per their historical and political theories, the necessity of a transfer of power to the Provisional Government that that committee was forming was not, for them, in dispute. But the Executive Committee's left-wing minority — three Bolsheviks, two SRs on the hard left of the party, one Mezhraionets — called instead for the formation of a 'provisional revolutionary government' without the Duma deputies. This was reminiscent of Lenin's pre-war position: then, while the Mensheviks had argued that the proletariat and Marxists should abstain from a (necessarily) bourgeois government, Lenin, by contrast, had advocated a provisional, proletariat-led revolutionary government as the best vehicle for the (again, necessarily) bourgeois–democratic revolution.

In fact the Executive Committee minority's call notwithstanding, the Bolsheviks as a party were not united in their approach either to the Soviet, of which some of their activists remained sceptical, or to questions of government power. That very day, when the left Bolshevik Vyborg District Committee circulated a proclamation in the chaotic streets demanding a provisional revolutionary government, the Bolshevik Party Central Committee clamped down on their ill-disciplined interventions.

The Soviet's Executive Committee, the Ispolkom, had allowed a single hour to discuss and decide the shape of post-revolutionary power. A ludicrous aspiration. The meeting dragged well over the allotted time. Under the dome of the Tauride Palace's great hall the hundreds of Soviet delegates, its general assembly, were awaiting the Ispolkom's report back. Their impatience grew loud. As noon slipped past, the Ispolkom sent the Menshevik Skobolev to plead for more time.

As he spoke, he was dramatically interrupted. The doors to the chamber flew open and a voluble group of uniformed soldiers piled in. As the newcomers clamoured, the Ispolkom got word and rushed to join the throng.

The anxious soldiers had come to ask the Soviet for guidance: how should they respond to Rodzianko's demands to surrender their arms? What should they do about their officers, against whom the popular mood remained ugly enough that there was a real danger of lynchings? And should they obey the Soviet, or the Duma Committee?

The raucous crowd left them in no doubt that they must keep their arms. That much was simple.

The decision to dissolve the Soviet's Military Commission into that of the Duma Committee, however, provoked more controversy. The left in the room were hollering, denouncing it as collaboration. For the Ispolkom, Sokolev, a former Bolshevik, defended the move on grounds of the military experience and 'historic role' of the bourgeoisie.

Out of the arguments echoing through the hall, a consensus began to emerge. Anti-revolutionary officers were not to be trusted, but the command of 'moderate' officers was valid – though only as regards matters of combat. As the back-and-forth continued, one soldier from the Preobrazhensky Regiment explained how he and his comrades had voted in an administrative committee from within their own ranks.

Elected officers. The idea spread roots.

At last the Soviet put together a draft resolution. It stressed that soldiers' committees were important. It proposed soviet democracy within units, combined with military discipline on duty. The soldiers, the gathering urged, should send representatives to the Duma Committee's Military Commission, and recognise its authority – *in so far as it did not deviate from the opinion of the Soviet.*

In that extraordinary conditional clause, radicalism and conciliation swirled together but did not mix.

Newly resolute, the soldiers went to present these decisions to the Military Commission's Colonel Engelhardt. They demanded that he pass an order for the election of, as he later recalled, 'the junior officers'. On behalf of the Duma Committee, however, Rodzianko immediately rejected this left compromise, leaving Engelhardt to placate the furious soldiers as best he could.

The jockeying was not yet done: later that evening, mandated by the Soviet, they returned to the Military Commision to request of Engelhardt that regulations regarding military organisation be drawn up, in collaboration with the Duma Committee. When he rejected this further overture, the soldiers took their angry leave.

'So much the better,' one exclaimed as they went. 'We will write them ourselves.'

At 6 p.m., in the Soviet, a packed Executive Committee, soon joined by several new delegates mandated by the soldiers – Bolsheviks, Mensheviks, SRs, independents, one lonely Kadet – resumed their discussions on power. Once again, the moderates called for active coalition with the Duma Committee. But the prevailing position, as put by Sukhanov, an independent intellectual close to the left Mensheviks, was that the Soviet's 'task' was, rather, to 'compel' the reluctant liberal bourgeoisie to take power. In the Menshevik model, they were the necessary agent, after all, of a necessary, and necessarily bourgeois, revolution. And excessively stringent conditions for compromise, of course, risked dissuading this timorous bourgeois liberalism from fulfilling its historic role.

On such a basis, the Ispolkom thrashed out nine conditions for its support of a provisional government:

1) an amnesty for political and religious prisoners;
2) freedom of expression, publication and strikes;
3) the introduction of a democratic republic by universal, equal, direct, secret – male – suffrage;
4) preparation for the convocation of a Constituent Assembly, towards a permanent government;
5) replacement of the police force by a people's militia;
6) elections to local administrative bodies as per point three;
7) abolition of discrimination based on class, religion or nationality;
8) self-government of the army, including election of officers;
9) no withdrawal from Petrograd or disarmament of revolutionary army units.

Crucially, as befitting its self-perceived role as overseer, the committee also voted, thirteen to eight, that its members should not serve in the cabinet of the provisional government the Duma Committee would create.

These were moderate demands. The left in the room was mostly quiet: all the upheaval had left the Bolsheviks, in particular, floundering somewhat, uncertain as to how to iterate their *differentia specifica* of consistent anti-liberalism.

The most radical points in the list were those concerning the army. These came from the soldiers' representatives, furious at Engelhardt's intransigence. And their anger was not yet spent.

The exhausted executive delegated a small group to join the soldiers in formalising their particular demands. They crowded together into a small room, Sokolov hunched at a dark desk, scribbling for them, translating into legalese. Half an hour later they emerged with what Trotsky would call 'a charter of freedom of the revolutionary army', and 'the single worthy document of the February Revolution', one put forward not by the Soviet Executive but by the soldiers themselves – Order Number 1.

Order Number 1 consisted of seven points:

1) election of soldiers' committees in military units;
2) election of their representatives to the Soviet;
3) subordination of soldiers to the Soviet in political actions;
4) subordination of soldiers to the Military Commission – in so far, again and crucially, as its orders did not deviate from the Soviet's;
5) control of weapons by soldiers' committees;
6) military discipline while on duty, with full civil rights at other times;
7) abolition of officers' honorary titles and of officers' use of derogatory terms for their men.

The order gave priority to the power of the Soviet over that of the Duma Committee, and put the weapons of the Petrograd Garrison at the Soviet's disposal. And yet that Soviet's Executive Committee, with its strange cocktail of Jesuitical Marxism and political hesitancy, did not want the power thus bestowed. However underenforced it would go on to be, whatever an embarrassment it might prove to the more cautious, in essence Order Number 1 was a severe rebuke to traditional military authority – and it would remain so, as a clarion.

Its last two points were a military articulation of the insistence on honour, on human dignity, for which the most radical workers had striven since 1905. Soldiers were, up to February, still subject to grotesque humiliations. They could not receive books or newspapers, belong to any political societies, attend lectures or the theatre, without permission. They could not wear civilian clothes off-duty. They could not eat in restaurants or ride in streetcars. And their officers referred to them by humiliating nicknames and using those superior linguistic forms. Hence this fight against belittling familiarity, the class spite of grammar.

Soldiers, like workers and others, demanded to be addressed with the respectful 'Citizen', a term spreading so widely it was as if it had been 'invented just now!' the poet Michael Kuzmin wrote.

The revolution and its language seduced him: 'Tough sandpaper has polished all our words.'

General Ivanov and his shock troops arrived late in Tsarskoe Selo, where the tsarina, dressed as a nurse, was tending her measles-infected children. She was fearful that Ivanov's presence might inflame the political situation, but his mission was already over: word came from Alexeev that he was not to proceed.

A little before 8 p.m., the tsar himself arrived at Pskov. Rodzianko had promised to meet him there, but now he sent apologies. He was, unknown to Nicholas, preparing for negotiations between the Duma Committee and the Soviet.

A General Ruzskii was in command of forces around the medieval city of Pskov. When he came to greet the tsar, the general arrived late, harassed, brusque, and wearing rubber boots. This was a borderline seditious lack of pomp. The tsar forbore. He gave the general permission to speak freely. He asked him for his assessment of the situation.

The old ways, Ruzskii offered carefully, had run their course.

Perhaps, he suggested, the tsar might adopt a formula such as 'the sovereign reigns and the government rules'.

A constitutional monarchy? The mere insinuation provoked in Nicholas a kind of glazed satori of his own limits. This 'was incomprehensible' to him, he muttered. To come around to something like that, he said, he would have to be reborn.

At 11:30 p.m., as the Soviet and Duma committees prepared to meet in Petrograd, Nicholas received a telegram that General Alexeev had sent him hours before, at the same time as he had called off the tsar's troops.

'It is impossible', Nicholas read, 'to ask the army calmly to wage war while a revolution is in progress in the rear.'

Alexeev begged the tsar to appoint a cabinet of national confidence, imploring him to sign a draft manifesto to this effect, that members of the Duma Committee had been hurriedly formulating and in support of which they had been collecting endorsements – pointedly including one from the tsar's cousin, Grand Duke Sergei Mikhailovich.

To the tsar, this – from the loyal Alexeev – was a severe blow. He pondered. At last he recalled Ruzskii and ordered him to relay to Rodzianko and Alexeev his consent – that the Duma should form a cabinet. Then he cabled Ivanov, rescinding his command and ordering him not to proceed to Petrograd.

By then, that order, of course, like the man who gave it, was redundant.

At midnight on 1 March, Sukhanov, Chkheidze, Steklov and Sokolov of the Soviet crossed from one side of the Tauride Palace to the other on a mission Sukhanov had initiated, one neither quite official nor quite unsanctioned. They were meeting their Duma counterparts, to discuss terms for the Soviet's support for the Duma in taking power.

Close to the left of the Mensheviks, Sukhanov was a clever, waspish, sardonic witness of this year, with an uncanny ability to be present at the key moments of history. In his memoirs, that night is vivid.

Below its high ceiling the Duma's meeting room was foul with cigarette butts, bottles, and the smell from plates of half-eaten food which made the famished socialists salivate. Ten Duma representatives were there, including Milyukov, Rodzianko and Lvov. Technically a Soviet man, Kerensky was also present. He kept uncharacteristically quiet. Rodzianko sulked and obsessively sipped soda water. For the most part it was Pavel Milyukov, of the Kadets, who spoke for the Committee, and Sukhanov who spoke for the Soviet.

The groups gauged the distance between them. On two key political questions, the war and the redistribution of land, they were quite divided. These issues, then, they avoided. Those aside, liberals and socialists – the latter disinclined to dissuade the former from taking power – were pleasantly surprised at how smoothly the negotiations proceeded.

Though he accepted that Nicholas himself must go, the Anglophile Milyukov dreamed of keeping the institution of the monarchy. Could Nicholas, he mused, be persuaded to abdicate in favour of his son, under the regency of the tsar's brother Michael? As if recollecting the present company of republican leftists, Milyukov hastened to describe the pair as 'a sick child … and a thoroughly stupid man'. That notion, Chkheidze told him, was unrealistic as well as unacceptable.

It was established that troublesome points could wait until the convening of a Constituent Assembly, so this question, too, was shelved. Point three of the Soviet's nine, about a 'democratic republic', was dropped.

To avoid trouble in the short term, Milyukov, with curled lip, agreed not to relocate the city's revolutionary troops. What he would not countenance, however, was the election of officers. For the liberals and for the right, what this would mean was the destruction of the army. And what of Order Number 1? Troops to obey the government only in so far as its orders did not conflict with the Soviet's? The idea was appalling.

Shulgin interjected. He was never as diplomatic as Milyukov. If the Soviet had the power implied in that order, he coldly suggested, they should immediately arrest the Duma Committee and set up government alone.

To actually take power was, of course, the last thing the flustered socialists wanted.

It was at that moment that an agitated group of army officers abruptly arrived to interrupt the discussion. They called Shulgin outside.

The revolution has its mysteries. This perfectly timed intervention is one. The identities of the officers remain unclear, as does their precise message. Whoever they were, they seem to have intimated to Shulgin that opposing Order Number 1, that night, would mean bloodshed. Perhaps even be a massacre of officers.

Whatever the source of the opaque intercession, it proved vital. On his return to the room, Shulgin agreed that the Soviet need not rescind Order Number 1, but that it would issue a second order to soften it.

The Duma Committee had its own demands. The Soviet Executive Committee, it insisted, must restore order and re-establish contact between soldiers and officers. Much as the fact might stick in the conservative craw, it was clear that the Ispolkom was the only body that might have the power to do this. And the Ispolkom must proclaim the Provisional Government, agreed between itself and the Duma Committee, legitimate.

Milyukov had girded himself for struggle on such points. He was agreeably surprised by the Soviet representatives' ready – even eager – acquiescence.

It was 3 a.m. on 2 March when the meeting adjourned. Not everyone, though, could afford to sleep: some still had other urgent business.

It was very soon thereafter that a strange truncated two-car train hauled out from Petrograd's Warsaw Station, shedding light into the night. Escorted by guards, it carried Shulgin and Alexander Guchkov, a conservative Octobrist politician, on a mission to reshape history. The two right-wingers had taken on themselves an unpleasant task: they had volunteered to go to meet the tsar, to try to persuade him to abdicate.

At station after station along the route, the platform and their train were invaded by crowds of soldiers and civilians, ignoring the cold, buoyed by insurgency, desperate for details, all in excited debate. At Lugin and Gatchina rebellious soldiers greeted the travellers enthusiastically: as representatives of the Duma, and thus, in many minds, of the revolution itself, Guchkov and Shulgin had to give speech after brief speech.

The early morning dragged, then the day, as the agitated, impatient men prepared for their task, not knowing it was already superfluous.

One reason the tsar had chosen to go to Pskov was its connection by wire to the capital. In a communications room deep in the Tauride Palace, there was a Hughes machine. Invented more than a half-century previously, this telegraphic apparatus was an intricate tangle of brass wheels, wires and wood, its lettered black and white keyboard designed to mimic a piano's. At such machines, as the print wheel turned, virtuoso operators would 'play' the text of messages, and at the other end of the connection, a long ribbon of words would emerge.

Russia's was an extensive empire of wires, running mostly through post offices and alongside railways. Along them passed events and opinions, information, dissent, order, confusion and clarity, spreading out in the staccato clatter of keys struck and unspooling paper, each party dictating one sentence at a time to trained operators at their keyboards.

At 3:30 a.m., very soon after Guchkov and Shulgin left, Rodzianko connected to Pskov on the Hughes machine. At the other end, through his own telegrapher, a bleary Ruzskii conveyed the good news that Nicholas, then fretfully scribbling in his diary in his private train carriage, had agreed at last to form a responsible ministry.

'It is obvious', responded Rodzianko, 'that His Majesty and you do not realise what is going on here.'

Stunned, Ruzskii watched Rodzianko's devastating message chatter out, word by word. The opportunity had been missed. The time for ministries was over.

Accordingly, at 5 a.m., with Rodzianko still only halfway through that momentous exchange, Milyukov met the lawyer Sokolov and the independent leftist Sukhanov from the Soviet, to formalise their collaboration.

The proclamation, Milyukov would later crow, enjoined the people to restore order, which was 'almost the same thing that [he, Milyukov] … had been telling the soldiers from the platform of the regiment barracks. And it was accepted for publication in the name of the Soviet!' There was no reference to the election of officers. Nor did the Soviet's Executive Committee interfere with the selection of the new cabinet. The Duma Committee offered positions to the two members of the Soviet to whom it had already made overtures, Chkheidze and Kerensky. Such government roles the Soviet had already in principle refused.

This decision would soon be dramatically overturned.

The long exchange between Rodzianko and Ruzskii continued. As was usual, it was also relayed to other relevant parties on the lines. The calamitous information spread out. At 6 a.m., one of the recipients, General Danilo of the northern front, ordered telegraphists to forward it to Mogilev, to General Alexeev.

Alexeev instantly understood the magnitude of what he read. At 8:30 a.m., he ordered Pskov staff to wake the tsar and relay to him the conversation's contents.

'All etiquette must be ignored,' he insisted. His urgency was not shared. The tsar, he was coldly informed, was sleeping.

Alexeev knew it would take representations from the army, one of the few institutions Nicholas respected, to make him understand, to bow to the inevitable. The general sent the text of the explosive discussion on to the commanders of Russia's fleets and fronts, asking them to respond with their recommendations to the tsar.

It was not until after 10 a.m. that the hapless Ruzskii at last brought to the tsar the transcript of his conversation with Rodzianko. He handed it over. The tsar read. When he was done, he gazed at the ceiling for a long time. He murmured that he was born for unhappiness.

Ruzskii, pale and terrified, read aloud Alexeev's mass telegram to the generals. There could be no mistaking its implication. The tsar must abdicate.

Nicholas remained silent.

Ruzskii waited. The tsar stood up at last. Apocalypse glowered. The tsar announced that he was going for lunch.

Some 1,400 miles away in Zurich, Lenin turned to page 2 of the *Neue Zürcher Zeitung*. There, a short report informed of a revolution in Petrograd. Lenin, too, looked up in thought, his eyes wide.

That morning, Milyukov came to the Tauride Palace's huge Ekaterina Hall to announce the Provisional Government to the revolutionary crowd gathered there. As he listed the cabinet, the room jeered in bewilderment at the names that were unfamiliar, and in disgust at those they knew.

There was one appointment, though, that drew applause: the role of justice minister had been filled by that popular SR (as he now declared himself) Alexander Kerensky. This despite the fact that the Executive Committee of the Soviet had agreed that its members would not take cabinet positions.

Milyukov was adroit. He deployed a few revolutionary slogans to win over his sceptical audience, fielding their barbs with aplomb. When the shout came, 'Who elected you?' he responded immediately: 'It was the Russian Revolution that elected us!' One thing, however, he could not sell: the continuation of the royal dynasty. When he announced 'only' Nicholas's abdication – to which, of course, Nicholas himself had not yet agreed – the incandescent crowd roared.

The tsar's departure was, of course, a calamity to some in the country. As Milyukov sparred with the revolutionaries, across the city ten-year-old Zinaida Schakovsky and her classmates were at assembly in the hall of the Empress Catherine Institute for Young

Ladies of the Nobility. Zinaida was confused: the older pupil leading the school prayers seemed to have skipped the usual wishes for the tsar and his family. Now she was stumbling over unfamiliar replacement words, unsure how to pronounce 'Let us pray for the Provisional Government.' The girl paused and began to cry. And as a bewildered Zinaida looked on, the teachers took out their handkerchiefs and wept too, and so did all the girls around her, and so did she, without knowing what it was she mourned.

No such sobs echoed through the Tauride corridors. Word began to reach the palace that soldiers were looting the houses of the rich and arresting any they considered royalists. Nicholas's intransigence was threatening national stability.

The workers thronging the corridors, fresh from Milyukov's announcement, hunted Soviet representatives, demanding to know from them whether it was true that the monarchy was still in place. And making it very clear that, if so, the task was unfinished.

That afternoon, the Petrograd Soviet gathered to debate what its Executive Committee had agreed with the Duma Committee. But not long after the stormy general session began, at 2 p.m., the proceedings were interrupted by a commotion. Kerensky. He came striding in, raising his voice, begging to speak. Chkheidze, in the chair, hesitated, but the gathered delegates demanded he allow the intervention.

Kerensky mounted the platform. He projected for the crowd. 'Comrades,' he said, 'do you trust me?'

Yes, the crowd shouted, yes, they trusted him.

'I speak, comrades, with all my soul,' he continued, tremulous. 'And if it is needed to prove this, if you do not trust me, then I am ready to die.'

Again, the crowd cheered his theatrics.

Kerensky had, he informed the room, just then received an invitation to be minister of justice in the Provisional Government. And he had been given five minutes to decide. Without time to consult the

Soviet, with no choice but to grab history by the tail, he had agreed. And now he had come to ask his comrades' approval.

As the historian Tsuyoshi Hasegawa has remarked, this was an extremely long five minutes: Kerensky had in fact received the invitation the previous day, and accepted earlier that morning.

His first act as minister, Kerensky exclaimed, had been to release all political prisoners – a measure which, in reality, had been agreed earlier by the Executive Committee with their Duma counterparts. Of course, having no formal Soviet authorisation to accept the position, he told the room, he hereby respectfully resigned his post as Soviet vice chair. However! He would – provided only that his comrades, and the masses for whom they spoke, wished him to do so – take up that role again. The choice was theirs.

Cheers. Ecstasy. He should, indeed, the delegates hurrahed, keep his Soviet position, too.

A few more histrionics later, Kerensky left, too rapidly for any challenge from his bewildered, outmanoeuvred colleagues on the executive. He had shrewdly banked on their unwillingness to risk a fight. With this mendacious *coup de théâtre*, his breach of the Ispolkom's directive post factum was mandated, and his position in the government backed by the Soviet assembly.

With many of their militants now released from jail, the so-called Russian Bureau of the Bolsheviks' Petersburg Committee, set up by Shlyapnikov in 1915 and recently reconstituted by him (despite the obstruction of police spies), began to function as something of an ersatz Central Committee. Initially under three members – Shlyapnikov, Molotov and Zalutsky – this operation continued while most of the formal members of the actual CC, including Lenin, Zinoviev, Stalin, Kamenev and others, were abroad or in Siberia.

In the Soviet, the Russian Bureau promptly introduced a resolution declaring the new Provisional Government to be 'representative of the grand bourgeoisie and big landowners', and thus incapable

of realising revolutionary aims. It appealed again, somewhat nebulously, for a 'provisional revolutionary government'. The motion
was slapped down.

And despite such radical declarations from some Bolsheviks –
especially those in the Vyborg ward of Petrograd – when the vote to
accept the transfer of power to the unelected Provisional Government came, of the forty Bolsheviks in the Soviet General Assembly,
only fifteen voted against. This illustrates the political confusion,
the degree of vacillation and moderation on the revolution's left
flank in those heady early days.

2 March, 2:30 p.m. The tsar paced the platform of the Pskov station.
Hovering at a respectful distance, keeping anxious watch, an entourage of nobles and sycophants.

Nicholas turned to them. He requested the presence of Generals
Ruzskii, Savic and Danilov. And they should bring, he said, all the
generals' telegrams.

He received the men in his private carriage. As the tsar walked
restlessly up and down, Grand Duke Nikolaevich begged him
'on his knees' to surrender the crown. All the generals cursed the
'bandits' of the Provisional Government, excoriated their perfidy,
railed against them – but, that denunciation done, they admitted
they faced a fait accompli.

Speak freely, the tsar urged them. They told him he must go.
There was no other option, Danilov said. Savic stammered, struggled to speak, concurred.

The tsar stopped by his desk and turned away to stare out of the
window at the winter. He was silent for a very long time. He grimaced.

'I have made up my mind,' he said at last, turning. 'I have decided
to abdicate the throne in favour of my son.'

The tsar crossed himself. His companions did the same.

'I thank you for your excellent and loyal service,' Nicholas said. 'I
trust it will continue under my son.' He dismissed them, so he might
compose the necessary telegrams to Alexeev and Rodzianko.

Count Vladimir Frederiks hurried through the carriage to tell the tsar's waiting retinue the news. They were thunderstruck. Some began to weep. Admiral Nilov decided that Ruzskii was to blame, and swore that he would execute him. Vladimir Voeikov, Commandant of Court, and Colonel Naryshkin rushed to the Hughes apparatus to stop the keys and wires doing their work, to demand the return of Nicholas's telegrams. But their world had passed: Ruzskii informed them that they were too late.

He was at least half-lying. He had sent the tsar's telegram to Alexeev, and, receiving it, the general immediately commissioned a manifesto of abdication. But when Ruzskii heard that the Duma men Guchkov and Shulgin were on their way, he kept back Nicholas's message to Rodzianko. It seems he wanted to hand it to them personally.

While his hangers-on floundered in rearguard action, the tsar himself was engaged in an urgent private conversation. His doctor was telling him plainly that the young haemophiliac Alexei, on whom the burden of the crown was now set to fall, was unlikely to live long.

Ruzskii gave orders for Guchkov and Shulgin to be brought to him without delay. But when at 9 p.m. they finally arrived, carrying a makeshift abdication act that Shulgin had scrawled en route, in one final spasm of court infighting and machination they were taken instead directly to the imperial salon car, without Ruzskii's knowledge. There commenced a last, bleak, Romanovian comedy.

Guchkov began to hold forth to Nicholas about the threat facing Russia. In tones verging on menace, he told the tsar there was only one course left. As he spoke, Ruzskii entered. He was aghast to see the two newcomers, let alone to realise that they were trying to persuade the silent tsar to do what he had already agreed to do.

Ruzskii interrupted, blurting out this information to the stunned men. As he spoke, Ruzskii handed Nicholas his signed, unsent telegram for Rodzianko – and his stomach pitched to see the tsar fold it up and put it absently away. To do with it who knew what?

'I deliberated during the morning and was ready to abdicate the throne in favour of my son, in the name of good, peace, and the salvation of Russia,' the tsar said. Ruzskii's heart lurched. 'But now, reconsidering the situation, I have come to the conclusion that because of his illness, I must abdicate at the same time for my son as well as for myself, since I cannot part with him.'

And to the bewilderment of all present, he named his brother Michael as his successor.

Shulgin and Guchkov floundered. Shulgin and Guchkov rallied. 'Your Majesty,' Guchkov said, 'the human feelings of a father have spoken in you, and politics has no place in the matter. Therefore we cannot object to your proposal.'

They must, though, they insisted, have a signed declaration. Embarrassed at the sight of Alexeev's professional abdication draft, Shulgin withdrew his own scrappy version. The details were finessed: 'Not wishing to be separated from Our beloved son, We hand Our succession to Our brother, Grand Duke Michael Aleksandrovich.' The declaration was backdated by hours, to avoid any implication that Nicholas had acted under pressure from the Duma Committee. As indeed he had. At 11:40 p.m., the tsar signed, and ceased to be tsar.

At 1 a.m. on 3 March, Nicholas Romanov's train left Pskov for Mogilev.

In a rare glimpse of something like an inner life, the erstwhile autocrat confided to his diary that he was suffering from 'gloomy feelings'.

Guchkov and Shulgin rushed back to Petrograd, where word of Nicholas's decision had set off a storm of intrigue among their colleagues. When their train arrived at the capital in the early light, they experienced the anti-monarchist mood first-hand.

The station was full of milling soldiers, eager for information.

They surrounded the returnees and pressed them into yet another speech. Shulgin held forth. He read out Nicholas's abdication impassionedly. But when he concluded, 'Long Live Emperor Michael III!' what cheers he provoked were distinctly underwhelming. Just then, in a moment of cruel, broad irony, he was called to the station telephone, where a cautious Milyukov begged him not yet to make public exactly the information he just had.

Guchkov, meanwhile, was also trying to drum up enthusiasm – to a meeting of militant railway workers. When he told them of Michael's ascension, the reaction was of such violent hostility that one speaker demanded his arrest. It was only with the help of a sympathetic soldier that he escaped.

Shulgin and Guchkov hurtled by car across the city to 12 Millionnaya, the sumptuous apartments of the Grand Duke's wife Princess Putiatina. There, at 9:15 a.m., Nicholas's brother met with the exhausted members of the Provisional Government and Duma Committee that had shaped it.

By now, it was only Milyukov – invoking Greater Russia, courage, patriotism – who was still bent on retaining the monarchy. Given the insurrectionary mood in Petrograd, most others were opposed to the Grand Duke's accession: when Shulgin and Guchkov arrived, their station stories gave the naysayers more weight. If he were crowned, Kerensky told the Grand Duke, 'I cannot vouch for the life of Your Highness.'

That morning, as at Tsarsko Selo Alexandra in her nurse's uniform was informed of her husband's abdication, and, weeping, she prayed that the 'two snakes', 'the Duma and the revolution', would kill each other, her brother-in-law debated with the first snake over how best to defeat the second.

At about 1 p.m., after hours of discussion and a long moment of solitude, of private soul-searching, Michael returned to his unwelcome guests. He asked Rodzianko and Lvov, another Kadet, whether they could vouch for his safety if he became tsar.

They could not.

'Under these circumstances,' he said, 'I cannot assume the throne.'

Kerensky leapt out of his chair. 'Your Highness,' he burst out, 'you are a noble man!' The other participants sat numb.

It was lunchtime, and the Romanov dynasty was finished.

That morning, the press, including the new Soviet paper *Izvestia*, proclaimed the new Provisional Government, constituted on the basis of the eight points agreed between Soviet and Duma Committee. *Izvestia* called for its support 'in so far as the emerging government acts in the direction of realising [its] obligations'.

'In so far as': in Russian, *'postol'ku-poskol'ku'*. A formulation key to Dual Power, and to its contradictions.

★

> Here, in the smoke of the wretched devil's sabbath
> In the noisy reign of petty demons
> They said, 'There are no fairy tales on earth.'
> They said, 'The fairy tale has died.'
> Oh, don't believe it, don't believe the funeral march.

A burst of re-enchantment. On 4 March, to the transported delight of vast swathes of the populace, the press made public Nicholas's abdication and Michael's refusal of the throne. This was the day that *Delo naroda*, the SR newspaper, told its readers that they had been lied to, that not only were fairy stories real but that they were living through one.

Once upon a time, it continued, 'there lived a huge old dragon', which devoured the best and bravest citizens 'in the haze of madness and power'. But a valiant hero had appeared, a *collective* hero. 'My champion', wrote *Delo naroda*, 'is the people.'

> The hour has come for the beast's end,
> The old dragon will coil up and die.

It was a new, post-dragon world. There came a flurry of far-reaching reforms, unthinkable scant days before. The Provisional Government abolished the loathed police department. No more Pharaohs. It began to dismiss Russia's regional governors. Cautiously, it probed concessions to and accommodations with the empire's regions and minorities. Within days of the revolution, the Muslims in the Duma formed a group calling for a convention on 1 May, to discuss self-determination. On 4 March, in Kiev, Ukrainian revolutionaries, nationalists, social democrats and radicals formed the Ukrainian Central Rada, or council. On 6 March the Provisional Government restored partial self-rule to Finland, reinstating the Finnish constitution after thirteen years of direct rule, and announced that a forthcoming Constituent Assembly would finally decide relations – such deferral emerging as the favoured technique for evading political difficulties. On the 16th it granted independence to Poland – though Poland being occupied by enemy powers, this was a symbolic gesture.

In these early days, the Soviet socialists attempted oversight of the government. 'Members of the Provisional Government!' exhorted the Menshevik paper *Rabochaya gazeta*. 'The proletariat and the army await immediate orders from you concerning the consolidation of the Revolution and the democratisation of Russia.' The masses' role, then, was to offer the liberal not only support, but obedience – but not unconditional. 'Our support is contingent on *your* actions.' This was support of the government *postol'ku-poskol'ku*. In so far as. As if that aspiration could be coherent.

In this context, the Soviet's proclamation of 5 March was telling. This was softening of the contentious Order Number 1 that it had promised the Duma Committee: Order Number 2.

What Guchkov had wanted was an unequivocal assurance from the Soviet that Order Number 1 only applied to troops in the rear. In fact, Order Number 2 was ambiguous on that point. It did stipulate that even in Petrograd, army committees should not intervene in military affairs; soldiers were 'bound to submit to all orders of the military authorities that have reference to the military service'. But the Ispolkom still implied support for the election of officers.

The following day, it agreed to install its own commissars in all regiments, to complement the link between soldiers and Soviet, and to exercise oversight of the government's relations with the forces. But with such relations and its own enshrined in documents such as Order Number 2 – equivocal, evasive, attempting to straddle compromise and conviction – the parameters of the commissars' power would not always be clear.

Far-left opposition to the Provisional Government – on the basis of the class coalition of its make-up, its defencist continuation of the war – was not initially unanimous, even among the Bolsheviks. On 3 March, the party's Petersburg Committee adopted what leading activists would later term a 'semi-Menshevik' resolution: for a republic, but withholding opposition to the Provisional Government *postol'ku-poskol'ku* – so long as its policies were 'consistent with the interests … of the people'. Such conciliationism would soon face a severe shock.

Marooned in Zurich, Lenin was urgently amassing information about the homeland where he had spent only a few months in the last fifteen years. On 3 March, he laid out his political position to his fellow Bolshevik Alexandra Kollontai, a provocative and brilliant thinker on a range of issues, most notoriously on sexual morality, regarding which her attitudes scandalised even many of her comrades.

'The first stage of the revolution', Lenin wrote to her, 'will not be the last.' And to that prediction he added: 'Of course, we shall continue to oppose the defence of the fatherland.'

This was not a given: many on the left, including plenty of former 'defeatists', saw the inauguration of a socialist-overseen democratic government as fundamentally changing the nature of the war. They would no longer oppose the defence of Russia. For Lenin, by contrast, revolutionary defeatism was constitutive of his anti-imperialism. And since Russia, he held, was still imperialist, its new government could not alter his opposition to its war. His ideas were hard but not unique in the party: it was in a similar vein, on the 7th, that the Russian Bureau of the CC – on the party's left – stated its own continuing defeatism, on grounds that 'the war is an imperialist one and remains so'. On 4 March, Lenin started to publicise his views in several theses co-written with Zinoviev, a member of the Bolsheviks since the 1903 split – an 'Old Bolshevik', as such activists were called – and one of Lenin's closest collaborators.

Lenin was desperate to return home, though he could not be sure of his reception there. He concocted madcap schemes to get through the war zone, to pass through Sweden to Russia; secret aeroplane flights; carrying a false passport, posing as a deaf mute, to avoid the dangers of speaking. As he schemed, he sharpened his political positions.

On 6 March, he cabled the CC in Petrograd: 'Our tactics: complete mistrust, no support for the new government. We especially suspect Kerensky' – who was, by freakish coincidence, the son of Lenin's old headmaster. 'The arming of the proletariat provides the only guarantee. Immediate elections to the Petrograd [Municipal] Duma. *No rapprochement with the other parties.*'

Between the 7th and the 12th, starting a week after the tsar's abdication, Lenin expounded his positions in a series of documents that would become known as the 'Letters from Afar'. These circulated in Switzerland, but what he most wanted was to disseminate them in Russia, among his Petrograd comrades, in their newly revived journal *Pravda*.

In Oslo, his comrade Kollontai was eager for word from him. 'We must get direction to the party in our spirit,' she wrote in her diary, 'we must immediately draw a sharp line between us and the Provisional Government along with the defencists ... I am waiting for directives from Vladimir Ilyich.' As soon as he had finished the first of his 'Letters from Afar' laying out his intransigent perspective, Vladimir Ilyich – Lenin – sent it to her. It arrived on the 15th, and

Kollontai, 'thrilled', she cabled him to say, 'by his ideas', set out on the long journey through Sweden, Finland, and on to Russia.

Lenin was not the only émigré anxious to return. Martov, then based in Paris, had come up with a scheme somewhat less eccentric than any of Lenin's, though in certain ways even more fraught. Through Swiss intermediaries, Martov suggested that exiled Russians ask the German government for safe passage across its territory, in exchange for the release of German and Austrian internees in Russia. This proposal was for what would soon become legendary as the 'sealed train'.

From Mogilev, Nicholas issued requests with stiff dignity. He asked the Provisional Government for permission to join his family at Tsarskoe Selo until his children were well, then to leave the country. Prime Minister Lvov sounded out the British about providing asylum.

But the Soviet and the people wanted the Romanovs brought to justice. The Provisional Government capitulated to this popular fury. At 3 p.m. on 8 March, four government representatives arrived at Mogilev station, to be greeted by a large and enthusiastic crowd, while Nicholas waited in his imperial train. He surrendered to the newcomers without resistance. 'Looking ashen,' one observer wrote, 'the tsar saluted, fingered his moustache as was his habit, and returned to his train to be taken by escort to Tsarskoe Selo where his wife was already under arrest. His entourage stood in silence on the platform as the train pulled out of the station.'

Some of the many onlookers saluted these new commissars of the revolutionary government. Others stared, pining, at the dethroned ruler.

Modernity was insurgent. The old machinery had stalled. The Provisional Government would impound the imperial train at Peterhof, for its finery to moulder on the sidings. It was soon to be overlooked by a new sculpture, an extravagantly expiring double-headed imperial eagle, its two necks craned, suspended, above a supremacist blast. Autocracy thrown down by a poised modernist explosion.

On 9 March, the United States became the first power to bestow the benediction of recognition on the Provisional Government. Britain, France and Italy soon followed. Such validation overstated certain realities. On the very day of the US recognition, Guchkov shared his frustration with Alexeev, who was now the reluctant commander-in-chief, complaining bitterly that 'the Provisional Government possesses no real power and its orders are executed only in so far as this is permitted by the Soviet ... which holds in its hands the most important elements of actual power, such as troops, railway and postal and telegraph service'.

The Soviet itself remained ambivalent about the power it held. Such uncertainty notwithstanding, the revolution, and the soviet form, spread in patchwork but accelerating fashion. On 3 March, one sixty-four-year-old resident of Poltava, Ukraine, recorded in his diary that 'people arriving from Petrograd and Kharkov reported that on 1 March there was revolution ... For us in Poltava it's quiet'. Less than a week later, his tone had changed: 'Events have been racing with such swiftness that there's no time to discuss or even simply write them down.'

The Moscow Soviet gathered as early as 1 March, more than 600 deputies, overwhelmingly working-class in composition, under a bloated seventy-five-person executive committee in which the Bolsheviks were a substantial left wing, and a seven-person presidium. In more inaccessible areas of the empire, the news, and new institutions, might take a long time to arrive. In remoter parts of the Volga countryside, it was only in the second half of March that rumours from telegraphs and conversations began to make real headway. Small communities dispatched messengers to travel to nearby towns to clarify details of the upheaval of which they were hearing. Villagers gathered into assemblies to begin, for the first time, considering not only local issues, but also national ones: the war, the Church, the economy. Ad hoc local committees sprang up in dizzying variety. A chaos of decentralisation. Some villages, towns and territories unconvincingly announced their independence. Very soon, countless soviets existed in the country, and their numbers were growing, but talk of 'the Soviet' usually designated the originatory, Petrograd Soviet.

The realities of the local soviets and of 'Dual Power' did not always obey the moderates' blueprints. In Izhevsk, in the Udmurt Republic, shop stewards set up a powerful soviet on 7 March, which quickly came to dominate local politics. In the provincial capital of Saratov, 60 per cent of the city's industrial workers elected deputies to their own hastily arranged soviet, which, by the end of the month, hammered out an ad hoc arrangement with the local Duma – which soon, however, faded into insignificance and stopped meeting. Dual, here, gave way to single power – that of the (moderate) soviet.

Sometimes political confrontation was obviated in a short-lived post-revolutionary burst of class camaraderie – what the journalist and historian William Chamberlin, soon to arrive in Russia, would call 'an orgy of sentimental speechmaking and fraternisation'. On 10 March, in Petrograd, the Soviet agreed with the factory owners that long-demanded eight-hour day, as well as the principle of worker-elected factory committees and a system of industrial arbitration. Such agreements were as much expressions of bosses' anxiety and workers' confidence as of consensus, of course: in many places, people were simply refusing to work longer than eight hours anyway, and were policing their new authority with direct action. Unpopular foremen were shoved in wheelbarrows and tipped into nearby canals. When the Moscow bosses resisted the eight-hour day, on 18 March the Moscow Soviet, recognising what workers were instituting as a fait accompli, simply decreed it, bypassing the Provisional Government. And their decree stood.

In Latvia, both radicalism and conciliation were visible: by 7 March the Riga Soviet comprised 150 delegates from thirty organisations, and the executive committee it voted in on 20 March consisted (temporarily) entirely of Bolsheviks. Their local line, though, was not yet as militant as that of their émigré Latvian Bolshevik comrades in Moscow. The Riga Bolshevik Committee – to their Moscow comrades' appalled shock – stated on 10 March that it 'fully submits to all decisions of the new government' reached in agreement with soviets, and that any 'attempts to create chaos' were the work of saboteurs.

On 6 March demonstrations in favour of the revolution shook Baku, Azerbaijan, the oil-rich city of Azeris, immigrant Russians, Persians, Armenians and others, a patchwork of medieval and modern edifices, watched over by the steep ziggurats of oil derricks. Fifty-two delegates met for the first session of the Baku Soviet. It was opened by the Menshevik Grigori Aiollo, and voted in as its chair Stepan Shaumian, a Bolshevik popular for his role in the legendary 1914 oil strike. But the Baku Soviet, too, was enthusiastic for social peace, and cooperated with the IKOO (Executive Committee of Public Organisations), the new self-appointed local administration born of the city government.

Such collaboration, as well as that between Mensheviks and Bolsheviks in many regions, or simply a certain indifference to the split, would not last. There were already exceptions. The sailors in Kronstadt, for example, disproportionately literate and deeply politicised, tended to join the most radical groups, and taking the most radical positions. The Kronstadt Soviet was controlled by Bolshevik hardliners, anarchists and anti-war Left SRs, already a distinct group.

The organisational infrastructure of the SRs as a whole accelerated, its newspapers, clubs, agitational schools and meetings and committees proliferating. It recruited so fast, by so many thousands, among workers and intelligentsia as well as the peasants and soldiers – 'peasants in uniform' – on whom the party traditionally particularly focused, that among some long-time activists 'March SR' became a snide shorthand for undependable political newcomers.

Traditional peasant uprisings were never far from the surface in these turbulent days. As early as 9 March, agrarian disorder rocked

Kazan Province. On the 17th, the Provisional Government insisted, rather nervously, that 'the land question cannot be solved by means of any kind of seizure'. That would not be its last such appeal. Eventually, on 25 March, it had to respond to inchoate upheaval on the land by proclaiming a state monopoly of grain, buying up all that was not needed for subsistence, animals or seed at fixed prices.

This could only ever be a stopgap. The land question remained unsolved.

'Democracy' was a sociological term in Russia in 1917, denoting the masses, the lower classes, at least as strongly as it did a political method. For many in those heady moments, Kerensky exemplified 'the democracy'. He was adored. Artists painted him, badges and medals celebrated him, poets immortalised him, in a torrent of kitsch.

'You personify the ideal of the free citizen, which the human soul has cherished throughout the ages,' the collective of the Moscow Arts Theatre told him. The celebrated writer Alexander Kuprin called him 'an inscrutable and divine spiritual receiver, a divine resonator, a mysterious mouthpiece for the people's will'.

'For us Kerensky is not a minister,' read one pamphlet, 'neither is he an orator for the people; he has ceased to be a simple human being. Kerensky is a symbol of revolution.' According to the cultish logic of the histrionic dialecticians, Kerensky's status as 'minister-cum-democrat', straddling government and Soviet, was more than mere addition, more even than synthesis. It was apotheosis.

Under Lvov, with pressure from the Soviet, the Provisional Government pursued social measures apace. On 12 March, it abolished the death penalty. The following day, it got rid of courts martial, except at the front. On 20 March, it eradicated legal discrimination on grounds of faith or nationality.

'A miracle has happened,' wrote the poet Alexander Blok. 'Nothing is forbidden ... almost anything might happen.' Every streetcar, every queue, every village meeting hosted political debate. There was a proliferation of chaotic new festivals, re-enactments of the February events. Tsarist statues were torn down, some having been put up for the purpose.

A 'Liberty Parade' in Moscow saw hundreds of thousands of marchers of all classes pray and party behind their banners. There was a circus, a camel and an elephant plastered with placards, a wagon bearing a black coffin labelled 'The Old Order', a leering dwarf labelled Protopopov, for the hated ex-minister. People read new books, sang various new versions of the Marseillaise and watched new plays – often lewd, crude retellings of the Romanovs' overthrow. Irreverence as revenge.

Gone was the obsequiousness of 1905. Citizens across the empire waged what Richard Stites called a 'war on signs', the destruction of tsarist symbols: portraits, statues, eagles. Revolutionary fever infected unlikely patients. Orthodox nuns and monks adopted radical talk, ousting 'reactionary' superiors. High-rankers in the Church complained of a revolutionary mood. The main religious newspaper took an 'anti-ecclesiastical' line so radical that one archi-mandrite, or high-ranking abbot, Tikhon, called it a 'Bolshevik mouthpiece'. At one monastery there was 'a little revolution', wrote the British journalist Morgan Philips Price, where 'monks had gone on strike and had turned out the abbot, who had gone off whining to the Holy Synod … They had already entered into an arrangement with the local peasantry. They were to keep enough land for them-selves to work, and the rest was to go into the local commune.'

Demonstrations voiced existential demands, even at the expense of income. 'No tips taken here', said the signs on restaurant walls. Petrograd waiters struck for dignity. They marched in their best clothes under banners denouncing the 'indignity' of tipping, the stench of *noblesse oblige*. They demanded 'respect for waiters as human beings'.

The government had equivocated over the issue of women's suffrage. Many even in the revolutionary movement were hesitant, warning that, though they supported the equality of women 'in principle', concretely Russia's women were politically 'backward', and their votes therefore risked hindering progress. On her return to the country on the 18th, Kollontai took those prejudices head-on.

'But wasn't it we women, with our grumbling about hunger, about the disorganisation in Russian life, about our poverty and the sufferings born of the war, who awakened a popular wrath?' she demanded. The revolution, she pointed out, was born on International Women's Day, 'And didn't we women go first out to the streets in order to struggle with our brothers for freedom, and even if necessary to die for it?'

On 19 March, a major procession descended on the Tauride Palace demanding women's right to vote – 40,000 demonstrators, mostly women, but including many men. 'If the woman is a slave', banners read, 'there will be no freedom.' Pro-war banners swayed above the marchers, too. This was a cross-class, broad-spectrum feminism, working women side by side with women in fine clothes; liberals and SRs and Mensheviks and Bolsheviks – though the latter, to Kollontai's disappointment, had not prioritised the march. The weather was dreadful, but the marchers were not put off. They came to fill the long street before the palace. There Chkheidze tried to claim that he could not come out to meet them because he had lost his voice.

They would not have it. He for the Soviet and Rodzianko for the Provisional Government had to bow to the movement. They launched a bill for universal women's suffrage, to be passed in July.

It was to the Soviet that the women marched – even those whose placards supported the war. The Soviet in which so many had vested their aspirations, despite its own ambivalence about power.

It strove to rationalise its structures, without much success. At its largest, that month, it had 3,000 boisterous members – a tiny number from the left (forty Bolsheviks, for example). Every thousand workers voted for a delegate – and every company of soldiers, initially large reserve companies, but quickly extending to those much smaller, skewing the representation heavily in the soldiers' favour. Ultimately 150,000 troops would have double the representation of

450,000 Petrograd workers. The soldiers' delegates were predominantly SR followers and, though often radical on the war, tended to be much less so on other issues than their proletarian counterparts.

One typical March day, the Petrograd general assembly discussed the following topics: a tsarist police plot against a union of Social Democrats; an anti-pogrom commission for the southern provinces; a call on Petrograd bakers not to interrupt work; a dispute over office space between two newspapers; taking over the Anichkov Palace; and posters explaining decisions of the central food committee. Then came some (intriguingly unspecified) negotiations with the Provisional Government; the idea of a soldiers' newspaper; an obscure point about the Fortress of Peter and Paul; a quarrel between workers and soldiers over bread distribution; the reception of delegations, plus wives, from the various garrisons; and the American Embassy. The list is not exhaustive.

Such enthusiastic bedlam might seem a nightmare, or a strange, faltering carnival, depending on one's perspective.

The Kadets, Mensheviks, SRs, and Bolsheviks all understood the key importance of the Petrograd garrison, and all created military organisations to promote their influence within it. What set the Bolsheviks apart was how early they did so – from 10 March – and with what intensity. The activists running the committee, Nevsky, Bogdatiev, Podvoisky and Sulimov, were all but the last from the party's left wing.

In these early days, they were not especially welcome among the soldiers. But they were tenacious. Less than two weeks after they started operations, Podvoisky and his comrades invited garrison representatives to a Military Organisation Constituent Assembly, out of which, on the last day of the month, the Bolshevik Military Organisation (MO) was born.

Almost immediately after the February revolution, one comrade had heard Podvoisky announce that 'the revolution is not over; it is just beginning'. The MO was in the hands of such independent-spirited, uncompromising Bolshevik 'lefts' from the start. More than once they would breach party discipline – sometimes with dramatic results.

There came, first, a boost to a more moderate party consensus on 12 March. That day saw the burial of perhaps 184 martyrs of the revolution – the numbers are uncertain – killed in the city's street fighting. These were mass graves. Long deep trenches in the hard earth of the Mars Field, the great park in the centre of Petrograd.

From early morning until long into the night came hundreds of thousands of mourners. Perhaps as many as a million filled the wide streets of the capital. From every part of the city, they converged slowly on the field, carrying their dead in red coffins. A new, religionless religion. They came with sad music. They came representing their units, their factories, their institutions, their civic groups, their parties. They came in ethnic groups – columns from the Jewish Bund, from the Armenian revolutionary Dashnaktsutyun, and others. A column of the blind came, carrying one of their own. They did not stop. No group stopped, no one made a speech. The marchers came carrying their cold comrades, solemnly passed their coffins to the burial workers and marched on, and a gun boomed in salute from the fortress across the river as the fallen were lowered. The living trudged through light snow, on wooden walkways erected between the maze of graves. Their dead were not victims, Lunacharsky's eulogies would claim, but heroes, whose fate engendered not grief but envy.

And as the mass of citizens sang and remembered the lost, three veteran party activists returned to the city from exile in Siberia. One was the Old Bolshevik Lev Kamenev, married to Trotsky's sister Olga Bronstein and a close comrade of Lenin, though always a party 'wet' (he had, in an almost incredible act he later shamefacedly denied, advocated sending a telegram to Michael Romanov praising his decision to decline the throne). With him were the erstwhile Duma deputy Muranov, renowned for having taken a hard defeatist line in defiance of the death penalty; and a member of the CC, one Joseph Stalin.

★

Stalin, of course, was not yet *Stalin*. Today, any account of the revolution is haunted by a ghost from the future, that twinkly-eyed, moustachioed monstrosity, Uncle Joe, the butcher, key architect of a grotesque and crushing despotic state – the -ism that bears his name. There have been decades of debate about the aetiology of Stalinism, volumes of stories about the man's brutality and that of his regime. They cast shadows backwards from what would come.

But this was 1917. Stalin had not turned forty. He was, then, just Stalin, Ioseb Jughashvili, known to his comrades as Koba, a Georgian ex-trainee priest and meteorological clerk, and a long-time Bolshevik activist. A capable, if never scintillating, organiser. At best an adequate intellectual, at worst an embarrassing one. He was neither a party left nor a party right per se, but something of a weathervane. The impression he left was one of not leaving much of an impression. Sukhanov would remember him as 'a grey blur'.

There is a rare hint at something more troubling about the man in the assessment of the party's Russian Bureau in Petrograd, which allowed him to join, but only as advisor, without the right to a vote – because, it said, of 'certain personal features that are inherent in him'. Would that the rest of Sukhanov's description had been accurate: that Stalin had remained no more than glimpsed, 'looming up now and then dimly and without leaving any trace'.

Almost immediately, the three returnees carried out something of a coup at *Pravda*, installing Muranov as editor on 13 March. The paper began to expound their decidedly moderate positions.

On 15 March, Kamenev wrote:

Our slogan is not the empty cry 'Down with war! – which means the disorganisation of the revolutionary army and of the army that is becoming ever more revolutionary. Our slogan is bring pressure to bear on the Provisional Government so as to compel it to make, without fail, openly and before the eyes of world democracy, an attempt to induce all the warring countries to initiate immediate negotiations to end the world war. Till then let everyone remain at his post.

The army, he further insisted, 'will remain staunchly at its post, answering bullet with bullet and shell with shell'.

Thus, as the Bolshevik Ludmila Stahl put it, the party 'groped in the darkness' – for with this line, *Pravda* differed not so much from the lefter Mensheviks or radical Left SRs. Setting themselves against agitation at the front, the troika were some way from Lenin.

Immediately on her arrival in Petrograd Kollontai delivered Lenin's 'Letters from Afar' to *Pravda*. The documents horrified and stunned his nervous comrades with their intransigence. The editors balked at publishing any but the first letter, and that, wrong-footed by its hard-left formulations, they assiduously bowdlerised, cutting it substantially.

The foregoing is a famous story of how Lenin's shocking letters stung the Old Bolsheviks. And a story is what it is.

In fact, *Pravda* published only the first letter because this was, almost certainly, the only one it received. And although it is true that it was heavily edited, those interventions did little to blunt Lenin's thesis or his provocative thrust. His argument that the revolution must continue remained clear, as did his exhortation to workers: 'you must perform miracles of proletarian and popular organisation to prepare for your victory in the second stage of the revolution' – a stage not of socialism, he would soon clarify, but of taking political power, of winning over the Soviet, to ensure the victory of the (necessarily bourgeois, democratic) revolution. At best, Lenin rather nebulously allowed (with an eye on the international context, where for him a revolution against and beyond capitalism *could* occur, inspired perhaps by Russian events), that might allow them to take faltering, initial steps towards socialism.

The Bolsheviks in Petrograd expressed enthusiasm for the letter. Lenin's sister Maria Ulianov, a party comrade who worked on *Pravda*, contacted him to express the 'full solidarity' of his comrades, as did the gratified Kollontai. The edits that the Bolsheviks performed on a piece written days previously, and a long way away, served to remove outdated references to a possible return of Tsarism and unconvincing insinuations of an anti-Nicholas plot among the allies, while correcting certain infelicities of language.

They also mitigated Lenin's typically splenetic denunciation of various enemies, including among liberals, the right, and non-Bolshevik socialists. The editors were judicious enough to delete insults directed at the Soviet Executive Committee's chair Chkheidze, at Kerensky, and even at the moderate liberal Lvov, head of the Provisional Government: they had reason to believe, after all, that they would need their help bringing the Bolshevik exiles – Lenin included – back into the country. They did not censor his attacks on Kadets and right Mensheviks who could not be of use to them. Not so much soft, then, as strategic.

The later myth of the bombshell 'Letters from Afar' seems to have been born out of a combination of misunderstanding of the *Pravda* edits and rather tendentious retellings – by Trotsky, among others – in the context of in-party jostling for position.

Yet while this particular conflict was largely a retrospective fiction, it undeniably gained in plausibility due to the way Lenin's formulations, including in his intemperate polemics, evinced an uncompromising tendency, a distinguishing political logic that would, in fact, be key to other real disputes within the party. Not ineluctible by any means, but chafing against Bolshevik moderation and coalition. The 'Letters from Afar' were thus 'continuity' Bolshevism, and yet contained seeds of a distinct and more trenchant position. One that would become clearer with Lenin's return.

On 15 March, the Soviet paper *Izvestia* printed the Declaration of the Rights of Soldiers, which had recently passed in the Soldiers' section of the Soviet. It declared the end of the hated and degrading system of tsarist military peonage. There would be no more compulsory saluting, censorship of letters, officers' right to impose disciplinary punishments. The declaration also gave soldiers the right to elect representative committees. To traditionalists, what this meant was the destruction of the Russian army.

Questions of armed power, of the soldiery, of policing, and thus of the new motley militias, were clearly central to the establishment and stabilisation of power – though this significance seemed to escape the SRs, whose paper *Delo naroda* featured next to no discussion of the issue. For their part, the Kadets stressed the necessity of setting up a City Militia for policing purposes – and, urgently, to replace the volunteer forces. At the same time, some among the radicals were beginning a careful consideration of the role of those armed workers' militias that had been so central in February, and of their relation to the soldiers themselves.

As early as 8 March, the Menshevik paper *Rabochaya gazeta* argued that while a trustworthy and preferably elected citizens' police force was a pressing need, a militia in the sense of 'the *armed people*' to defend the revolution was both impossible and unnecessary, given the existence of the revolutionary army. In their writings, the Bolsheviks opined that the nascent City Militia was unsatisfactory and the continued existence of the revolutionary army could not be taken for granted, and hence – marking a recurrent distinction between their position and that of other socialists – stressed the centrality of self-organisation. On 18 March, the Bolshevik intellectual Vladimir Bonch-Bruevich published 'The Armed People' in *Pravda*, in which he called for a permanent, disciplined, democratic militia of the working class, trained by the revolutionary soldiers. Such a group, in exhortation, he named 'a Red Guard of the Proletariat'. This name, this concept, this controversial body, would soon crop up again.

Order Number 2 notwithstanding, neither Order Number 1 nor the soldiers' declaration reduced suspicion between the ranks. As one young captain lamented in a letter home: 'Between us and the soldiers there is an abyss.' And now the abyss was dangerous. He sensed in the men a new attitude of recalcitrance and overt resentment, 'revenge for centuries of servitude', which sometimes manifested in the murder of unpopular officers at the front.

Certainly some activists attempted systematic politicisation in the army, but most of what came to be called 'trench Bolshevism' was simply a disgust at the soldier's lot, a loathing of officers, and a reasonable desire not to fight and die in a hated war. After February, rates of desertion spiked. Armed men simply walked out of the trenches laden with whatever equipment they did not discard, trudging back to the towns and cities, back to the country, the mud of the fields.

In the growing anti-war mood, despite fervent attempts by the patriotic to stoke bellicose nationalism, such desertion was not always felt as shameful. 'The streets are full of soldiers,' complained one official of the town of Perm, near the Ural Mountains, in mid-March. 'They harass respectable ladies, ride around with prostitutes, and behave in public like hooligans. They know that no one dares to punish them.'

On the 17th, Lenin declared Martov's plan to be his 'only hope' for getting out of Switzerland, a place he roundly cursed. He was well aware that by travelling with German help, he risked being accused of treason – as, in due course, he was. For the Provisional Government, Milyukov declared that anyone who entered the country in such fashion would be subject to legal action. Regardless, 'even through hell', he said, Lenin was determined to go.

With the intermediation of the Swiss Socialist Party, he tried to minimise the dangers of perceived fraternisation with German authorities, insisting that there would be no passport controls on the journey, no stops or investigations along the way, and that the Germans would have no right to enquire as to the passengers' details. The 'sealed train' would not technically be sealed: much stranger, it would be an extraterritorial entity, a rolling-stock legal nullity.

On 21 March, the German Embassy accepted his terms. Courtesy of the Reich, Lenin and several other revolutionaries were headed home.

★

Given its incoherent organisation, the range of its activities and its own unease about its authority, it might seem astonishing that the Petrograd Soviet had any sway at all. But the chagrin of the Provisional Government about the rival power was warranted: the Soviet's announcements could directly impact government policies, most notably with respect to the war itself.

As early as 14 March, the Soviet issued a manifesto written with the help of the celebrated writer and leftist Maxim Gorky. This called for a just peace, and for 'the peoples of the world' 'to take into their own hands the question of war and peace', and to 'oppose the acquisitive policy of the ruling classes'.

The international reception of such outreach was precisely nil. Within Russia, however, the manifesto had a propagandistic impact in its refusal of annexations or indemnities, which seemed a step towards peace; a series of military congresses endorsed it, soldiers declaring for the Soviet. A week later, the Soviet officially adopted this 'Revolutionary Defencism' as its position.

Such a call for peace while maintaining revolutionary Russia's right to defend itself contained a certain ambiguity, leaving the door open to a continuing, even intensifying, war effort. Still, the Soviet declaration was anathema to right-wing liberals like Milyukov, now foreign minister, both on patriotic principle and because he believed the autocracy's overthrow had revitalised Russia and its military power. The country could now fight effectively, he thought, if only it was allowed to.

On 23 March, during a press interview, Milyukov pointedly mentioned that he looked to a peace conference to verify Russia's claims over the Ukrainian parts of the Austro-Hungarian Empire, and that he expected, in fulfilment of a long-held Russian expansionist dream, to gain Constantinople and the Dardanelles Straits. His absurd claims of 'pacifist aims' notwithstanding, this was a major provocation, and the Soviet was duly provoked. In response to the Soviet's outrage, on 27 March the Provisional Government was forced to publish a statement of war aims very close to the Soviet's own, invoking the 'self-determination of nations' and implicitly voiding the claims to Turkish and Austrian territories. But the incorrigibly off-message Milyukov openly told the *Manchester Guardian* that this did nothing to alter Russia's – hardly very 'revolutionary' – commitments to its allies. The Soviet reacted with more fury. Its leaders – particularly Viktor Chernov, head and chief intellectual of the SRs, soon to return to Petrograd – insisted that the government's 27 March declaration, which struck a very different tone to the foreign minister's, be forwarded to the allies as a 'diplomatic note'. Urged by Kerensky, a harsh rival to Milyukov, the Provisional Government felt constrained to comply. Further confrontation on this issue was not avoided, however: only postponed.

The same day as the government's statement, a motley mix of revolutionaries met at the Zurich station. They boarded a train, checked their baggage and stowed their food. The travellers were six members of the Bund, three followers of Trotsky and nineteen Bolsheviks. A gathering of revolutionary heavyweights, including Lenin and Krupskaya; Zinoviev, the intelligent, hard-working, tousled-haired man viewed as Lenin's henchman; Zlata Lilina, Bolshevik activist and the mother of Zinoviev's young son Stefan; and the remarkable, controversial Polish revolutionary Karl Radek. Here too was Inessa Armand, the French-Russian communist, feminist, writer and musician, Lenin's close collaborator and comrade, with whom, rumours have long suggested, his relationship was at various points more than platonic.

At the Swiss border, the exiles transferred to a two-coach special: one carriage for the Russians, one for their German escorts. The journey across Germany began. Lenin spent hours writing and making plans, breaking off late at night to complain to his boisterous comrades about their noise. To disperse the loud crowd outside the toilet, he instituted a system of slips for its use, either for its intended function or to have a smoke, in the proportions, he decided, three to one. 'This', Karl Radek remembered drily, 'naturally evoked further discussions about the value of human needs.'

Far from being 'sealed', every time the train stopped, the German authorities had their hands full keeping local Social Democrats from trying to meet and socialise with the famous (and unwilling) Lenin. He asked his comrades to tell one persistent trade unionist to go to 'the devil's grandmother'.

As the train crawled on, in Russia, Kamenev and Stalin consolidated their position at an all-Russian conference of party workers. There was, however, resistance to what some comrades saw as their conditional support for the government, and still more to what was, essentially, revolutionary defencism. The Muscovite Old Bolshevik Viktor Nogin, later a party moderate, now argued that 'we ought not now to talk about support but *resistance*'; Skrypnyk agreed that 'the government is not fortifying, but checking the cause of the revolution'. But the powerful and respected party right, particularly Stalin, went so far in the direction of moderation as to support a merger of Bolsheviks and Mensheviks – the proposal of Irakli Tsereteli, the outstanding Menshevik intellect and orator, recently returned from Siberian exile and now in charge of the Petrograd Soviet.

Immediately on arriving in the city on the 21st, Tsereteli gave a speech that was admirably clear with a right-Menshevik analysis of history and the party leadership's position on the Soviet's relationship to the government. It also sounded a warning about his attitude to excessive radicalism. He congratulated the workers for not attempting proletarian revolution – he considered this an achievement *as great* as overthrowing tsarism: 'you weighed the circumstances ... you understood that the time has not yet come'.

'You understood that a bourgeois revolution is taking place,' he continued. 'The power is in the hands of the bourgeoisie. You transferred this power to the bourgeoisie, but at the same time you have stood guard over the newly gained freedom ... The Provisional Government must have full executive power in so far as this power strengthens the Revolution.'

The Mensheviks commanded the respect and affiliaton of many

activists, and Tsereteli, Chkheidze, Skobolev and the top brass did not by any means speak for them all. Within two weeks, insinuations of their move towards conciliationism, 'defencism' and political moderation would leave Martov, the great left Menshevik, still in exile, 'plagued by doubts' and hoping that the rumours were 'questionable'.

Within Petrograd, however, it was Tsereteli's proposal of unity that the Bolsheviks considered.

The day after the party workers' conference opened in Petrograd, so did an All-Russian Conference of Soviets, bearing impressive witness to the spread of the soviet form: 479 delegates from 138 local soviets, seven armies, thirteen rear units and twenty-six front units were represented.

Nomenclature was tangled: Russia that year was riddled with committees, caucuses, congresses, permanent and semi-permanent, standing and not-standing. Meetings proliferated ad well-minuted infinitum. This first conference of soviets was intended in part to plan the first *congress* of soviets, to take place in June. The Petrograd Soviet, now with delegates countrywide, technically became the All-Russian Soviet of Workers' and Soldiers' Deputies. After the conference, the growing Ispolkom, the Soviet Executive Committee responsible for day-to-day decisions and administration, now including representatives from the provinces, was formally renamed the All-Russian Central Executive Committee, or VTsIK. Any and all of these names might be used.

For the Mensheviks, it was at the soviet conference that Tsereteli made his mark, coordinating discussions, instilling a new professionalism, solidifying the positions of *postol'ku-poskol'ku* and a muscular revolutionary defencism. Until the peoples of other countries, he declared, overthrew their own governments or compelled them to change tack, 'the Russian Revolution should fight against the foreign enemy with the same courage which it showed against the internal forces'. For the Bolsheviks, Kamenev instead put forward a version of the party's internationalist insistence not on defence of the nation, but on the necessary export of the revolution, transforming the Russian experience into 'a prologue for the uprising of the peoples of all the warring countries'.

His position was an affair of nuance and aspiration rather than an expression of any stark, concretely distinct policy. Even so, it was defeated by 57 votes to Tsereteli's 325. Nevertheless, while Bolshevik powerbrokers tacked right, some other socialists in the Soviet tacked left, enabling both camps to meet in the middle. On relations between the Soviet and the Provisional Government, the official Soviet position, moved by the Menshevik Steklov, insisted so sternly on vigilant oversight that a satisfied Kamenev withdrew the alternative Bolshevik resolution.

Such convergence had only a very few days left to run.

On 29 March, the 'sealed train' arrived in Berlin via Stuttgart and Frankfurt. From there it headed coastward. All the way through Germany, Lenin wrote. Secluded in his cabin, fortified by refreshments from the unlikely restaurant car, he scribbled on as trees and towns rushed past. Thus, in March, in a stateless train, were born what would become known as the April Theses.

By the wild shores of Germany's Jasmund peninsula, at the town of Sassnitz, a Swedish steamer awaited the travellers. It was dusk when they stumbled down the swaying gangplank into Sweden's southernmost town of Trelleborg. Their journey had become news, and journalists trailed them. The mayor of Stockholm welcomed the party before it continued on to the Swedish capital, where Lenin went shopping for books, scorning his comrades' pleas that he buy new clothes, and found time to attend a meeting of Russian leftists.

On the last day of the first full month of revolutionary Russia, the comrades climbed into traditional Finnish sleighs, and slipped across the crisp snow out of Stockholm towards Finland – Russian territory.

4

April: The Prodigal

In the muck, ideologues and true believers like the murderous Black Hundreds – ultra-monarchist pogrom enthusiasts, proto-fascists and mystics of hate – skulked and schemed behind closed doors, biding their time. The early days of the revolution were remarkable for how submerged and scattered that hard right was. Most of its high-profile figures had left the country or been arrested after February. Only the erratic Purishkevich remained at large, more or less powerless, tolerated and toothless. The political integument of Petrograd in particular had lurched leftward, repositioning radicals as moderates and moderates as right-wingers. In those days everyone was, or claimed to be, a socialist. No one wanted to be bourgeois.

Until the eve of revolution, the Kadets were a party of occasionally even bracing liberalism, harried by reaction, not without heroes. They entered April 1917 fresh from their congress, committed to a democratic republic. But now, history – revolution – made them conservatives. On the party's right, Milyukov was an early outlier of this trend, a function of the strong tactics of weak liberalism in fractious times.

For now, though, as April began, not even the far left had unanimously declared itself an enemy of the Provisional Government. That was to come, with the train from Finland.

★

On 2 April, the Bolsheviks got word from Lenin that he would be back in Petrograd the next day. The leader was coming. They hastened to prepare. So it was that the following evening, at the little Belo Ostrov border station where Finland and Russia met, a small, select group of Bolsheviks awaited the train: Kollontai, Kamenev, Shlyapnikov, Lenin's sister Maria, a few others.

They were not the only ones who had heard that Lenin was returning. Some hundred eager workers were on the platform too, to greet the train that wheezed slowly in. As his comrades watched, while the engine idled for half an hour, those gathered mortified Lenin by calling him out of his carriage and parading him jubilantly on their shoulders. 'Gently, comrades,' he muttered. At last they let him go and he took his seat again with relief, joined now by his excited party escort.

They were in for a shock.

As best he could, Lenin had kept up with his comrades' writings on the war and the Provisional Government. 'We had hardly got into the car and sat down,' said Raskolnikov, a Kronstadt Bolshevik naval officer, 'when Vladimir Ilyich burst out at Kamenev: "What's this you're writing in *Pravda*? We saw several issues and really swore at you."' This was his greeting to an old comrade.

The revolutionaries rocked homeward through a darkening landscape. Was he at risk of arrest? Lenin asked uneasily. His welcome party smiled at that. He would soon understand why.

When the train pulled in to Petrograd at 11 p.m., the Finland Station echoed to a vast cheer of welcome. Lenin at last began to grasp his own standing in the revolutionary capital. His comrades had arranged a showcase of the party's strength, convoking friendly garrisons, but the excitement of the crowd clamouring for him was quite real. The station was festooned with vivid red banners. As he stepped, dazed, onto the platform, someone handed Lenin an incongruous bouquet. Thousands had come to salute him: workers, soldiers, Kronstadt sailors.

A throng of well-wishers propelled Lenin into the splendid chamber still called the 'Tsar's Room'. There, officials from the

Soviet waited for their own chance to greet him. The Soviet chairman, the Georgian Menshevik Chkheidze, a serious, honest activist, had lost his usual amiable veneer. When the Bolshevik leader entered, Chkheidze launched into a welcome speech that was neither welcoming nor a speech. Sukhanov, who was of course present, called it a 'sermon', and a 'glum' one.

'Comrade Lenin, in the name of the Petrograd Soviet and of the whole revolution we welcome you to Russia,' said Chkheidze. 'But we think', he continued anxiously, 'the principal task of the revolutionary democracy is the defence of the revolution against attacks from without or within. We consider this end to require not disunity, but the closing of democratic ranks. We hope you will pursue these objectives with us.'

The flowers dangled half-forgotten from Lenin's fingers. He ignored Chkheidze. He looked up at the ceiling. He looked everywhere but at the beseeching Menshevik.

When Lenin at last replied, it was not to the Soviet chair, nor to anyone from its delegation. He spoke instead to everyone else present, to the crowd – his 'dear comrades, soldiers, sailors and workers'. The imperialist war, he roared, was the start of European civil war. The longed-for international revolution was imminent. Provocatively, he praised by name his German comrade Karl Liebknecht. Ever the internationalist, he concluded with a stirring call to build from this first step: 'Long live the worldwide socialist revolution!'

His Soviet hosts were stunned. They could only watch numbly as the crowds demanded a further speech. Lenin hurried from the station, climbed onto the bonnet of a car and began to hold forth. He denounced 'any part in shameful imperialist slaughter'; he excoriated 'lies and frauds' and the 'capitalist pirates'.

So much for *postol'ku-poskol'ku*.

February and March were festive bursts of architectural expropriation. Revolutionary groups captured and occupied government buildings, along with various sumptuous others. The Provisional Government and the Soviet had little option but to tolerate such appropriations. On 27 February, as the city convulsed, the legendary ballerina Matilda Kshesinskaya and her son Vladimir had fled her modern mansion at 1–2 Kronverkskiy Prospect on the Neva's north side, below the towering minarets of Petrograd's main mosque: almost immediately, revolutionary soldiers had taken it over.

The house displayed a striking, strange asymmetry of interconnected structures, stairwells and halls. In mid-March the Bolsheviks had decided it would make an excellent headquarters, and had moved in without ado. On the night of 3 April, it was in its main meeting hall, amid precise art nouveau stylings, that Lenin made his views clear to the comrades who had gathered to welcome him home.

It had been the last day of the All-Russian Conference of Soviets. There, the Bolshevik caucus had unanimously approved their leadership's policy of 'vigilant control' over the Provisional Government, and had broadly accepted Stalin and Kamenev's opposition to 'disorganising activities' at the front. The next day, unity talks between the Mensheviks and Bolsheviks were due to start. Such was the mood music that Lenin interrupted.

'I will never forget', said Sukhanov, 'that thunder-like speech, which startled and amazed not only me, a heretic … but all the true believers … It seemed as though all the elements had risen from their abodes, and the spirits of universal destruction … were hovering around Kshesinskaya's reception room above the heads of the bewitched disciples.'

What Lenin demanded was continual revolution. He scorned talk of 'watchfulness'. He denounced the Soviet's 'revolutionary defencism' as an instrument of the bourgeoisie. He raged at the lack of Bolshevik 'discipline'.

His comrades listened in stricken silence.

The next day at the Tauride Palace, Lenin intervened again, twice. First at a session of Bolshevik delegates from the Soviet Congress;

then, with breathtaking audacity, at a Bolshevik–Menshevik meeting scheduled to discuss unity. Aware of his isolation, he made it clear that he was expounding personal opinion rather than party policy, as he presented his seminal document of the revolution: the April Theses.

Among its ten points was the wholesale rejection of 'limited support' for the Provisional Government and the 'no opposition' pledge of the Bolshevik Petersburg Committee. Lenin repudiated without 'the slightest concession … "revolutionary defencism"' – continuing to advocate fraternisation at the front. He demanded the confiscation of landlord estates and the nationalisation of land, to be disposed of by peasant soviets; a single national bank under the Soviet's control; and the abolition of the police, army and bureaucracy. For now, he said, the order of the day was to explain the imperative of a struggle to take power from the government, and to replace any parliamentary republic with a 'Republic of Soviets'.

His speech unleashed bedlam. The impact of the Theses was electric, and Lenin's isolation almost total. Speaker after outraged speaker denounced him. Tsereteli, the prominent Menshevik Lenin anathematised, accused him of breaking with Marx and Engels. Goldenberg, a Menshevik who had once been a leading Bolshevik, said Lenin was now an anarchist, 'on Bakunin's throne'. Lenin's words, yelled the furious Menshevik Bogdanov, were 'the ravings of a madman'.

Chernov, the SR leader, who reached Petrograd from exile five days after Lenin, after a dangerous sea journey through submarine-infested waters, saw Lenin's 'political excesses' as so complete that he had marginalised himself. The evening of the prodigal's shocking speech, another Menshevik, Skobelev, assured Milyukov that Lenin's 'lunatic ideas' disqualified him from being a danger, and told Prince Lvov that the Bolshevik leader was 'a has-been'.

And what of the Bolsheviks? How appalled were they?

It is often claimed that on 18 April the party's Petersburg Committee rejected the Theses by thirteen to two, with one abstention. The story, however, is based on inaccurate minutes. Two of those present, Bagdatev and Zalezhsky, later insisted that the committee voted to *approve* the Theses, but by thirteen to two rejected Zalezhsky's rather fawning motion that these be accepted without criticism or reservation. The Committee instead reserved the right to dissent on specifics and details.

And dissent they did. After Lenin's speech at the Kshesinskaya Mansion, his comrades were not backward in coming forward with concerns.

The wrangles were mostly over tactical issues, such as Lenin's suggestion that they change the name of the party, or his new political emphasis on the soviets rather than the more traditional propagandist stress on convening the Constituent Assembly. A particular point at issue was that Lenin adamantly opposed, almost as *distasteful*, making 'impermissible, illusion-breeding "demands"' on the Provisional Government, which would and could never accede to them. Instead he advocated 'patient explanation' in the soviets that the government could not be trusted. By contrast, Bagdatev, Kamenev and various others saw such 'demands' as a proven method of *puncturing* illusions, precisely because the government would fail to meet them. Kamenev called this 'a method of exposure'.

A continuity, then, between 'Old Bolshevism' and Lenin's theses could certainly be argued, as it was by many activists, such as Ludmila Stahl. But a permeable membrane exists between tactics and analysis – and emphasis. There was kinship, certainly, but the stress in the uncompromising theses was more than 'mere' rhetoric. It was no surprise that some in the party, both on Lenin's side and against, considered them a break with Bolshevik tradition. Such debates could simultaneously be misunderstandings of the depth of shared ground, *and* symptomatic of real divergence more substantial than that supposedly in the 'Letters from Afar'.

Bolshevik concerns at Lenin's tack were widespread. The Kiev and Saratov organisations rejected the Theses outright. Lenin had been out of Russia too long, their members said, to understand its situation. Zinoviev, his comrade-in-exile and close collaborator, called the Theses 'perplexing'; others in the party were not so kind.

At first the board of *Pravda* were hesitant to reproduce the Theses, but Lenin insisted, and they were published on 7 April – swiftly followed by Kamenev's 'Our Disagreements', distancing the Bolsheviks from Lenin's 'personal opinions'. 'Lenin's general scheme appears to us unacceptable,' he wrote, 'inasmuch as it proceeds from the assumption that the bourgeois–democratic revolution is *completed*, and builds on the immediate transformation of this revolution into a socialist revolution.'

The party, more than many on the left, had always focused on the agency of the working class in collaboration with the peasantry. The post-1905 'Old Bolshevik' hope for the revolution in Russia was steadily, if rather nebulously, pinned on that 'democratic dictatorship of proletariat and peasantry' destined to sweep away the muck of feudalism and oversee what could only be a move to a bourgeois–democratic system, including on the land. As late as 1914, Lenin was still writing that a Russian revolution would be limited to 'a democratic republic … confiscation of the landed estates, and an eight-hour working day'. Now, though, he was dismissing Kamenev's formula as 'obsolete', 'no good at all', 'dead'. In the April Theses Lenin wrote that Russia was, right now, 'passing from the first stage of the revolution … to its second stage, which must place power in the hands of the proletariat and the poorest sections of the peasants'.

This was a shift. As regards the 'second stage', Lenin was clear that it was not 'our *immediate* task to "introduce" socialism', prior to a European socialist revolution, but to place power in the hands of working people, rather than to pursue political class collaboration as advocated by the Mensheviks. 'Let the bourgeoisie continue to trade and build its mills and factories,' the Bolshevik activist Sapranov later glossed it to young Eduard Dune, 'but power must rest with the workers, not with the factory owners, traders, and their servants.' Still, there is not necessarily a neat firewall between 'trading and building' on the one hand and 'power' on the other, and there was in Lenin's position at least a tendential implication going further, an eye on a horizon. There is a political logic, after all, implicit in taking power. There was something pregnant even in Lenin's emphasis – it was not an *immediate* task to introduce socialism – but …

No wonder Lenin was accused by his own party of falling into Trotsky's heresy of 'permanent revolution', of folding February into, or at least edging determinedly towards, a full socialist insurrection.

But more Bolshevik exiles were returning. And they tended to be more radical than those who had remained. The economic hardships in the country were worsening, the inadequacies of the Provisional Government growing clear, the brief honeymoon of cross-class collaboration souring, and the Bolsheviks were recruiting from a mostly young, disillusioned, angry, even impetuous milieu. It was in this context that Lenin began a campaign to win over his comrades.

And his stubbornness did highlight a certain instability of the party's current 'quasi-Menshevik' position, according to which some on the Bolshevik right seemed to imply that history was 'not ready' for socialism, while insisting that the bourgeois government could not deliver.

Ten days after Lenin's return, the First Petrograd City Conference of the Bolsheviks convened. There, Lenin developed his argument, insisting that the Provisional Government could not be '"simply" overthrown', that it was necessary first to win the majority in the Soviet. Still, delegate after delegate accused him of anarchism, schematicism, 'Blanquism' – a modern iteration of the radical conspiracies of the nineteenth-century French socialist Auguste Blanqui. By now, however, a week and a half after his return, he had gained supporters, too. Those stalwartly on his side, like Alexandra Kollontai and Ludmila Stahl, remained vocal. And he must have had a good deal of shy support, too, because though the majority of speakers spoke against him, his resolution on opposing the Provisional Government passed by thirty-three votes to six, with two abstentions.

This shift in the party cadres would soon make trouble for the Provisional Government.

★

In these April days, a remnant of the social carnivalesque of March continued, but now with a harder and more bitter edge. First signs of a general crisis were not hard to find.

In early April, thousands of soldiers' wives – *soldatki* – marched through the capital. These women had started the war disadvantaged, browbeaten and precarious, desperate for charity and inadequate state support. But the absence of their husbands could also mean an unexpected liberation. In February their demands for food, support, respect, had started to take on a radical bent. That trend continued. In Kherson province, one observer saw the *soldatki* forcing their way into homes and 'requisitioning' any luxury they thought was undeserved.

> Not only did they flout laws and intimidate the authorities wherever they possibly could, there were also direct acts of violence. The state flour trader who did not want to offer them his goods at discounted price was beaten by a band of soldiers' wives, and the *pristav*, the local police chief, who wanted to hurry to his help, escaped the same fate by a hair's breadth.

On the land, the exuberant and pandemoniacal spread of soviets and congresses and conferences and peasant assemblies, amid established local bodies like *volosts* and township *zemstvos*, was beginning to take ominous forms. As early as March, in the Volga, pugnacious rural communes began disputing with landowners over rent and rights to the commons. Gangs of peasants were increasingly wont to make their way into private woods with axes and saws and fell the estate's trees. Now, in April, particularly in the north-west districts – Balashov, Petrovsk, Serdobsk – that movement surged. Sometimes peasants simply began to mow the gentry's meadows for their own use, paying only the prices they reckoned were fair for seed.

That sense of 'fairness' was crucial. Certainly there were moments of crude class rage and cruelty. But the actions of village communes against landlords were often scrupulously articulated in terms of a moral economy of justice. Sometimes this entailed the presentation of their demands in quasi-legal form, through manifestos and declarations formulated by sympathetic local intellectuals, or in the careful prolixity of autodidacts. This was an ad hoc realisation of the traditional chiliastic yearning for equal shares of the land for all who worked it – 'black repartition', as this redistribution was known – and the freedoms that should ensue.

'Cabinet, appanage, monastery, church, and major estate owners' lands must be surrendered to the people without compensation, for they were earned not by labour but by various amorous escapades,' 130 illiterate peasants of Rakalovsk Volost in Viatka Province had their scribe write to the Petrograd Soviet, in a collective letter of 26 April, 'not to mention through sly and devious behaviour around the tsar'.

It was one of a torrent of letters from the newly politicising, the engaged and eager, across the empire. Ever since February they had crossed the country, addressing themselves to the Soviet, to the government, to the land commissions, to the newspapers, to the SRs, to the Mensheviks, to Kerensky, to anyone or any organisation that seemed as if it might have some power or importance. In these first months some still took a tone so careful as to be almost cowed, though they were often hopeful, joyful, even, if unsure. Injunctions, entreaties, offers, queries and lamentations of curious people. They came in the great unparagaphed underpunctuated blocks of text, the urgent, rushing metaphors, and that stilted quasi-legalese of those not used to writing. There were poems and prayers and imprecations.

Outraged workers in the Tula Brass Cartridge Factory defended their output in *Izvestia*. The peasants of Lodeina village in Vologda wrote to the Soviet pleading for socialist newspapers. In the Menshevik press, the 'Committee of Workers' Elders' in the Atlas Metal Factory decried alcoholism. Soldiers of the 2nd Battery Assembly of the Caucasus army sent a letter directly to 'deeply respected deputy' Chkheidze, lamenting their own lack of education and pleading with the Menshevik leader for books. Transport Repair Workshop Number 2 in Kiev wrote to him too, enclosing forty-two roubles for the martyrs of the revolution.

Over the months such letters would grow angrier and more desperate. Many were already angry now, and many more were impatient.

'We are sick and tired of living in debt and slavery,' the Rakalovsk peasants had their chairperson write. 'We want space and light.'

On 18 April, the Provisional Government cabled its foreign allies with their official 'Revolutionary Defencist' war aims, as the Soviet demanded after Milyukov's provocative interview the previous month. But Milyukov was seemingly determined to wreck any such move, to undermine what he considered inexcusable treason. To the document, the reiteration of the 'Declaration of March 27', he appended a note 'clarifying' that the cable did not mean Russia was planning to leave the war. That the country remained determined to fight for the 'high ideals' of the Allies.

The 'Milyukov Note', as it was swiftly known, was not the machination of one rogue right-wing Kadet. His draft and the plans for its communication were approved by the cabinet in a compromise between the Provisional Government's left and right wings – precisely to undermine the Soviet.

On 19 April, when the Soviet Executive Committee discovered the note's content, Chkheidze denounced Milyukov as 'the evil genius of the revolution'. And the Ispolkom was not the only group so incensed. When on the 20th the text appeared in various newspapers, spontaneous, furious demonstrations instantly broke out.

In the Finland Regiment served the dashing sergeant Fedor Linde, a politically unaligned romantic who had played an important, undersung part in February, rousing the 5,000-strong Preobrazhensky Regiment to mutiny. Now the Milyukov note inflamed him as a betrayal of the revolution's promise to end the war. As a revolutionary defencist, Linde feared that the note could demoralise and agitate the army in a profoundly unhelpful way.

When Milyukov's intervention went public, Linde led a battalion of his regiment to the splendid neoclassical Marinsky Palace, where the Provisional Government met. He fully expected that the Soviet Executive, of which he was a member, would endorse his actions, assert its power, and arrest the perfidious government. Soldiers from the Moscow and Pavlov regiment joined his demonstration, and soon 25,000 men were angrily protesting outside the palace.

To Linde's surprise and dismay, the Soviet condemned him. It insisted, rather, that it must help the Provisional Government restore its authority.

The Milyukov note and the escalating demonstrations against it caused uncertainty and tension among the Bolsheviks. Lenin's resolution on the issue, passed that morning at an emergency session of the First Bolshevik Petrograd City Conference, was uncharacteristically equivocal. It condemned the note, and suggested that the end of the war would become possible only by transferring power to the Soviet – but it did *not* call workers and soldiers to come out.

However, thousands of soldiers and workers were already on the streets, demanding the resignations of Milyukov and Guchkov. When the Soviet ordered them to disperse, most, including the disconsolate Linde, obeyed. But the demonstrators were still carrying their placards reading 'Down with Imperialist Policy', and, tellingly, 'Down with the Provisional Government'.

And such slogans went down well with some Bolshevik district delegates. There was a mood on the party left for such spectacles and interventions. Already that day, at the conference, Nevsky of the Military Organisation had argued for the mobilisation of troops to agitate for a Soviet seizure of power. Ludmila Stahl implored her comrades not to be 'further left than Lenin himself', and the delegates ultimately agreed to call for 'solidarity with the resolution of the Central Committee', meaning Lenin's own, rather evasive motion.

But the next day, demonstrators were out again in their thousands, though with fewer soldiers among them. There was that surge again. Overthrow the government? The thought gained traction among Bolsheviks.

Hundreds of copies of a leaflet were scattering in the wind, some being trodden underfoot, many caught up and read: the anonymous thoughts of a troublemaker. 'Down with the Provisional Government!' was the heading. The comrades whispered that Bogdatiev, a far-left Bolshevik Putilov worker and candidate for the Central Committee, was the culprit. The redoubtable Kronstadt Bolsheviks were firmly in favour of overthrow. They were ready, they announced, 'at any moment to support with armed force' such demands.

On the afternoon of the 21st, demonstrations spread to Moscow, too. In the capital, workers once more took over Nevsky Prospect, shouting for the end of the Provisional Government. But this time as they marched forward they began to make out banners that were not their own. Another crowd milled outside the Kazan Cathedral, between its curving rows of columns like outflung arms. A Kadet counterdemonstration.

The Kadets stared pugnaciously and chanted their own slogans. 'Hurrah for Milyukov!' 'Down with Lenin!' 'Long Live the Provisional Government!'

Clashes broke out in the shadow of the dome. People wielded their placards like weapons. They grabbed and swung. Then a series of shocking rat-tat-tat echoes. Gunfire, starting a panicked stampede. Three people died.

At 3 p.m., as workers marched again towards the Winter Palace, General Lavr Kornilov, in charge of the Petrograd Military District, ordered his units to take up position in the great square before it, surrounding the soaring Alexander Column.

Kornilov was a career soldier of Tatar and Cossack stock, celebrated for his escape from Austro-Hungarian captivity in 1916. Aggressive, dashing, unimaginative, brutal, brave, he had the unenviable task of re-establishing military discipline in Petrograd. As if to prove to him the scale of that commission, the soldiers now snubbed his order. Instead, they followed the Soviet's command to stand down.

Kornilov was a hothead but not a fool. He swallowed back his fury and contempt, and avoided confrontation by rescinding his own instruction.

Rather than try to solve the crisis with violence, the Soviet issued an edict against unauthorised military presence on the streets. This was effectively a directive to wind down these disturbances, the April Days. That evening the Soviet Executive, the Ispolkom, voted, thirty-four against nineteen, to accept the Provisional Government's 'explanation' of Milyukov's note – an explanation that was tantamount to a withdrawal.

Activists' blood was still up. That evening, at a meeting of the Bolshevik Petersburg Committee's Executive Commission, a motion for the government's overthrow was gaining support. Having scandalised Bolshevik moderates, Lenin now moved to dampen the worrying ardour of his party's 'ultra-lefts'.

'The slogan "Down with the Provisional Government"', stated his resolution of 22 April, 'is an incorrect one at the present moment', because there was not yet a majority on the side of the revolutionary working class. Absent such weight, 'such a slogan is either an empty phrase or, objectively, amounts to attempts of an adventurist character'. He reiterated that 'only when the Soviets ... adopt our policy and are willing to take power into their own hands' would he advocate such a transfer.

The April Days had imparted an important, if unintended, lesson. It had become absolutely clear that the Soviet possessed more authority over the Petrograd Garrison than did the Provisional Government or the officers, whether the Soviet wished it or not.

The upsurges of the April Days may have been precipitous in the capital, but all over the country the tide of progress and change was still very strong. Across the immensity of Russian territory, the boisterousness and experiment thrown up by February went on, developing into particular shapes, channelling into more serious, formal investigations of liberation. In the nations and minorities unrest stirred, and moves for autonomy.

The predominantly Buddhist Buryat region of Siberia had seen waves of Russian immigration since the Trans-Siberian Railway reached its main city of Irkutsk in 1898. More than once in subsequent years it had been rocked by Buryat revolts against discriminatory laws, and it had faced chauvinist cultural and political threats from the Russian regime. In 1905 a Buryat congress had called for rights to self-government and linguistic–cultural freedom: it had been suppressed. Now, with the new wave of freedoms, came a new Congress in Irkutsk – which voted in favour of independence.

In Ossetia, in the Caucasus mountains, locals called a congress to establish organs of self-rule in the newly democratic state. In the Kuban, a region of southern Russia on the Black Sea, the local Cossacks in the Rada, its head hitherto appointed by the tsar, declared it the supreme local administrative power. Buoyed by the February revolution, and feeling it vindicated their own programme, members of the progressive, modernising Muslim Jadidist movement set up an Islamic Council in Tashkent, Turkestan, and across the region, helping to dismantle the old government structures – already undermined by the spread of local soviets – and enhancing the role of the indigenous Muslim population. At the end of the month, the council convened the first Pan-Turkestan Muslim Congress in the city. Its 150 delegates recognised the Provisional Government, and unanimously called for substantial regional autonomy.

Nor were such probings towards progress only in the arena of nationhood. The All-Russian meeting of Muslims, called for by Muslim Duma deputies immediately after the February revolution, was fast approaching – but before this, on 23 April, delegates gathered in Kazan in Tatarstan for the All-Russian Muslim Women's Congress. There, fifty-nine women delegates met before an audience 300 strong, overwhelmingly female, to debate issues including the status of Sharia law, plural marriage, women's rights and the hijab. Contributions came from a range of political and religious positions, from socialists like Zulaykha Rahmanqulova and the twenty-two-year-old poet Zahida Burnasheva, as well as from the religious scholars Fatima Latifiya and Labiba Huseynova, an expert on Islamic law.

Delegates debated whether Quranic injunctions were historically specific. Even many proponents of trans-historical orthodoxy interpreted the texts to insist, against conservative voices, that women had the right to attend mosque, or that polygyny was only permitted – a crucial caveat – if it was 'just'; that is, with the permission of the first wife. Unsatisfied when the gathering approved that progressive–traditionalist position on plural marriage, the feminists and socialists mandated three of their number, including Burnasheva, to attend the All-Russian Muslim Conference in Moscow the next month, to put their alternative case against polygyny.

The conference passed ten principles, including women's right to vote, the equality of the sexes, and the non-compulsory nature of the hijab. The centre of gravity of the discussions was clearly Jadidist, or further left. A symptom of tremulous times.

Petrograd was recovering from Linde's adventure. From 24 to 29 April, immediately after the April Days, the Seventh All-Russian Conference of the Russian Social Democratic Workers Party, the RSDWP – since 1912, the Bolsheviks' official name – took place. There, Lenin added his new 'right' critique of the left to his left critique of the Bolshevik right. The April Days, he said, should not have been a battle. Rather, they were an opportunity for 'a peaceful reconnaissance of our enemy's forces' – that enemy being the Provisional Government. The Petersburg Committee in its enthusiasm had committed the 'grave crime' of moving, he said, 'a wee bit to the left'.

Stalin was one of several who now shifted from their original more moderate position to vote with Lenin. There was continued vocal opposition to the April Theses from the more consistent Kamenev, among others, and from a minority further to the right clinging to the position of 'watchfulness' over the Provisional Government. Nonetheless, Lenin's call for 'all power to the soviets', as expounded in a corrective to Bogdatiev and his adventurers, was overwhelmingly adopted. As was Lenin's position that imperialist war and 'revolutionary defencism' should both be opposed.

Considering the horror which had greeted his proposals barely three weeks earlier, the shift was remarkable. Lenin's stock was rising in his party, and fast.

The Bolsheviks were hardly monolithic, however. Lenin felt obliged to dilute his motion 'On the Current Moment' with concessions to Kamenevism, and still it only passed by seventy-one to thirty-nine votes, with eight abstentions. The Bolshevik right gained four places, one taken by Kamenev, on the nine-seat Central Committee, enough to hold Lenin's feet to the fire. And on the question of the Second International, which had disgraced itself with its pro-war leanings, Lenin was entirely alone in voting to break with it.

Even so. When the congress closed on 29 April, Lenin could be cautiously pleased with his progress.

On the 26th, the Provisional Government issued a frank, emotional appeal. It admitted, as the April Days had shown, that it was not in control in Russia. It invited 'representatives of those creative forces of the country which until then had not taken a direct and immediate part' to join the administration.

This was a direct plea to the Soviet for formal collaboration. It wavered, riven by debates over how to respond.

The positions of Guchkov, the minister of war, and the hated Milyukov had become untenable. They resigned on the 29th.

During all the drama of the month, the Soviet had been attentive to the plights of various revolutionaries stranded abroad, prevented from returning home to Russia, possibly being held in conditions of questionable legality. The Soviet demanded the intercession of the government. One of Milyukov's last tasks as foreign minister was to intervene with the British and Canadians on the matter of a Russian national detained by the British at a camp in Nova Scotia, considered a threat to the Allies. The prisoner's name was Leon Trotsky.

Guchkov believed Dual Power was unsustainable, and instead sought a right-wing coalition linking the bourgeoisie in the Provisional Government with those 'healthy' parts of the armed forces, such as General Kornilov, along with various business leaders. This, of course, the Soviet would not countenance. But that did not mean it knew what to do with its own whip hand. It was still absurdly committed to 'watching over' a government that frankly proclaimed it could not govern.

The same day Milyukov and Guchkov resigned, the Soviet's Executive Committee rejected coalition with the Provisional Government by a hair: twenty-three to twenty-two. Regional soviets – in Tiflis, Odessa, Nizhni Novgorod, Tver, Ekaterinburg and Moscow, among others – remained firmly set against the participation of socialists in the bourgeois government. Meanwhile, many further to their left, like the Bolsheviks, were growing dismissive of the Provisional Government *tout court*.

At the same time, however, pressures for collaboration mounted. Representatives of the patriotic socialist parties of the Allied countries, representing the international left wing of the pro-compromisers, agitated strongly for entry into the Russian government. These, in Zimmerwald parlance, were the social patriots. They came to Russia in their numbers, intent on convincing the Russian people to support the war. Albert Thomas from France, Arthur Henderson and James O'Grady from Britain, Emile Vandervelde and Louis De Brouckère from Belgium, France's Marcel Cachin. They toured the country and the front, joining forces with Russian generals to bolster fighting spirit for what one French socialist, Pierre Renaudel, said it was now possible to describe 'without blushing' as 'the war of justice'.

Most of those they sought to convince, exhausted by the war, ranged between indifference and hostility. To this their visitors seemed blind. In one particularly unedifying moment of theatre, Albert Thomas, addressing a crowd from a balcony, supplemented the French-language exhortations few understood with a ludicrous charade, like a mime at a children's party. He twirled imaginary Kaiser moustaches, choked an imaginary Russia, and, mistaking his audience's audible disgust at this buffoonery for praise, closed with a flourish of his bowler hat.

For the workers, peasants and soldiers who supported the soviets, and who were not implacably antagonistic to the government, common sense might suggest that having socialists within that government could only be a good thing. Gradually, certain provincial authorities began to make this argument. Kerensky was already a member of the cabinet, was he not? And Kerensky was popular, was he not? How could more Kerenskys be bad?

In the SR party, the tide began to pull in this direction, manifesting in a widening of the split between the left and right flanks. Rank-and-file soldiers demanded that the government conduct the war 'in a revolutionary manner'. Military units in Petrograd – even including the pro-Bolshevik armoured car division – now announced in favour of coalition, on such grounds.

And to this species of 'left' entryism was, in strange arithmetic, added that of a certain 'right' socialism. Where radicals wanted coalition with the government out of faith in the soviets, those to their right, including many of the 'official' socialists in the moderate parties and in the soviets themselves, were coming to wonder if those soviets were finished – if power must now revert to more traditional forms.

Within the Petrograd Soviet, despite their numbers, the moderate SRs tended politically to trail the Menshevik leaders. There was diminishing distance between the dominant wings of the two organisations, and Dan, Chkheidze and Tsereteli of the Mensheviks were of a different class in ability to most of the SR figureheads. Since his return, even the esteemed Chernov, traditionally to the SR left, tacked quickly towards former party opponents such as Gots, and 'revolutionary defencism'. He adopted the moderation of those SR intelligentsia previously to his right, arguing for a consolidation of February's 'revolutionary gains', and against radical moves which might risk reactions. Decrying disorganisation on the left, and holding 'propertied elements' as better placed to govern, Chernov espoused socialist–liberal collaboration and support for the Provisional Government.

Excluding the rejectionist anarchists, Bolsheviks, Left SRs and left Mensheviks and maximalists of various traditions, the upshot was that both left-left and right-left began to turn towards coalition.

April ended with a rudderless government, lacking a minister of war, and with socialists in the Soviet committed to the success of a bourgeois revolution from the institutions of which they remained absent, and from which the bourgeoisie themselves were resigning. Small wonder that Kerensky prophesied entropy, confusion, doom. Disorganisation, he warned his Soviet comrades, would spread. The army would soon be unable to fight.

Thus it was with the war as key to the argument that the concerns of revolutionary defencists dovetailed with those of the country's imperialists. They merged in Kerensky's predictions of Russia's impending collapse.

5

May: Collaboration

On 1 May, only two days after its previous vote on the matter, the Soviet Executive Committee turned again to the principle of coalition with the Provisional Government. This time, by forty-four to nineteen, with two abstentions, it voted in favour. In vain did a furious Martov, committed to class independence and abstaining from power as the far left opposition in a bourgeois revolution, cable his Menshevik comrades that participation in coalition government was 'impermissible'.

Negotiations began immediately. The Soviet set conditions for its support. It insisted on a serious effort to end the war, on the principle of self-determination without annexations; democratisation of the army; a degree of control over industry and distribution; labour protections; taxes on the wealthy; a democratic local administration; an agrarian policy aimed at 'the passing of the land into the hands of the toilers'; and moves towards the convocation of that much-vaunted Constituent Assembly.

Some of these desiderata might have sounded unacceptably radical to the guardians of bourgeois order imploring the Soviet to join them in ruling, but in fact these conditions were obligingly elastic, their time frames long, often indeterminate. The mainstreams and rights of the Mensheviks and SRs, particularly the leadership and intellectuals – including many a one-time radical terrorist – were coming to feel that the only alternative to coalition with the government was the dangerous current to their left. The culturally weighty SR right undermined the activist Left SRs of Petrograd and the Northern Regional Conference, denouncing them as 'party Bolsheviks'. Its new paper, *Volia naroda*, bankrolled by Breshko-Breshkovskaya, wrote that the choice was now 'openly and definitely between joining the Provisional Government – that is, energetic support to the state revolutionary government – and frankly declining – that is, rendering indirect support to Leninism'.

For their part, as with their debates in February, the liberals and right extracted concessions from the socialists in turn. The Kadets demanded at least four ministers in any cabinet. On the central issue of the war, the Provisional Government insisted that the Ispolkom recognise in it the ultimate authority, the sole source of command of the armed forces.

The Soviet approach to foreign policy and the war was too pacific for Kadet tastes, but the agreed programme accommodated the Kadets in one crucial respect: it allowed the army to prepare offensive, as well as defensive, operations. In fact, with the international prestige of revolutionary Russia severely dented by its equivocal and ineffective military policy, even some within the Soviet were growing less opposed to an offensive.

On 4 May, the final day of negotiations on the composition of a cabinet, the First All-Russian Congress of Peasants' Soviets convened in Petrograd. That same day saw the long-delayed return to the city, with his family, after a protracted, conspiracy-snarled, police- and incarceration-interrupted trip from the US, of Lev Davidovich Bronstein – Leon Trotsky.

Trotsky was remembered as a leader of the Soviet in 1905, and commanded general respect on the left, if not trust. He was much spoken of, but in an uncertain tenor. His maverick theories, bitter and brutal polemics, abrasive personality and inveterate contrariness meant that 'both Mensheviks and Bolsheviks regarded him with rancour and distrust', recalled Angelica Balabanoff, the cosmopolitan Italian-Russian Bolshevik. In part, she thought, this was 'fear of competition': Trotsky was universally considered brilliant, a painful thorn in the flesh of any opponents, and his only current allegiance was to the scintillating but tiny left group, the Mezhraiontsy. As to what he might do now, no one was certain.

On 5 May, the new government was born: the Second Provisional, or First Coalition, Government. Other than Prince Lvov, who stayed on as president and minister of the interior, it was all change. Among the new ministers were six socialists and ten others, including the Kadet Michael Tereshchenko, a young millionaire sugar manufacturer from Ukraine, replacing Milyukov. Tereshchenko was a known Freemason, and in that febrile, whispering, parapolitical atmosphere, it was easy to suspect conspiracies behind his appointment. Such Mason-obsessed speculation is still rife in discussions of the revolution today. In fact, whether nepotistically advanced or not, Tereshchenko would prove reasonably adept at the impossible task of managing relations with both the Allies and the Soviet.

The cabinet socialists included one from the Populist Socialist Party, A. V. Peshekhonov, in charge of food supplies; two Mensheviks, Tsereteli and Skobelev, for posts and telegraphs and for labour; and three SRs, Chernov himself in agriculture, Perverzev as justice minister, and, by far the most important, the new minister of war (and another noted Freemason): Alexander Kerensky.

At a plenary session of the Petrograd Soviet, the six socialist ministers asked the Soviet for their support in the venture of coalition. This the Soviet granted. The only organised opposition from the left, the Bolsheviks, garnered 100 votes against.

It was now that Trotsky entered the Tauride Palace hall, and the stage of 1917, to enthusiastic applause.

At the sight of him, the new minister Skobelev called out: 'Dear and beloved teacher!'

Trotsky took the floor. He spoke haltingly at first. The great orator was not himself. Nerves made him shake. The gathering grew quiet to listen to him. He gained in self-assurance as he offered his reading of the situation.

Trotsky eulogised the revolution. He dwelt on the scale of the impact it had had and could still have, too, on the wider world. It was in the international arena, after all, that the revolution must be completed.

Sugar sprinkled, Trotsky then dosed with bitter medicine. 'I cannot conceal', he said, 'that I disagree with much that is going on here.'

Sharply, with growing confidence, he condemned the entry of the socialists into the government, the fallacies of Dual Power. He recited to the gathering 'three revolutionary articles of faith: do not trust the bourgeoisie; control the leaders; rely only on your own force'. What was needed, what he called for in the silent room, was not a dual but a *single* power. That of workers' and soldiers' deputies.

'Our next move', he said, 'will be to transfer the whole power into the hands of the Soviets.' The formula could have been Lenin's.

When he left the hall, Trotsky was applauded far more tepidly than when he had come in. Bolshevik ears, though, had pricked up at his words.

No surprise that five days after his provocative appearance, Lenin offered Trotsky's Mezhraiontsy a seat on the board of the journal *Pravda* if they would join the Bolsheviks. He even mooted making the same offer to the left-wing Menshevik–Internationalists. Their leader Martov had, after long delay and without much help from his Petrograd comrades, returned to the city by a similar method to Lenin (in a considerably larger train).

For his part, although Trotsky no longer objected to such joining of forces in principle, he could not accept *dissolving into* the Bolsheviks. He proposed instead the formation of some new amalgam between the two, tiny as the Mezhraiontsy ranks were compared to those of the Bolsheviks. Lenin declined this arrogant suggestion. He could wait.

From the 7th to the 12th, the Mensheviks held their first All-Russian Conference in Petrograd – midway through which, their left leaders Martov, Axelrod and Martynov arrived to join them.

Martov was appalled by what he described to a friend as his party's 'ultimate stupidity' of joining the government, without even extracting a commitment to end the war. The conference had already validated this the day before he arrived, and now his émigré internationalists were soundly beaten on the question of defencism, too, with Tsereteli speaking forcefully in favour. The tiny Menshevik–Internationalist group refused to be bound by these decisions.

When Martov attempted to speak from the platform, the audience howled contumely on him. The horrified left understood how marginalised they were. Particularly in Petrogard, some on the Menshevik left, like Larin (also a Mezhraionets), argued for a split. Martov decided instead to remain within the party as an opposition bloc, hoping to win over the majority in time for a party congress scheduled for July.

The stakes were high, the mountain to climb even higher. 'Down with him!' the delegates had shouted. 'Out with him!' 'We don't want to hear him!'

These ferocious disagreements on collaboration in the liberal government notwithstanding, both wings of the party were as yet in accord that the workers themselves were in no position to take power. On the ground, this doctrine could give Menshevik organisers, particularly moderates, a certain, somewhat abstract, even quietist political mien.

The young Bolshevik Dune regarded the cadre of Mensheviks within his Moscow workplace with respect, as 'older, thoughtful and widely read comrades', 'the most skilled workers', a 'workers' aristocracy' with impressive knowledge and experience – but as those whose 'revolutionary ardour had cooled'. During the post–April Theses factory debates, those Mensheviks of course spoke out against soviet power, at length and with citations, on the grounds that the country was not yet mature, and because 'before workers could come to power they had to learn a great deal'. As Dune recalled,

> The meeting listened carefully to all the speakers but with less attention to [Menshevik] arguments about the socialist and bourgeois–democratic revolutions, supported by citations from the works of Bebel and Marx ...

The Bolsheviks spoke in a way that was more comprehensible. We must preserve and strengthen the power we had won during the revolution, not give
any of it away to the bourgeoisie. We must not liquidate the soviets as organs
of power, but transfer power to them.

★

Tensions in the country continued to grow as the month stretched
on. An uneasiness, a dangerous ill temper escalated among soldiers,
workers, and, most dramatically, peasants. For the most part it did
not, yet, take explicitly politicised forms, but it was protean, destructive and very often violent.

In the regions, bouts of rural insurgency occurred with ominous
and increasing frequency. 'Russia', said the Kadet organ *Rech*, 'is
turned into a sort of madhouse'. Groups of angry peasants, often
with soldiers among them, were looting manor houses in growing
numbers. Soldiers, despite theatrical imprecations and blandish-
ments from the war minister Kerensky, continued to desert in
enormous numbers. Their columns stalked the countryside. They
crowded the cities. Traumatised by the war, conspicuous objects
of moral panic, on the wrong side of the law, many now broke it to
survive, and for darker ends.

They were not the only ones. Crime rates soared: that year came
countless more murders in Petrograd than in the last, and some were
spectacular and particularly horrific, spreading angst and terror.
Deserters broke into a house in Lesnoi, choked a servant to death
and savagely beat a young boy before making off with money and
valuables. A young woman from the city's 10,000-strong Chinese
minority was found hacked to death, her eyes gouged out. The
middle classes in particular were in a panic – they felt more vulnerable than the rich, who could afford protection, or those in the
tight-knit working-class areas, where workers' militias were more
effective than was the city's own. It is no wonder that in this month,
the phenomenon of *samosudy*, lynchings and mob justice, 'took', in
the words of *Petrogradsky listok*, 'a sharp turn'. The *Gazeta-kopeika*
began to run a regular column entitled 'Today's Mob Trials'.

No less angry than the soldiers, though generally more politicised, was the mood among the workers. Strikes multiplied, as did those wheelbarrow-to-canal journeys for abusive overseers. And not only in Petrograd, or among the industrial workers most commonly associated with such agitation: in the town of Roslavl in Smolensk province, for example, it was milliners who made a stand. These mostly young Jewish women, with a tradition of militancy stretching back to 1905, came out for the eight-hour day, a 50 per cent wage increase, a two-day weekend plus paid holidays, and other demands. And they did so with no obsequious niceties.

On 13 May, the Kronstadt Soviet declared itself the only power on the naval island. It announced that it would not recognise the Coalition Government, and would deal only with the Petrograd Soviet. This radical repudiation of Dual Power, though heavily influenced by local Bolsheviks, was slapped down as adventurism by the Petrograd Bolshevik Central Committee. It was not the time, the CC insisted, for such toytown insurrectionary power grabs. The Bolsheviks, wrote Lenin in one pamphlet, must 'set [themselves] free from the prevailing *orgy of revolutionary phrase-mongering* and really stimulate the consciousness both of the proletariat and of the mass in general'. The party's task was to explain their reading of the situation 'skilfully, in a way that people would understand'. Accordingly, the CC summoned to Petrograd the leading Kronstadt members, Raskolnikov and Roshal.

Lenin remonstrated with them. To no avail. Nor did an appeal from the Petrograd Soviet itself to the Kronstadt forces on 26 May resolve the matter. It would, in fact, require the intercession of Trotsky, on the 27th, to broker a compromise that allowed the Kronstadt Soviet to back down with dignity. Even after that, it remained the only effective government on the island.

In those heady days, as the Coalition Government struggled not to lose control of the country, its critics on the left had trouble controlling their own supporters.

★

The subordinated nations of the empire were stretching, feeling out new possibilities.

Between 1 and 11 May, Moscow hosted the convention demanded by Muslim Duma deputies in February. Nine hundred delegates from Muslim populations and nations arrived in the city – Bashkirs, Ossets, Turks, Tatars, Kirghiz and more.

Almost a quarter of those present were women, several fresh from the Women's Muslim Congress in Kazan; one of the twelve-person presidium committee was a Tatar woman, Selima Jakubova. When one man asked why men should grant women political rights, a woman jumped up to answer. 'You listen to the men of religion and raise no objections, but act as though you can grant us rights,' she said. 'Rather than that, we shall seize them!'

The conference was riven on several axes. But a powerful programme of women's rights was adopted, and, as the left at the Women's Congress had advocated, polygyny was banned, if only symbolically. Against the plans of the powerful Tatar bourgeoisie for extraterritorial cultural–national autonomy, and against pan-Islamic aspirations, the conference advocated a federalist position of cultural autonomy. This could, and indeed would, mature into calls for national liberation.

Similar demands were on the rise. On 13 May, a Kirghiz–Kazakh congress sent greetings and solidarity to the Petrograd Soviet from Semipalatinsk, a province on the border with China with a largely nomadic population. This congress likewise asserted its right to 'cultural–national self-determination' and 'political autonomy'. In Finland, February had energised a push for autonomy, and perhaps more. The government in Petrograd implored the Finns to wait for a Constituent Assembly: they were setting a bad example for other nationalities. In Bessarabia, there was a contest for the souls of Moldovan peasants. The left took on the fractious new Moldovan National Party, whose leaders demanded the 'broadest autonomy'. Between 18 and 25 May, Kiev hosted the First Ukrainian Military Congress. Over 700 delegates attended, representing nearly a million people, from the fronts, the rear, and the fleets. A voice for national self-determination.

According to the Menshevik journal *Rabochaya gazeta*, now, post-revolution, 'the Provisional Government [had] cut itself off completely from imperialist influences' and was racing towards 'universal peace'. On 6 May, the Soviet's *Izvestia*, though heavy-hearted that Russian soldiers must continue to fight, asserted that they could at least do so 'with all their energy and courage ... in the firm belief that their heroic efforts will not be used for evil ... [but] serving one and the same goal – the defence of the revolution from destruction and the earliest possible conclusion of universal peace'.

Alongside such appeals to the war's new legitimacy, the Coalition Government knew that its international standing, certainly among the Allies, was heavily dependent on whether it was seen to be doing its bit to win the war – and doing so on those Allies' decidedly unsocialist terms. Some were clear-sighted that this was a contradiction, and, continuing to laud the anti-imperialist necessity of the war's continuation, they were entirely cynical. Among the many socialists who were not, who were sincere, the mental contortions were unbearable and tragic. And they grew more painful as the government prepared the army for an offensive.

On 11 May, Kerensky published the document 'On the Rights of Soldiers'. The edict retained much of the content of Order Number 1 – a necessary sop to popular opinion – but, crucially, reinstated the authority of officers at the front. This included the right to appoint and remove lower-ranking officers without recourse to the soldiers' committees, and the right to use corporal punishment. The Bolsheviks immediately derided this degrading return of traditional hierarchies as the 'Declaration of the Rightlessness of Soldiers'.

Kerensky was a born performer. He set out to rally troops for a massive push, the offensive for which everyone was braced. It was a quixotic and grotesque campaign.

In the bomb-swept wilds of the front, the 'persuader-in-chief', as he was known, called on all his showmanship. He trudged smiling through the shit, mud and blood of battle lines, attired in immaculate quasi-military outfits. He assembled the soldiers, praised them warmly, met their eyes. He pressed a great deal of flesh. Standing on boxes and stumps and the bonnets of battered military cars, he delivered his shrill oratory to the massed troops, demanding sacrifice, working himself up into such a passion that he would sometimes faint.

And in limited fashion, for a limited time, these interventions worked. When Kerensky arrived, soldiers threw flowers. They carried the beaming leader on their shoulders. When he called for them to do so, they hurrahed. One last push, he exhorted the soldiers, would mean peace. At these words, they prayed and wept.

Or some of them did. The testeria of the reception was genuine, but it was neither deep nor lasting. Kerensky sincerely convinced himself that the army was ready and eager for an offensive. It was not. Perspicacious officers, like the thoughtful General Brusilov, with whom Kerensky replaced Alexeev as commander-in-chief on 22 April, knew this.

Besides, Kerensky only orated before certain troops. He was kept away from those where to attempt it would have been to invite injury or worse. Where he did speak, he soon left, and when the brief narcotic of his sermons ebbed, the soldiers were still stuck scant yards from enemy lines, in freezing filth, in the sights of machine guns. His best speeches notwithstanding, at several stops Kerensky was heckled. The rates of desertion remained astounding, the habits of mutiny assertive. Anti-war agitation, Bolshevik and other, did not abate.

The old guard at the army's top were deeply bitter at the direction of the war and the erosion of old nostrums. On his first day in charge, Brusilov went to greet the staff at Stavka high command. Their 'frosty feelings', he said, were palpable. For these stiff and unreconstructed officers, his willingness to work with soldiers' committees made Brusilov a traitor. He appalled the senior officers with a cack-handed attempt to show his democratic credentials, greeting the privates on arrival, reaching out to shake their hands. The startled men fumbled with their weapons to respond.

Still, irrespective of plunging morale, distrust at the top and desertion at the bottom, the momentum towards an offensive would not slow. No more would counterpressure for rebellion.

The First All-Russian Congress of Peasants' Soviets took place in Petrograd over almost the entirety of May. Reflecting the overlap between peasantry and soldiery, close to half the 1,200 accredited delegates were from the front.

A sizeable minority of delegates (329) had no affiliation. The majority of the 103 Social Democrats were Mensheviks. The SRs, predictably in this peasant country, dominated, with 537 representatives. Even without an absolute majority, they were able to push through their policy of support for coalition with the Provisional Government, their positions on war and peace and the nationalities question. But it was a reflection of the fractious and hardening mood in the country that such triumphs did not always come easily.

Despite the Bolsheviks' tiny presence – a minuscule group of nine, accompanied by a caucus of fourteen 'non-party' delegates who tended to vote with them – their influence was growing. This was, in particular, because of their harder, more coherent and clearly expressed positions on the two key questions of war and land, as laid out in an open letter from Lenin to the Congress on 7 May.

On the 22nd, he addressed the delegates in person, hammering home his support for the poorest peasants and demanding the redistribution of land. Seemingly in response to this upstart stealing the thunder of the peasant party from the left, the SRs hurriedly added to their programme a provision that 'all lands must without exception be placed under the jurisdiction of the land committees'. Later, Lenin would not hesitate to filch policies from the left wing of the SRs: for now, he provided the party with material.

It was a reflection of the fractiousness within the SRs that at their own Third Congress, held late that month, Chernov came under bitter assault from high-profile Left SRs like Boris Kamkov, Mark Natanson and the celebrated Maria Spiridonova herself. Spiridonova, after eleven brutal prison years, was freed in February, and had recently arrived in Petrograd in dramatic and triumphal style. Promptly elected mayor of Chita in Siberia, near where she had served time, on getting out, she immediately ordered the blowing up of the prisons. Now she and the other Left SRs accused Chernov of having 'mutilated' the party programme. They put forward their own proposals for land seizures, immediate peace and socialist government.

The left's groundswell of support – 20 per cent of the delegates, and up to 40 per cent on some votes – could not win them more than one place (Natanson) on the Central Committee, and it was the moderates' policies that the party officially represented at the Congress of Peasants' Soviets. The SR radicals quietly inaugurated an 'informational bureau' to coordinate their activities. When rumours of this reached an alarmed Chernov, the Left SRs formally and falsely assured him that they had set up no such thing.

The assiduous push of Lenin and the Bolshevik radicals (not counting the party's most adventurist wing) for intransigent political positions was starting to bear fruit, including among seemingly unlikely constituencies. That month, Nina Gerd, the organiser of the Committee for the Relief of Soldiers' Wives in the Vyborg district, a liberal but an old friend of Krupskaya, surrendered to her the organisation. Three years before, in the recollection of one philanthropist, the *soldatki* had been 'helpless creatures', 'blind moles', pleading with the authorities for help. Now, as she relinquished the committee, Gerd told Krupskaya that the women 'do not trust us; they are displeased with whatever we do; they have faith only in the Bolsheviks'. Soon the *soldatki* were self-organising in their own soviets. And this dauntless spirit was spreading.

At the time, though, for most of the empire, it is fair to say that local conditions, complicated as they often were by national questions and often steered by moderate activists, encouraged less radical positions than the Bolshevik hardliners would like. At the start of May, for example, the Georgian Bolsheviks Mikha Tskhakaya and Filipp Makharadze arrived from Petrograd in Tiflis, Georgia, to urge their comrades to break immediately with 'collaborationist' Mensheviks, and unite only with the left Menshevik–Internationalists. Their injunctions were received with scepticism.

In Baku, too, the local Bolsheviks worked with the Mensheviks, and Lenin's April Theses still caused consternation: discussion of them in the Social Democratic press was hedged with disclaimers. A citywide conference of Social Democrats in mid-May, with a pro-Bolshevik majority, did oppose the Coalition Government, but would not vote to support a position of 'all power to the soviets'. And in the Baku Soviet itself, resistance to leftist positions remained stiff. On 16 May, the Bolshevik Shaumian's no-confidence resolution in the new government was roundly defeated: by 166 to nine, with eight abstentions, the soviet passed a Menshevik–SR–Dashnak (a leftist Armenian party) resolution supporting the inclusion of Petrograd Soviet members in the Provisional Government.

Among the most important exceptions to the tendency of regional moderation was Latvia. In the early days, its Bolsheviks, influenced in part by a strong tradition of local unity with Mensheviks, had taken a mild position, as with the Riga Committee's 'submissive' statement of March. Since then, chivvied by their harder, Russia-based Central Committee, their ranks swelled by the return of more militant émigrés, attitudes had changed. The sheer dominance of the local Bolshevik party in the soviets, its outmanoeuvring of liberals within provisional elected councils, gave it so powerful a hand that, in the words of the historian Andrew Ezergailis, 'the peculiarity of the institutional framework emerging in Latvia after March was that ... the concept of dual power simply did not obtain'.

Key to this shift were the Latvian riflemen. The soviet of these soldiers had moved very rapidly leftward in only a few weeks, and at a congress on 15 May, it passed a resolution on the 'Present Situation' which laid out a Leninist position on the war, the Provisional

Government, and the soviets. Julijs Danisevskis, who moved the document, pre-prepared it with his Bolshevik comrades in Moscow, from where he had only recent arrived. Two days after it passed, the soldiers elected a new Executive Commitee, of which only one member was not a Bolshevik.

Notwithstanding Brusilov's sincere efforts to embrace certain democratic norms, Kerensky's reimposition of traditional military discipline, combined with the ongoing threat of transfer to the front, provoked immense anger among soldiers. This was particularly true of those in revolutionary Petrograd – among whom Bolshevik influence was slowly increasing.

The First All-Russian Congress of Soviets of Workers' and Soldiers' Deputies was scheduled for 3 to 24 June, in the capital. The prospect of an opportunity to show its military strength appealed to the hard-left Bolshevik Military Organisation (MO). It prepared to flex its muscles. On 23 May, the MO agreed that several regiments – the Pavlovsky, Izmailovsky, Grenadier and First Reserve Infantry – were 'ready to go out on their own', to come onto the streets in a large armed demonstration against Kerensky's military measures.

In the discussion that ensued among the MO activists, the question was never whether the demonstration should occur – on that there was no disagreement – but only how, under what parameters, whether it needed to attract the majority of the soldiers. The organisers decided to hold a meeting with representatives from Kronstadt early the following month. On the basis of that they would decide how and when this show of force should take place.

The repercussions of this decision would be profound.

On 30 May, yet another conference opened: the First Conference of Petrograd Factory Committees, the Fabzavkomy. Such committees had sprung up at the start of the February Revolution, mostly in the publicly owned defence plants, from where they had spread to private industry. In the early, heady post-February days, managers had agreed with the Soviet Ispolkom to introduce them to all plants in Petrograd, and in April they had been empowered to represent workers.

Initially they had tended to issue relatively moderate economic demands, along the kind of radical trade unionist lines that the socialist left might term 'syndicalist'. Then, as shortages continued and social tension ratcheted up, the Fabzavkomy turned left, hard. While Mensheviks controlled most of the national trade unions, already in May it was the Bolsheviks who commanded more than two-thirds of the delegates to the Factory Committee Conference. Now those committees provocatively demanded that workers be given a decisive vote in factory management, and access to the firms' accounting books.

The industrial working class as a whole was growing militant more quickly than were the peasants and soldiers. On the 31st, in the Workers' Section of the Petrograd Soviet, a symptomatic motion was won by 173 to 144 votes, insisting that all power should be in the hands of the Soviets.

Such a vote would not have passed in the Soviet as a whole. Nonetheless, this Bolshevik formula was a slap in the face to advocates of Dual Power and to the moderates in the Soviet itself, let alone to the Coalition Government.

6

June: A Context of Collapse

On the first day of June, the Bolshevik Military Organisation met with representatives of the Kronstadt party and approved plans for a garrison demonstration. To the Central Committee, the MO sent a list of regiments it was confident it could persuade to take part. Together they numbered 60,000 men.

At that moment the CC was focused on affairs of state: from 3 to 24 June, that First All-Russian Congress of Soviets of Workers' and Soldiers' Deputies – the gathering planned at the All-Russian Conference of Soviets, at the start of April – was meeting in Petrograd. Its 777 delegates comprised 73 unaffiliated socialists, 235 SRs, 248 Mensheviks, 32 Menshevik–Internationalists, and 105 Bolsheviks. The congress quickly elected a new SR- and Menshevik-dominated executive committee.

Almost as soon as proceedings opened, a visibly furious Martov went on the attack – against fellow Mensheviks. He deplored Tsereteli's collaboration with the Provisional Government, particularly over the recent deportation of his Swiss comrade Robert Grimm. He appealed to the Mensheviks in the hall: 'You, my past comrades in revolution, are you with those who give *carte blanche* to their minister to deport any category of citizen?'

From the Mensheviks came an extraordinary response: 'Tsereteli is not a minister, but the conscience of the revolution!'

Then, Sukhanov wrote with admiration, Martov – 'slight, meek, somewhat awkward' – bravely faced down the 'voracious, screeching monster' of the crowd. The attack by his own party was so ugly that Trotsky himself, hardly a close comrade, ran forward to offer solidarity to the embattled internationalist. 'Long live the honest socialist Martov!' he shouted.

Tsereteli's speech, by contrast, provoked 'rapturous, never-ending applause' from his fraction. Here was evidence of an ongoing shift among the leading party moderates towards being *gosudarst-venniki* – 'statists', of a sort. The crisis of April had strengthened the beliefs of those Mensheviks who saw socialist participation in power as necessary for authoritative government, and as a way to push their policies. With which, *pari passu*, grew their sense of themselves as custodians of the state itself – a state that might get things done.

It was not as if that state powered from success to success. After a month of governmental coalition, the mood in the country was hardening. Unrest in the countryside, the cities and at the front was increasing to the point of provoking serious social alarm. Urban crime and violence were still rising. Shortages grew worse. Hauling themselves feebly through the traffic on the streets of Petrograd in these high summer days, the horses were skeletal. The people were famished.

Despite all this, to the impatience of some on the left of his party, Lenin stuck to his patient programme of 'explaining' Bolshevik opposition to coalition, and of what he insisted was the real reason for social problems. 'The pilfering of the bourgeoisie', he told the congress, 'is the source of the anarchy.'

Against such intransigence, on 4 June, Tsereteli, the minister of posts and telegraphs, justified the Soviet's collaboration with the bourgeoisie to the gathered delegates. 'There is', he said, 'no political party in Russia which at the present time would say "Give us power".'

To which from the depths of the room an immediate heckle came back.

'There *is* such a party,' shouted Lenin.

★

On the 4th, the Bolshevik left showed its strength. On Petrograd's Mars Field, the party held a rally in honour of the fallen of February. Alongside the Kronstadt sailors, the MO had organised hundreds of troops from the Moskovsky, Grenadier, Pavlovsky, Finlyandsky, Sixth Engineer, 180th Infantry, and First Machine Gun regiments. In his speech on behalf of the MO, Semashko pointedly praised the radicalism of Kronstadt – to an audience that included Krylenko of the Bolshevik CC, which had chided the soldiers, and the caution of which was provoking such exasperation among radicals.

Two days later, at a joint meeting with the CC and executive of the Petersburg Comittee, the MO again proposed an armed demonstration. At this point Lenin was in favour; Kamenev, ever cautious, was against, as were several others on the Petersburg Committee, including Zinoviev. Even Krupskaya, unusually, took a different line from Lenin – in her view the demonstration was unlikely to be peaceful, so perhaps, given the risks of it escalating beyond the party's control, it should not go ahead.

In the end the leadership made no decision. A decision would soon be made for them.

The Bolsheviks were the most organised and largest group on the far left, but they were not the only one. To their own left were groups of anarchists of various sizes, inclinations and degrees of influence. Decidedly a minority current, anarchism nonetheless enjoyed localised support across the empire, with various strongholds, such as Odessa – and Petrograd.

There in the capital, the most radical and influential were the Anarchist–Communists. Some of their leaders were held in esteem, like Iosif Bleikhman, a fiery, unkempt, charismatic figure who spoke his native Russian with what Trotsky described as a 'Jewish-American accent' which his audiences enjoyed, and Shlema Asnin, a respected militant with the First Machine Gun Regiment, a dark-bearded former thief who dressed like a gothic cowboy, wide-brimmed hat, guns and all.

In the same chaotic expropriatory post-February wave during which the Bolsheviks moved into the Kshesinskaya Mansion, revolutionaries had taken and retooled the Vyborg summer home of the official P. P. Durnovo. Its gardens were now a park, with facilities for local children, and the building was hung with black banners reading 'Death to all capitalists'. The house was the headquarters of several groups including the district bakers' union, some far-left SR-Maximalists, and an Anarchist–Bolshevik group grandly styling itself the Soviet of the Petrograd People's Militia. This last, desiring better facilities to produce its leaflets, on 5 June decided with staggering chutzpah to send eighty gun-toting members to occupy the press of the right-wing *Russkaya volia*. After only a day, two regiments easily forced them out. But the authorities were ruffled. Up with these anarchists, they decided, they would not put.

On the 7th, Minister of Justice P. N. Perevezev issued them a deadline of twenty-four hours to vacate their villa. The anarchists appealed to Vyborg workers for protection. It is a measure of the moment, and of the respect these anarchists commanded, that the next day saw sizeable armed demonstrations in support. Several thousand workers came out on their behalf, closing twenty-eight factories.

The contradictions of the Soviet immediately resurfaced. The Ispolkom, the Executive Committee, lobbied by workers' delegations, asked Perevezev to rescind his ultimatum while they looked into the matter: simultaneously, they drafted an appeal to the demonstrators to return to work. Meanwhile the delegates to the All-Russian Congress of Soviets overwhelmingly voted for full cooperation with and support for Lvov's government, and prohibited armed demonstrations without Soviet authorisation.

Such a commitment to maintaining order was, to the Bolsheviks, an irresistible opportunity for agitation: the party hurriedly brought forward to the evening of that day, the 8th, a discussion between the CC, the Petersburg Committee, the MO, and representatives of regiments, trade unions and factories of the MO's proposal. Now, by 131 votes to 6, with 22 abstentions, the meeting agreed that the moment was propitious for organising a demonstration.

The size of this majority, though, disguised unease. Asked to vote on whether there was a general inclination among people to come out, and also on whether the masses would do so against Soviet opposition, the results were much less clear-cut. To the first question, the ayes had it, but only by fifty-eight to thirty-seven, with almost as many abstentions – fifty-two – as voted yes. To the second question, the affirmative margin was tiny: forty-seven to forty-two. And this time, among a group of militants not renowned for sitting on their hands, there were almost as many abstained as voted for yes and no *combined*: eighty. This bespoke immense uncertainty about the demonstration's chances in the face of Soviet disapproval.

Still, the decision was made. The demonstration would go ahead at 2 p.m. on Saturday 10 June, which left only one day to organise. The call was to go out the next morning. A special edition of the MO daily paper, *Soldatskaya pravda* – a starker, blunter publication than *Pravda*, with a less educated reader in mind – was quickly prepared, containing routes, instructions and slogans. The key demand would be the end of *dvoevlastie*, Dual Power, and the transfer of all power to the Soviet.

That night, in an unrelated crackdown against militants, the authorities arrested Khaustov, editor of the Bolshevik MO's front-line paper, *Okopnaya pravda*, and charged him with treason for writing against a military offensive. His incarceration would not, as we shall see, be without consequence.

The Anarchist–Communists, of course, were fully behind the upcoming demonstration. Late in the afternoon, the Mezhraiontsy were informed of the plans, and with Trotsky supporting them and over the objections of Lunacharsky, they voted to join the preparations. Across the capital, within military units and factories, Bolshevik agitators tabled resolutions in favour of coming out – and, for the most part, they won them, not least because, given that they were a minority within it, their call for all power to the Soviet did not appear partisan.

However, one important group remained in the dark. Almost unbelievably, in what was either a lamentable oversight or some ill-thought-through machination, the party's organisers failed to alert their own Bolshevik delegates to the All-Russian Congress of Soviets.

At around 3 p.m. on the 9th, Bolshevik leaflets about the demonstration hit the streets. At once, the Coalition Government appealed for law and order, and warned that force would be met by stern force. It was only now, as word spread, that the Bolshevik Congress delegates got wind of the plans. Tacking somewhat to the right of their Petrograd comrades in general, many had concerns at the politics behind the decision: besides which they were, unsurprisingly, incandescent at their treatment.

At an emergency meeting with representatives from the CC, including Viktor Nogin, they made their fury clear. 'Here I, a representative, only now found out that a demonstration was being organised,' one said. They insisted that Nogin – who was himself opposed to the coming-out – dissuade the CC from its planned course.

The Soviet's Executive Committee, too, was doing its utmost to prevent it. Many in the Soviet were terrified that any such armed provocation would provoke bloody clashes with the right, strengthening reaction; they also feared that this presaged some Bolshevik attempt to take control. And there was in fact a minority on the party left, including Old Bolsheviks Latsis, Smilga and Semashko, who wondered if the action might not indeed be a way to seize the city's communications – perhaps even power.

Evening fell amid a flurry of rushed debates, miscommunications, preparations. False rumours spread that Kerensky had mobilised military forces to crush any march. Chkheidze, Gots, Tsereteli and Fydor Dan of the Soviet Congress presidium appealed desperately for order. Lunacharsky and other Mezhraiontsy tried to stop the congress from declaring action against the demonstration, stalling, it seems, in the hopes that caution would prevail among the Bolsheviks.

At 8:30 p.m., Zinoviev, Nogin and Kamenev reached the Kshesinskaya Mansion and reported the fury of the party's delegates. The Bolshevik leadership hastily convened a meeting. In view of the tense situation, the naysayers vociferously counselled cancellation. But, despite the growing opposition, the meeting voted fourteen to two to go ahead.

Within a few hours, the Soviet Congress, meeting late and excluding Bolsheviks and Mezhraointsy, was unanimously condemning the Bolsheviks for their plans. It ruled that 'not a single demonstration should be held today', and prohibited any such action for three days. To police this, the Congress quickly inaugurated the splendidly named Bureau for Counteracting the Demonstration. The forces ranged against the plans were growing in anger and strength.

At last, at 2 a.m. on the 10th itself, the increasingly agitated Lenin, Zinoviev and Sverdlov met once again with Nogin, Kamenev and the Bolshevik delegation to the Congress, who demanded of the rump CC present – only five members – that it cancel the plans.

The CC voted. Kamenev and Nogin held firm to their opposition. Zinoviev had earlier switched sides, to support the proposal: now in these last tumultuous minutes he switched back again. And Sverdlov and Lenin abstained.

With what can only have been anxious relief, the Central Committee cancelled the demonstration, by three votes to none, with those two key abstentions.

The vote was ludicrously small. No members of the Petersburg Committee or the MO itself were present. Had there been any opposition to this final-second decision, the process could easily and reasonably have been denounced as inquorate and undemocratic. But Lenin made no objection. The demonstration was off.

An undignified, pell-mell rush. The unhappy Bolsheviks scrambled to inform party organisations and cadre, and the Anarchist–Communists themselves, that the action was cancelled. At 3 a.m., party printers got word. Urgently they rejigged the layouts of

Pravda and *Soldatskaya pravda*, shuffling and reconfiguring stories, removing instructions for the demonstration. At dawn, party militants raced to factories and barracks to argue against what they had so keenly promoted scant hours before.

Delegates from the Soviet Congress, too, spread through Petrograd, pleading with workers and soldiers not to come out. Some local committees passed resolutions insisting that though they stood down, they did so in response to the Bolsheviks' request, not to that of the Soviet Congress or the Coalition Government.

Not that the Bolsheviks could avoid censure. In the factories, barracks and courtyards of Vyborg, militants were furious at the volte-face. They inveighed against the party. Incredulous members, reported the Bolsheviks' own *Izvestia*, heaped insults on their leaders. *Soldatskaya pravda* washed its hands of the decision: the order, it stressed, came from above. Stalin and Smilga proffered their resignations from the CC, in protest at the highly questionable vote from which they had been absent (their resignations were rejected). A disgusted Latsis reported members tearing up their party cards. In Kronstadt, one prominent Bolshevik, Flerovsky, described the wrath of his fellow sailors that morning as 'among the most unpleasant' hours of his life. He was able to dissuade them from a unilateral demonstration only by suggesting that a delegation sail to Petrograd to find out from the CC precisely what was going on.

The Bolshevik leadership had a lot of explaining to do.

At a special commission of Mensheviks and SRs on 11 May, Tsereteli gave voice to the rage of the moderates. The recent events, he said, were evidence of a shift in Bolshevik strategy from propaganda to an overt attempt to seize power by arms, and thus he called for the party's suppression.

The debate continued at a meeting of the Congress.

Fyodor Dan was in his late forties, a committed high-profile Menshevik, a doctor who had served in the war as a surgeon, though he had been an anti-war 'Zimmerwaldist', close to the Menshevik left intellectually and personally – his wife Lydia was Martov's sister. After February, however, he took a revolutionary defencist position, contending that newly revolutionary Russia had the right and the duty to hold out in the war. Notwithstanding certain leftist leanings, Dan was also, as he saw it perforce, an advocate of the 'democracy' – the democratic masses – working with the Provisional Government, and he supported Tsereteli's ascension to minister for posts and telegraph in May. But despite that solidarity with his party comrade, and the vitriolic attacks it had earned him from the Bolsheviks, now, along with Bogdanov, Khinchuk and several others of his party, he opposed Tsereteli from the left.

On principles of revolutionary democracy, rather than of any particular support for the Bolsheviks, he argued against Tsereteli's punitive stance. Dan's group proposed a compromise. Armed demonstrations should be prohibited, and the Bolsheviks condemned rather than officially suppressed.

In Lenin's absence, it was Kamenev who responded for the Bolsheviks – an interesting choice, given his consistent opposition to the demonstration that never was. He now insisted, not very persuasively, that the march was always to have been peaceful, and would have made no calls to seize power. Besides which, it had been cancelled at Congress's request. What, he wondered, butter not melting in his mouth, was all the fuss about?

Between Dan's suggestion of slapped wrists, and Kamenev's wide-eyed ingenuousness, the situation seemed to be defusing. But then, out of order, Tsereteli took the floor again.

'He is white as a sheet,' *Pravda* reported, 'and very excited. Tense silence reigns.'

Tsereteli launched into a brutal attack. The Bolsheviks were conspirators, he said. To stand against their plans, he demanded once more that they should be disarmed and legally repressed.

The mood was electric. All eyes turned to Kamenev as he rose to respond. If Tsereteli stood by such claims, he rather splendidly exclaimed, let him immediately arrest and try Kamenev himself. With that riposte, the Bolsheviks swept from the hall.

The debate was splenetic in their absence. On the side of Tsereteli were Avksentiev, Znamensky, Liber, and many other right social-ists – including Kerensky. Ranged against them were centrist and Left SRs, Trudoviks and Mensheviks, and the far-left Mezhraiontsy. Some argued their case, like Dan, from principles of democracy; some affirmed that Tsereteli's claims of conspiracy were unproven; some – most eloquently Martov – underlined that the mass of workers supported the Bolsheviks on many issues, and that the task of socialists to their right had, therefore, to be to win those workers over, not to make martyrs of the left.

When it came to the decision, the SRs and Mensheviks narrowly agreed to Dan's compromise. Tsereteli's suppressive resolution was withdrawn.

At an emergency meeting of the Bolshevik Petersburg Committee, Lenin tried to put the case behind the cancellation. Again he stressed the necessity of 'maximum calmness, caution, restraint and organisa-tion', but now he further implied – as, from a very different political position, had Tsereteli – that the revolution was entering a new phase.

Except in the most abstract possible way, Lenin did not apologise or admit to error. To do so was never his style. He argued, rather, that the CC had had 'no alternative' but to call a halt to the action, for two reasons: because the Soviet itself had 'formally banned' it, and because, according to reliable sources, a formidable group of Black Hundreds had intended a violent response, to unleash counterrevolution.

The former argument was quaint, coming from a man who had never hesitated to break an order or a law if he considered it advan-tageous so to do. As to the latter, Latsis pointed out that everyone had been aware of the possibility of a counterdemonstration. 'If we were not ready for it,' he said, 'we should have approached the ques-tion of a demonstration negatively from the very beginning.'

The fact is that Lenin had blinked. And his abstention on the vote to cancel was not only uncharacteristic, but uncharacteristically evasive of responsibility: if, as he now claimed, there had been no choice, why had he not voted against the action? If the intent behind abstention had been to inoculate himself from criticism for backing down, it did not work.

Volodarsky, Slutsky, the irrepressible Latsis, and various others derided the CC as, in Tomsky's words, 'guilty of intolerable wavering'. Naumov, of the Soviet's Bolshevik delegation, voiced the ultra-left mood, insisting bullishly that he was glad the leadership was undermined, because 'it is necessary to trust only in oneself and the masses'. 'If the cancellation was correct,' he added, 'when did we make a mistake?'

The question was pertinent. While it may not be alone in this, the socialist left has always tended to exaggerate its successes – the vinegary humorist Nadezhda Teffi quipped, 'If Lenin were to talk about a meeting at which he, Zinoviev, Kamenev and five horses were present, he would say: "There were eight of us"' – and it does not have a good record of acknowledging its failures. The fear, perhaps, is that fallibility undermines authority. The left's typical method has been to brazen out errors; then, as long as possible after any dust has settled, remark *en passant* that 'of course', everyone knows 'mistakes were made', back in the mists of time.

On 12 June, Kerensky persuaded the All-Russian Soviet Congress, against the opposition of Bolsheviks and a few others, to resolve that 'the Russian revolutionary democracy is obliged to keep its army in a condition to take either the offensive or defensive …[to] be decided from a purely military and strategic point of view'. This was permission to resume military operations – including advances. In other words, 'defencism', even in its 'revolutionary' variety, even undertaken in good faith to protect the gains of the revolution, could segue into 'traditional' war. Chernov was clear about this: 'without an offence', he said, 'there is no defence'.

That done, Congress went on to pass Dan's censure of the Bolsheviks. Then Dan, Bogdanov and Khinchuk proposed another way to take wind out of the left's sails. The moderates in the Soviet were committed to channelling the city's radical energies in their own direction, away from the radicals, through a sanctioned outlet to tap and shape the popular mood. Therefore, Congress scheduled for Sunday 18 June a mass demonstration of its very own. That, the moderates decided, would show the Bolsheviks who had a handle on the Petrograd masses.

At the front, the war crawled on. A strange infrastructure of death.

Beyond fields of rye and potatoes and grazing cows, deep in thick woods, Red Cross tents loomed in forest clearings. Dugouts and low log cabins; rough, jury-rigged chapels; and a staccato tinnitus of mortars. Trench-drenched soldiers the colour of the ripped-up earth taking what hours of respite they could, drinking tea from tin mugs. Alternate rhythms of boredom and terror, fire rising to meet German planes blasting overhead scattering propaganda, or fire of their own. The desperate jocularity of fraternisation, yells in halting German and Russian back and forth across those yards of no-man's-land. The rage of machine guns, the visitations of bad spirits, twelve-inch shells nicknamed for the witch Baba Yaga, screaming in to tear the world apart.

Soldiers stumbled, snared by the war's predatory metal, the barbed wire that grasped as if with its own purpose. Behind the lines huddled terrorised men – and a small number of women combatants, too – from across the empire, a debased cosmopolitanism of the conscripted, fingering bayonets in these premonitory graves.

All the while behind the front, inflation and inadequate supplies meant living conditions were collapsing. The peasants' impatience grew more violent. A slow increase of reports of expropriation, less according to some rude, careful sense of village justice, now, than by sheer force, destruction, arson, sometimes murder.

Breakdown was widespread. On 1 June, in Baku, a thousand Azerbaijanis crowded the city hall, demanding grain, as relations soured between them and Armenians. In Latvia, landless peasants kept up pressure on the Land Council, demanding the expropriation of baronial estates. In Ukraine, on the 13th, after repeated attempts to negotiate with Petrograd, the Ukrainian Rada (parliament) issued its 'First Universal', announcing an 'autonomous Ukrainian republic' – just short of formal separation, but bad enough as far as the Russian right were concerned. The Coalition Government, though, had no choice but to allow it.

Some on the left had little sensitivity to tangled local tensions. In Baku, the *Izvestia* of the Soviet polemicised against Muslim nationalism without mentioning its counterpart among local Armenians, Jews or Russians. The local Bolsheviks, though they opposed the 'bourgeois' nationalist federalist demands of the Muslim National Committee, criticised such soviet myopia; they strove to keep communication open with the Muslim 'democratic' movement.

The two great wings of social democracy were moving further and further apart. In early June, those Baku Bolsheviks, following their Georgian comrades in Tiflis, terminated all association with the Mensheviks. At last the regional organisations were swinging behind Lenin's call for schism.

In part in an effort to dilute the dangerous energies of nationalism and radicalism with Russian patriotism, and, more, to reassure the Allies, the government sped up its plans for what was now a Soviet Congress-authorised military offensive. On 16 June, at the southern front near Lwów, Russian heavy artillery began a pounding two-day onslaught. Kerensky, once more the persuader-in-chief, announced to Russian troops in Galicia that an offensive was about to commence. On the 18th, it would begin – on the very same day as the Soviet's planned march.

The Mensheviks and the SRs inaugurated yet another organising committee, and their papers pushed hard for their demonstration. Briefly, with impressive perversity, the anarchists tried instead to build for one of their own, on the 14th. An irritated *Pravda* declared such plans 'ruinous', and they faded to nothing.

154

The Bolsheviks and Mezhraiontsy, too, agitated, according to the Bolshevik CC's aspiration 'to transform the demonstration, against the will of the Soviet, into an expression of support for the transfer of all power to the Soviet'. They hoped for what Zinoviev called 'a demonstration within a demonstration'. By their good fortune, from 16 to 23 June, the All-Russian Conference of Bolshevik Military Organisations was scheduled in Petrograd, lending the party the skills of around 100 experienced activists.

The Soviet's own rather vague slogans for the march declared for the 'Democratic Republic', 'General Peace' and 'Immediate Convocation of a Constituent Assembly'. The Bolsheviks reverted to the combative slogans intended for the aborted march of 10 June: 'Down with the Tsarist Duma!' 'Down with the Ten Capitalist Ministers!' (those non-socialists in the cabinet); 'Down with the Politics of the Offensive!' 'Bread! Peace! Land!' On the 14th, *Pravda* announced that Bolshevik supporters should come out under these slogans even if the rest of their factories did not. The Soviet leadership, to the hooting derision of the left, made a half-hearted attempt to insist that only official slogans would be permissible. The Bolshevik Fedorov embarrassed them by crowing that his party's main slogan would be: 'All Power to the Soviets!'

Still, those moderates were combative. On the 17th, Tsereteli mocked Kamenev. 'Tomorrow', he taunted, 'not separate groups but all the working class of the capital there will demonstrate, not against the will of the Soviet but at its invitation. Now we shall all see which the majority follows, you or us.'

Indeed.

Sunday 18 June: a clear, windy morning. Workers and soldiers assembled early. That day sister demonstrations were planned in Moscow, Kiev, Minsk, Riga, Helsingfors (Helsinki), Kharkov, and across the empire.

At 9 a.m., a band struck up the Marseillaise, the French national anthem that had become an international hymn to freedom. The parade began its procession down Nevsky Prospect.

Its colossal size became slowly clear. The march filled the wide vista for miles. Some 400,000 people had taken to the streets.

The great column traced a route via the tomb of the February martyrs, to pay its respects. At its head walked the organisers from the Ispolkom, Mensheviks and SRs from the presidium of the All-Russia Congress, including Chkheidze, Dan, Gegechkori, Bogdanov and Gots. As they approached the Mars Field, they peeled away. A platform had been raised near the burial place. They ascended, to look out over the crowd.

Horror crept over them.

Sukhanov surveyed the mass of jostling banners. 'Bolsheviks again,' he later remembered thinking. 'And there behind them is another Bolshevik column … Apparently the next one, too.' His eyes widened. He turned his head to take it all slowly in. Here and there, he glimpsed an SR or an official Soviet slogan. But they were 'submerged by the mass'. The overwhelming majority of banners advancing towards the aghast organisers – like, he said, Birnam Wood towards Macbeth – were Bolshevik.

Seas of 'Down with the Ten Capitalist Ministers!' Wave after wave of 'Peace! Bread! Land!' And – a strange taunt to the Soviet conciliators – endless iterations of 'All Power to the Soviet!'

Tsereteli had looked forward to the Soviet march being 'a duel in the open arena'. Now blowback blew back, very hard. The results were devastating, unambiguous, crushing. 'Sunday's demonstration', wrote Gorky's paper *Novaya zhizn*, 'revealed the complete triumph of Bolshevism among the Petersburg Proletariat.'

As they came past, Bolshevik after Bolshevik broke away from their fellows to rush up to Chkheidze. Kaustov, the recently imprisoned editor of the party's front-line paper, they demanded, must be released from custody. Chkheidze made placatory noises. Soon the matter would be out of his hands.

Early afternoon. An extraordinary column of workers marched into sight, as precise as highly trained soldiers. 'What district is this?' came a shout.

'Why, can't you see?' the group's leader said proudly. 'Exemplary order! That means it's Vyborg.' The militant district came led by their heavily Bolshevik soviet. The Vyborg red flags were interspersed with black banners, the irrepressible anarchists demanding 'Down with Government and Capital!' Ignoring official pleas, many Vyborg workers carried weapons.

At 3 p.m., 2,000 Anarchist–Communists and sympathetic soldiers broke away from the march and made rapidly for the bleak brick sprawl of Vyborg's notorious riverside prison, Kresty. At its entrance gates they raised their weapons at the guards, and demanded Kaustov be let out. His terrified jailers plunged into the keep-like maze to fetch him out. Freed from his cell, Kaustov, with lordly front and without missing a beat, demanded that several other political prisoners also be released. Only when their comrades had emerged did the daring anarchists disperse.

That afternoon, as the exultant left celebrated the day, the minister of justice, Perevezev – one of the ten capitalist ministers against whom the banners had railed – called an emergency government meeting. He wanted full power to recapture all escaped prisoners. He demanded the right to employ any means necessary. He got it.

At three the following morning, 19 June, soldiers, Cossacks and armoured cars surrounded the Durnovo villa. They shone their lights on the walls in that eerie White Night, one of the city's midsummer skies, dark but dimly glowing, a haze like a dirty sunset. The soldiers blared through a megaphone, shouting for the sixty anarchists within to hand over those they had broken out of jail the previous day. Most, including Kaustov, were long gone: still, the anarchists refused to cooperate. They ducked below the windows of the besieged building and hurled out bombs that did not explode. The troops stormed the doors.

A noisy, confused fracas. Asnin – so went the claim in the official enquiry – tried to grab a soldier's rifle. There was a shot. Asnin was dead.

Word of his martyrdom spread fast through the district. That morning, the factories nearest the villa – the Rozenkrants, the Fenisk, Metalist, Promet and Parviainen plants, among others – came out in militant protest. Crowds gathered. Asnin's grieving comrades displayed his body at the villa, and mourners lined up to pay respects.

Furious workers lobbied the Ispolkom, which begged for calm and implored the strikers to return to work. It set up an investigation. It demanded that the government release all those detained that night who were not accused of specific crimes. But such measures did little to mollify the militants. Anarchists from the Rozenkrants factory sent representatives to the radical First Machine Gun Regiment and the Moskovsky Regiment, to propose a joint demonstration against the government. The soldiers deflected the suggestion, but the seed of an idea was sown, rage stoked. From here began to accelerate a wave of protests in Petrograd.

That day, the 19th, also showed how divided and politically febrile Petrograd was. The same Nevsky Prospect that had, the previous day, vibrated with Bolshevik slogans under hundreds of thousands of boots, now hosted a parade organised by officer cadets. It was a largely middle-class demonstration, a fraction of the size of that of the 18th, but, nonetheless, it bespoke a certain genuine upsurge of patriotic enthusiasm. The marchers chanted, hurrahed for the troops. They sung nationalist songs and waved portraits of Kerensky. In the eyes of the right, Russian honour seemed to be on its way to a restoration: they were out on the streets to celebrate an event whose echoes had just reached the city: the advance of the army. A shift in the war, a long-mooted wager taken by those in charge. The June, or Kerensky, Offensive.

In Galicia, the Eighth Army broke through lines of demoralised Austrian troops across a twenty-mile front. The offensive, undertaken to reassure the Allies, to shift the war, to discipline the restive and troublesome rear, seemed a devastating success. On the central and northern fronts, the Seventh and Eleventh Armies rapidly took more than 18,000 prisoners. As the advance continued, patriotism swept the country, including among many socialists within the Soviet. An official proclamation from the All-Russian Congress burbled enthusiastically, demanding bread from the peasants and support from the citizenry for Russia's heroic soldiers.

But such rah-rah did not last long. Word very soon began to drift back from the front that things were not going as planned.

In working-class areas in particular, unrest began to return. Several regiments and factory committees went as far as explicitly condemning the offensive in the Bolshevik press.

On 20 June, the First Machine Gun Regiment in Petrograd received orders to supply 500 machine guns to the front. The regimental committee agreed to this, but a mass meeting of the regiment felt differently. It was unwilling to lose weapons from the revolutionary capital, even to help their fellow soldiers. To the vigorous approval of the far left, the soldiers voted for another demonstration against the government, to be held as soon as possible. They approached other garrisons, and at 5 p.m. won the support of the Grenadier Guards.

The Soviet urgently denounced their actions as 'a stab in the back' of their comrades at the front. They begged the machine-gunners to reconsider. When, the next morning, the regiment was ordered to relocate two-thirds of its members to the front, it would only agree to send ten of the thirty detachments, and that only when 'the war has taken on a revolutionary character'. Given Order Number 1, the machine-gunners insisted, such a forced transfer of units from Petrograd to the front was illegal, and the command was a calculated attempt to break the radical Petrograd garrison. They added, with ominous resolve: 'If the Soviet ... threatens this and other revolutionary regiments with forcible dissolution in response we will ... not stop at using armed strength to break up the Provisional Government and other organisations supporting it.'

They were not intimidated by the Soviet's authority. Even so, later that day the machine-gunners elected to wind down their agitation – possibly, if perhaps counterintuitively, at Bolshevik request. Because throughout this tumult, at the Conference of Bolshevik Military Organisations, Lenin and a cautious party leadership were striving to restrain their militants from 'excessive' insurgent action. Having yanked the party to the left in April, now Lenin was trying to tug it right.

On the 20th of the month, an agitated and perturbed Lenin addressed the conference. Startling those who assumed he would approve of their 'revolutionary spirit', he stressed that all talk of an immediate seizure of power was premature. Their enemies were trying to bait them, at a time when they did not have the mass support they would need for such a venture. The present priority, he said, was assiduously to increase that support – to build up influence in the Soviet.

'This is no longer a capital,' wrote Gorky, amid a sense of slow apocalypse, 'it is a cesspit ... The streets are filthy, there are piles of stinking rubbish in the courtyards ... There is a growing idleness and cowardice in the people, and all those base and criminal instincts ... are now destroying Russia.'

The strike wave continued. On 22 June, Bolshevik delegates to the VTsIK – the All-Russian Soviet Ispolkom, or Executive Committee – warned that workers at the Putilov metalworks were likely to come out, and that they would not restrain them. On the 23rd, representatives of several labour organisations resolved that, as higher wages were not compensating for rising prices, they wanted control of production. At repeated mass meetings, the Kronstadt sailors determined to free those soldiers who had been arrested along with the anarchists. These were not secretive conspiracies: on the 25th, the sailors openly warned the justice minister of their plans.

All this while, the offensive demanded more and more men. Soldiers over forty, who had already served and been furloughed from the front, were starting to be recalled. To have risked their life once was not enough. In provincial towns like Astrakhan and Yelets, the call-up provoked riots.

The Bolsheviks were busy preparing their Sixth Congress, as well as the second City Conference of the Petersburg Committee, slated for early July. As they did, their in-party debates continued. Within the Petersburg Committee, Kalinin and other moderates won, nineteen to two, an appeal to eschew isolated revolutionary actions, resolving instead to build up political influence in the movement and the Soviet. But Latsis managed to amend the resolution: 'if it proved impossible' to restrain the masses, the Bolsheviks should take the movement into their own hands.

In the pages of *Pravda*, Lenin and Kamenev stressed caution, care, the slow building up of forces; simultaneously, *Soldatskaya pravda* continued to fan flames of more impatient dissent, pointedly declining to validate what their leaders described as a need to overcome 'petty-bourgeois illusions'. On 22 June, at an informal meeting of members of the CC, the MO and the Petersburg Committee with the regiments supporting the Bolshevik party, Semashko – effectively in command of 15,000 radical machine-gunners – chided the CC for underestimating the party's strength.

During those turbulent late June days, out of the boisterous energies of Petrograd's most militant groups, particularly the increasingly legendary First Machine Gun Regiment, a tentative collective plan began to emerge. The protean notion grew more distinct as the days passed.

Determined to batten down the surge of unrest, and provoked by the ill discipline of the First Machine Gun Regiment, on 23 June the All-Russian Congress of the Soviet called on all garrison units to immediately obey orders. But the Soviet's manoeuvering was uncertain. That same day, its vacillation with regard to the creaking Russian Empire came to the fore, when the Finnish parliament issued its *Valtalaki* – a 'power act' declaring its intent to legislate on domestic issues. The celebrating Finns were astonished when the leaders of the Soviet, having previously approved the negotiation of a treaty of independence – of which this fell short – reacted with outrage. Unilateral declarations of even limited autonomy had clearly not been what they had had in mind.

And meanwhile, on this last day of the Bolshevik MO Conference, its *Biulleten* reported a serious dispute between radicals and moderates – here the Leninists! – over whether to actively pursue agitation at the front while the offensive was proceeding successfully. The very premise of the debate, however, was mistaken. The offensive was not proceeding successfully.

After the first two, three exhilarating days of the offensive, its degeneration was swift. The scavenger birds of the front were gathering over what was becoming a catastrophe.

As early as 20 June, the exhausted, ill-equipped Russian troops ceased advancing. They refused to obey orders to attack. The next day, a German counterattack began. Panic spread through the Russian forces. On the 24th, a desolate Kerensky wired the Provisional Government that 'in many cases, the breakthrough turned out to be unstable, and after the first days, sometimes even after the first hours of battle, there was a change of heart and spirits dropped. Instead of developing the initial successes units … began drawing up resolutions with demands for immediate leave to the rear'.

In the diaries of his AWOL years, *A Deserter's Notes*, the young Ukrainian Aleksandr Dneprovskiy execrated the patriotic press in the last months before the offensive as 'tubs of printed slop … poured over the heads of long-suffering humanity'. Despite the newspapers dutifully recycling patriotic blather, the miserable truth of events leaked quickly across the country. Often at first hand.

The situation had long ceased to be a matter of individuals, or even whole battalions, disobeying orders. Now there was mass movement of Russian troops in both directions: forward from the trenches, not belligerently but in more fraternisation, shouting greetings, picking a way through the landscape of cataclysm to share liquor and make-do conversation with the Germans they were supposed to kill; and, in vast numbers, in retreat from the front. Mass desertions. Thousands simply walked away.

That summer, the great poet and critic Viktor Shklovsky set out for the Galician war zone, a Soviet army commissar. He came the last miles on foot, through swampy spruce goves near Austrian lines.

> While going through the forest, I kept running into stray soldiers with rifles, mostly young men. I asked, 'Where are you off to?'
>
> 'I'm sick.'
>
> In other words, deserting from the front. What could you do with them? Even though you know it's useless, you say, 'Go on back. This is disgraceful.' They keep going.

The scale was staggering. A ramping up of already enormous numbers. On a single night near Volochinsk, shock battalions of the Eleventh Army arrested 12,000 deserters hiding or wandering numbly in the dark. This was a mass movement. Officially, 170,000 soldiers ran away during the offensive: the real number is very much higher.

Soldiers stormed trains from the front. The creaking engines rocked under their weight, screeching on the rails as men clung to roofs and buffers, as, rammed sullen and exhausted together, they swayed with the sluggish carriages. Near the northern front, thousands of the runaways set up what they announced was a 'soldiers' republic', a strange new polity in an encampment near a Petrograd racecourse. They flooded the capital, hustling for cash. By the hot days of July, more than 50,000 deserters were in the city.

The men found work as casual labourers. They scavenged off the land. They became violent bandits, ripping and reconfiguring their old uniforms with a ragged swagger. Their desertions were the result of fear, of course, but that was by no means always all.

'The mass desertions', Trotsky wrote, 'are ceasing in the present conditions to be the result of depraved individual wills' – that would be a severe and unsympathetic assessment at any time – 'and are

becoming an expression of the complete incapacity of the government to weld the revolutionary army with inward unity of purpose.'
Among these hundreds of thousands, increasing numbers were in
the mould of the eloquent Dneprovskiy, whose desertion inspired
him to write, who combined a desperate desire not to die in stinking
runnels of blood with political rage and despair, with critical lucidity
in the analysis of the hated war.

One 'Worker Zemskov' described himself in a letter to Kerensky
– matter-of-factly, without apology – as 'a deserter ... hiding in the
Kuban steppes for more than two years'. 'To hell with it, though,' he
protested,

> what kind of freedom is this, when millions of voiceless slaves are still being
> led like sheep to the cannons and machine guns and the officer is still treating
> the slave as if he were a mere thing, when still only crude coercion restrains
> the multimillionfold army of grey slaves, when the new government (exactly
> like the old) has the authority to send the entire male population into this
> bloody abyss (war)?

Some deserters now took to parading through Petrograd with
placards, demanding what they called their 'liberation'. This was
desertion as a social movement.

Even before the offensive, the loathing the war engendered, the sense
from soldiers, their families, their supporters, workers and peasants
in vast numbers, that it must be ended immediately, gave the Bolsheviks political traction. From late June in particular, they ramped
up their propaganda in the crumbling army: their networks of speakers and agitators were reaching 500 regiments along the front.

Lenin's intention had always been to forge a perception of the
Bolsheviks as the most unapologetic and absolute opposition to the
war, but perhaps, as his left critics had cautioned, the details of his
revolutionary defeatism had indeed been ambiguous. Perhaps they
had been evasive, had elided distinct positions, and perhaps that had

confused some audiences. In any case, the specifically (and ambiguously) 'defeatist' phraseology had, since Lenin's return, been considerably less prominent. The party's anti-war reputation was still, sure enough, growing.

On occasion this could become closely associated with the person of Lenin himself: thus, even before the offensive, soldiers of the Fifth Army on the northern front declared him the only authority they recognised. As the war grew ever more hated, people remembered the Bolshevik party's unwavering opposition to it.

This was thanks in particular to the unstinting work of Bolshevik cadres, especially the undersung middle-level activists. They were the backbone of the party organisations across the empire. They worked hard, and grew more expert. Eduard Dune, in Moscow, travelled with his comrades far into surrounding country districts to give talks. Few of the several hundred in his local party were natural public speakers. But after February, they improved their skills, got to know their audiences – and their own strengths.

'We began to specialise,' he wrote. One comrade, Sapronov, was in his element in large meetings of thousands: a gentle soul called Kalmykov, ragged as a mendicant, toured the small workshops to deliver warm effective homilies; another, Artamanov, 'either because he had an impressive bass voice or because he spoke the dialect of the Moscow suburbs or possibly for some other reason ... was a great hit with peasant audiences'.

And such villagers in particular 'listened willingly enough to speeches against the war and for peace'.

Even the more perspicacious of the party's enemies could see the appeal and logic of its unflinching antinomianism towards the war, compared to the negotiations of the moderates. General Brusilov, no intellectual but a thoughtful man, would later recall: 'The position of the Bolsheviks I understood, because they preached "Down with the war and immediate peace at any price," but I couldn't understand at all the tactics of the SRs and the Mensheviks, who first broke up the army, as if to avoid counterrevolution, and at the same time desired the continuation of the war to a victorious end.'

On 26 June, delegates from the Grenadier Regiment, one of many that had refused to advance against the Germans, returned to the capital. They told the reservists' battalion the truth about the front – including that their own commanders drove them into battle at the points of machine guns. They appealed for help, and demanded all power to the soviets. *Soldatskaya pravda* pledged them full support.

Across the city and the empire, as news spread of the calamitous push that bore his name, the remnants of the Kerensky cult turned to dust.

After all his urgent and frenetic interventions, Lenin was exhausted to the point of illness. His family were concerned. His comrades persuaded him that he needed to take a rest. On the 27th, accompanied by his sister Maria, he left Petrograd. They travelled together across the border to the Finnish village of Neivola, where his comrade Bonch-Bruevich had a country cottage. There they spent the days relaxing, swimming in a lake, strolling in the sun.

As they did so, the machine-gunners received new orders for a substantial transfer of men and weapons. On the last day of the month, the military section of the Petrograd Soviet sent one G. B. Skalov to discuss these matters with them.

Provoked by the fury of their men, the Regimental Committee, controlled by SRs and Mensheviks, was pushed to hold the talks in the halls of the Tauride Palace. There the soldiers themselves, many of them anarchists or Bolsheviks – including Golovin, a leading light of the rebellion-that-never-was of the 20th and 21st – protested that these new orders were a prelude to treachery or sell-out.

The machine-gunners would not allow the regiment to be either disarmed or disbanded. They were of one mind. The room rang with their declarations. Openly, they began to discuss how to prevent this. In the sedate surroundings of the palace, the soldiers mooted the necessity of the force of arms, on the city streets.

7

July: Hot Days

Deep in the Vyborg district, a shouting crowd dragged a man behind them. They hauled him through the uneven streets and he howled and left a red trail behind him. It was not only his blood. He was a wheeler-dealer, a middleman, a food speculator in a hungry city. The meat he sold was old and rotten. The locals had caught him and pelted and smeared him with his own decaying wares, so that he left behind him a trail of rancid flesh and blood. 'The surge is coming to the surface,' Latsis wrote in his diary at the start of the month. 'It is beginning. There is uneasiness in the district.'

'Russians returning, *Russians*, mind you, simply throw up their hands and describe it as bedlam.' *Swallows and Amazons* had yet to be born behind Arthur Ransome's eyes: these days he was the correspondent of the *British Daily News*, a man keen to express the delirium of Petrograd. The uneasiness in the districts. 'One lives the whole time in an atmosphere of mental conflict of the most violent kind.'

On 1 July, the Soviet issued a plaintive call to the First Machine Gunners to return to their barracks and await further instructions. But the gunners continued formulating plans for an armed demonstration-cum-uprising. That day, as tensions boiled up in the forms of crime, industrial upheaval and violent conflicts over shortages of food and fuel, the Bolshevik Petrograd Second City Conference opened in the Kshesinskaya Mansion.

Tensions between the wings of the party were sharpening. The enthusiasts and the ultra-left confronted the cautious. The MO had learnt of the gunners' plans, and fervently insisted to the CC that the regiment could overthrow the government. That, in any case, a movement of the soldiers was inevitable: the question, therefore, was not whether it should 'be allowed', but how the party should relate to it.

The leadership, certain that the time was not ripe for insurrection, continued to urge restraint. They ordered the MO to try to prevent any outbreak.

Years later, Nevsky of the MO described how he discharged this duty. 'When the Military Organisation, having learned of the machine-gunners' demonstration, sent me as the more or less most popular Military Organisation orator to talk the masses into not going out, I talked to them, but in such a way that only a fool could come to the conclusion that he should not demonstrate.' Nor was he the only MO comrade to perform this leftist ca'canny, discharging the letter of orders against their spirit. The Anarchist–Communists, of course, resorted to no such subterfuge. They were quite open in their support for an armed uprising.

On the afternoon of the 2nd, there was a concert at the city hall known as the People's House. It was not the usual farewell to front-bound troops: this event was sponsored by the Bolsheviks themselves, to raise money for anti-war literature for soldiers to *take to the front with them*. An astonishing provocation.

Before of an audience of 5,000, musicians and poets performed, interspersed with speeches from leading Bolshevik and Mezhraiontsy activists – the latter now caucusing with the Bolsheviks so closely as to be effectively indistinguishable. The event became a wild anti-government, anti-war rally, and rang with denunciations of Kerensky. To the crowd's delight, Trotsky and Lunacharsky demanded all power to the soviets. Such gatherings could only instil resolve in the machine-gunners.

That evening, the cabinet of the government met to discuss Ukraine's declaration of independence. The Rada had pledged loyalty to revolutionary Russia and agreed to forgo a standing army, but having acquired broad legitimacy, it was now implicitly recognised as the voice of Ukrainians – and this was a loss of authority too far for the Kadet ministers.

After a long, rancorous debate late into the night, one Kadet, Nekrasov, voted for the proposal to accept the Ukrainian proposal, quitting his party to do so. The other four voted against, and quit the cabinet instead.

Six moderate socialists and five 'capitalists' remained. The coalition was collapsing.

From the first moments of 3 July, the air was tight and strained as a stretched skin. In the very early hours, Petrograd postal workers struck over pay. Then, at mid-morning of that warm day, a thousands-strong protest of the 'over-forties', those soldiers being recalled to the war, marched in protest down Nevsky.

The main demonstration business of the day began at around 11 a.m. As the First Machine Gun Regimental Committee discussed the troop and weapon transfers, preparing for negotiations with the Soviet, a mass meeting of several thousand activist machine-gunners under Golovin, supported by the Bolshevik MO, formulated their own position.

Bleikhman, the energetic Anarchist–Communist, exhorted them. He insisted that it was time to overthrow the Provisional Government and take power – directly, not even handing it to the Soviet. And as to organisation? 'The street', he said, 'will organise us.' He proposed a demonstration at 5 p.m. In an ambience of combative enthusiasm, the suggestion was unanimously passed.

The soldiers quickly elected a Provisional Revolutionary Committee, under the popular Bolshevik agitator A. I. Semashko, now directly disobeying his party's injunctions. Soldiers' delegates set out in boats for Kronstadt, and went racing through the city in their armoured cars, waving banners from their windows, spreading the word, garnering support from the Moskovsky, Grenadier, First Infantry, and Armoured Car Divisions – as well as from workers in their Vyborg factories. Not all their appeals were rewarded with explicit support: sometimes they met with 'benevolent neutrality'. No signs of a countermovement, of active opposition, were visible, however.

Mid-afternoon. A seething, angry mass started to gather in the city's outskirts, heading slowly for the centre.

Gone, now, were the uptown types. Vanishingly few of those present were the better-dressed, more affluent protestors who had taken part in the February marches. This was the armed anger of workers, soldiers – those Bonch-Bruevich had called to be Red Guards.

As the demonstrations began to converge on the Tauride Palace, around 3 p.m., the Bolshevik delegation to the Soviet convened the Workers' section without notice. The party's members turned up en bloc, outnumbering those Mensheviks and SRs who had scrambled to attend. The Bolsheviks were able to promptly pass a motion calling for all power to the Soviet. Their outflanked opponents walked out in protest.

At Kshesinskaya, the Bolshevik Second City Conference was into its third day. Heated disagreements continued. As the Petersburg Committee debated whether to override Lenin's opposition and establish a separate newspaper – on the grounds that *Pravda* was not meeting their needs – two MO machine-gunners burst into the chamber, and announced that they were marching on the Provisional Government.

Chaos descended. Volodarsky excoriated the soldiers for going against party wishes; they witheringly replied that it was better to leave the party than turn against their regiment. With that, the machine-gunners walked out, and the meeting was abruptly terminated.

The All-Russian Central Executive Committee of the Soviet of Workers' and Soldiers' Deputies, and its counterpart for Peasants'

Deputies, were already assembled in the Tauride Palace: they had been trying to work out how best to offer their support to the diminished, Kadet-less Provisional Government. It was at around 4 p.m. that reports of the swelling demonstration got through to them. The Soviet leadership understood immediately that this was an existential threat to their authority – possibly even to their persons.

Quickly they mandated the Menshevik intellectual Wladimir Woytinsky to arrange the palace's defence. They dispatched telegrams to all garrison troops, and to the Kronstadt base, sternly reiterating the ban on demonstrations. They drafted a proclamation condemning the march as treachery, warning that it would be dealt with by 'all available means'. Members of the Soviet fanned out across Petrograd to try to calm the streets.

News of the demonstration had reached the Bolshevik CC, also meeting in Tauride, a few doors down. There was quick and fractious debate. The CC, by now including Trotsky, maintained its cautious 'Leninist' line – that the time for such an adventure was not right – and voted against joining in. Urgently the leadership sent activists to try to hold the machine-gunners back. Zinoviev and Kamenev prepared an appeal for the front page of next day's *Pravda*, imploring the masses to show restraint. The CC relayed its decision to their Second City Conference.

At that conference, however, dissent exploded.

Though expressions of support for the rebels were defeated and the CC position did pass, it was criticised by many high-profile delegates. The conference left called for a meeting with representatives from factories, the military, the Mezhraiontsy and Menshevik–Internationalists, to 'take the temperature' of the city. This demand was, and was understood to be, pressure on the CC to pitch left.

A compromise was rush-cobbled together, but though couched in the party's usual tough language, it was in fact formalised floundering. It would take days, weeks, for the radicals to make sense of what was about to come – events that would lead them to shift their

positions, discard the sloganeering call for Soviet power and envisage something new, more combative still.

'We will see', announced Tomsky, articulating the party's hesitant stance at that moment, 'how the movement develops.' For
now neither firestarters nor firefighters, the Bolsheviks could only
commit to keeping on watching. 'We will see.'

From the start, the demonstration was violent. Shouting marchers
heaved together to overturn trams, tipping them out of their runnels
to lie on their sides in their own shattered windows. On the bridges,
revolutionary soldiers set up machine gun posts. The mood was
insurrectionary.

And not only among the left. 'Black Hundreds, hooligans, provocateurs, anarchists and desperate people introduce a large amount
of chaos and absurdity to the demonstration', said Lunacharsky. In
volleys of shots and frantic punches and hurled and broken glass, the
left and the hard right clashed. The city rang to the sounds of guns
and hooves. Beside the City Council on Nevsky Prospect, bloody
fighting erupted.

Bullets from machine guns took men down. Wounded demonstrators staggered to escape along Petrograd's impassive streets and
rounded colonnades. The faces of lions watched from the grand
facades of which they were part, their mouths carved shut but the
dirty city air giving them smut tongues. In the canals, gliding under
the bridges, barges laden with wood from the endless forests continued their deliveries, as if the streets were not full of whinnying
and screaming, as if armoured cars did not hurtle overhead, and
the bargemen did not have to duck at the whine of missiles. Black-
bearded men from the villages frowned up from the cuts where their
low boats puttered.

At 7:45 p.m., a truck bristling with weapons pulled up at the Baltic
Station: the men within had come to arrest Kerensky, who they had
heard would be there. But they had missed him by moments. He had
departed the city. Three battalions of the Machine Gun Regiment set

out through Vyborg. 'Down with the Ten Capitalist Ministers!' their placards read. News of the Kadet resignations from cabinet had not reached them yet – with them out, only six remained. Massed militants seized munitions from the Mikhailovskoe Artillery Academy, and stormed across the Liteiny Bridge, where one section of the crowd joined the Sixth Engineer Battalion and headed for Tauride – and another peeled off for the Kshesinskaya Mansion.

There, the Bolshevik leaders were still debating what to do, when word reached them that the armed masses were approaching. Someone in the room gasped: 'Without the sanction of the Central Committee?'

To be a radical was to lead others, surely, to change their ideas, to persuade them to follow you; to go neither too far or too fast, nor to lag behind. 'To patiently explain.' How easy to forget that people do not need or await permission to move.

A great militant crowd spread out at the junction of the road and river, filling the space between the mosque and the mansion. For the party, Podvoisky, Lashevich and Nevsky emerged onto the mansion's small low balcony. Standing only a few handspans above the multitude, they shouted greetings at them – then, absurdly, urged the enraged thousands to return to Vyborg.

But this movement could not be reversed. The question for the Bolsheviks, then, was whether to shun it, join it, or attempt to lead it.

A turning point: the militant MO at last got its way, as, scrambling to catch up, the party gave its hurried and flustered blessing to a march on the Tauride Palace, in an effort to spread its aegis over a fait accompli. The demonstrators set back out south across the city's bridges and east along the river. It did not take them long to reach the palace, or to surround it.

Within, the Soviet was buzzing in an emergency session. There could be no holding back this sea of armed protestors, and a delegation from the First Machine Gun Regiment pushed their way inside. Storming through the corridors in their heavy boots, they found Chkheidze. As he stared at his unwanted visitors in alarm, the men informed him coldly that they were disturbed to hear that the Soviet was considering entering a new coalition government. That, they said, was something they could not allow.

Some among the throng were ready to be less polite. From the city outside, from beyond the palace fence, came voices hollering for the arrest of the leaders of the Coalition Government. The arrest of the Soviet itself!

But there was no plan and no direction. The streets, despite Bleikhman's confidence, organised no one.

Darkness came at last, and though the tension had not abated, the massed crowds dispersed. For then.

That evening, the remaining 'capitalist ministers' of the coalition huddled with General Polovtsev in the Stavka headquarters near Palace Square. The Winter Palace and the Stavka were guarded by the only troops they had at their disposal: the loyalist war-wounded. Reinforcements were due to join them the next evening. That was a long time to wait.

The night stretched out. A few Cossack detachments roved the city, engaging insurrectionaries. Woytinsky, responsible for the Ispolkom's protection, was on edge: the guard was inadequate to see off any serious attack on Tauride, and he knew it. And the Mensheviks and SRs also knew, notwithstanding a degree of wavering from the less radical regiments who had come out, that morning would bring more protests, heightened uncertainty. They denounced the Bolsheviks, condemned the 'counterrevolutionary' demonstrations, protested 'these ominous signs of disintegration'.

As dawn approached, the Soviet delegates crept out to brave the streets, with the unenviable task of going to the regiments and factories, to try to talk them down.

In the small hours, the Bolshevik CC urgently dispatched M. A. Saveliev to Bonch-Bruevich's dacha to bring back Lenin. By 4 a.m., they were distributing a hastily printed leaflet drafted by Stalin, one that seemed, if anything, designed to stress their own relevance. In tones of equivocal vagueness – 'We call upon this movement … to become a peaceful, organised expression of the will of the workers, soldiers and peasants of Petrograd' – it pretended to a unity of purpose and analysis, an influence, that the party did not possess.

Playing catch-up, the Bolsheviks, who felt they had little choice, gave the militant MO its head, freed it to become part of whatever this was. Of course, now that the party line had switched, Zinoviev and Kamenev's injunction in *Pravda* not to come out was worse than ineffectual: it was an embarrassment. But there was neither time nor focus to replace it. And who could be sure of what, exactly, should be put in its place? What was the party's direction? In the absence of answers, the offending words were simply cut.

On the 4th, the second and more violent of the July Days, *Pravda* appeared, and the centre of its front page was blank. A white, text-less hole.

The 4th. A warm damp dawn. Across the city, shops stayed shut. Insurgents' trucks rushed through the streets. Soldiers squared off against real or imaginary enemies, gunfire sounding repeatedly in the morning quiet. The streets began to fill. By mid-morning, Petrograd thronged again with demonstrators. Half a million people would come out that day.

At 9 a.m., the dilapidated train carrying Lenin, his sister Maria, his comrades Bonch-Bruevich and Saveliev, crossed the Sestra river dividing Finland and Russia, through the border town of Belo-Ostrov. Though part of the Russian empire, the Finnish border was marked by checks. Bonch-Bruevich held his breath as an inspector examined their documents. With Petrograd in these throes, he was fearful that they would be intercepted. But the man waved them on, and the conclave continued back to the city.

As they approached, so too at the Neva's mouth did a naval gallimaufry. A mad patchwork flotilla. Eight tugs, a torpedo boat, passenger ferries, three trawlers, three gunboats, a pair of barges, a scattering of civilian craft. On their decks, waving from their railings, guns aloft, the sailors of Kronstadt, riding the current. Thousands came, commanded by the energetic Bolshevik Raskolnikov, editor of the Kronstadt *Pravda*. They sailed for the mainland to join what they believed would be the culmination of their revolution. The fury of Kronstadt, the revolution's redoubt, came in whatever they had been able to commandeer.

As they powered and tacked closer, the Soviet's Executive Committee sent out its own tug to hail the bizarre arrivals. On its deck stood a messenger, begging them to leave, bellowing across the water that the Soviet did not want them. The motley armada left him bobbing in their overlapping wakes.

Kronstadt's February had been bloody and desperate, an act of revolutionary hope on an isolated island, in expectation of counter-revolution by dawn. No officer held sway in their base now. The sailors' soviet had had no qualms about completing its own local revolution, and their arrival meant more than just more men in Petrograd. They were, rather, emissaries from a red fortress. A living collective, a political premonition.

Their vessels swung into the city. The Kronstadt men moored near Nikolaevsky Bridge, tied up and raised their arms in greeting to the city. Demonstrators in the streets by the water's edge watched and cheered, and exhorted the newcomers to overthrow the government. But Raskolnikov was not ready to head for the Tauride Palace yet. First, he announced, he would lead his sailors along the embankment, across the bridge north and past the long blank walls of the Peter and Paul Fortress, and thence to Kshesinskaya Mansion, on the wrong side of the river for the palace. But there at Kshesinskaya he would present the ranks to the Bolsheviks, or vice versa.

As they came ashore, there, waiting eagerly to address the celebrated sailors, stood Maria Spiridonova.

Spiridonova, the near-legendary SR, who had killed for the people and paid the price, whose torture and imprisonment in 1906 had shocked even liberal consciences. Her courage, sincerity and sacrifice

— and doubtless her striking beauty — had made her something of a popular saint. Still implacably on her party's hard and restive left, she was a fierce opponent of Kerensky and the government.

It was in a needless moment of petty sectarianism that Raskolnikov would not give Spiridonova — the great Spiridonova! — a chance to speak to the Kronstadt sailors. Instead he left her standing, humiliated and aggrieved, as he led his men away to the beat of their band.

The sailors marched across Vasilievsky Island and the Stock Exchange Bridge, carrying banners that read 'All Power to the Soviets'. Their column arrived at last outside the mansion, where from the balcony Sverdlov, Lunacharsky and Nevsky addressed them. The anarchists and Left SRs among the congregation, furious at Spiridonova's uncomradely snubbing, left this partisan gathering in protest.

Raskolnikov and Flerovsky made their way inside, where, holed up within, they found the newly returned Lenin.

The two Kronstadt Bolsheviks implored him to speak, to greet the militant visitors. Lenin, though, was troubled.

He was not happy with the day's events, and he tried to decline, hinting at his disapproval of this huge precipitous provocation. But the demonstrators would not disperse or leave, and nor would they stop their shouting for him. The demands were audible through the mansion walls.

At last, before the tension reached some dangerous point, Lenin surrendered to the insistent crowd. He stepped out onto the balcony to a roaring ovation.

His hesitancy, though, was evident. His speech was uncharacteristically brimstone-free. He greeted the sailors with surprising mildness, hoped, rather than demanded, that 'All Power to the Soviets' would become a reality. He appealed for self-restraint and vigilance.

Even many party faithful were nonplussed. In particular, as one Kronstadt Bolshevik put it, they were taken aback by his emphasis on the necessity of a peaceful demonstration to 'a column of armed men, craving to rush into battle'.

★

'Looking at them,' said the British ambassador's daughter of the insurgent Kronstadt soldiers on the streets, 'one wondered what the fate of Petrograd would be if these ruffians with their unshaven faces, their slouching walk, their utter brutality were to have the town at their mercy.' What indeed? Did they, in fact, not so have the town? But this was something more than a demonstration, something less than an insurrection.

The MO agitated among the garrison at the Peter and Paul Fortress, where amid shouting and wrangling they drew 8,000 men to their side. Radicals with weapons in their hands spread out through the city, took control of anti-Bolshevik newspapers and set up guards at stations. The noise of bullets kept up, as right and left skirmished bloodily.

Mid-afternoon. Some 60,000 people processed by a church on the corner of Sadovaya and Apraksina streets. From above came pounding shots, sending the marchers scattering in panic. Five were left dead on the ground.

At 3 p.m., the huge sailors' demonstration clogged the channel between the smart facades of Nevsky and Liteiny Prospects, where shop windows displayed proud support for the army's offensive and for the government. The curious monied watched the marchers from above. From somewhere came another shot. A black-flag-carrying anarchist fell dying. The crowd stampeded again, ducking and zigzagging to safety, amid counterfire and chaos. Sailors broke into overlooking houses in rough search parties, hunting for arms and sometimes finding them. Blood had been spilt and blood was up, and the men spilt blood in revenge, lynching some of those they overcame.

Fired up, firing, fired upon, the marchers converged on the Tauride Palace. Again and again they shouted their demand: *all power to the soviets*. The skies released torrential rain, whipping up the end-of-days atmosphere among the many who stayed. As darkness started to fall, someone fired a sodden weapon at the palace, spreading panic. The Kronstadters were demanding to see Perverzev, the minister of justice, to hear from him why the anarchist

Zhelezniakov, who had been taken into custody at Durnovo, had not been released.

At the very moment that the crowd began to break down doors to look for him, in fact, Perverzev was in his offices, greeting journalists and representatives from Petrograd military units. He had, he said, something to show them. Evidence that the government had been amassing for some time. Evidence that purported to prove that Lenin was a German spy.

Besieged in the Tauride Palace, the Soviet leaders were panicking. After quickly conferring, they sent out the SR leader Chernov as their emissary, to placate those howling and chanting for Perverzev. An amiable, erudite man, once held in general respect, they thought he could calm the demonstrators with a typical quotation-peppered speech.

But when he appeared, someone yelled, 'Here is one of those who shoots at the people!' Sailors began to grab for him. Startled and alarmed, Chernov clambered atop a barrel and began gamely to orate.

He must have thought it a crowd-pleasing touch to mention the four Kadets who had quit the government, and to declare, 'Good riddance!'

'Then why', came an answering shout from the crowd, 'didn't you say so before?'

The mood grew ugly. Chernov shrank precariously back as suspicious men and women surrounding him jostled closer to where he balanced. A big worker pushed his way through and came up close and shook his fist in Chernov's face.

'Take power, you son of a bitch,' he bellowed, in one of most famous phrases of 1917, 'when it's given to you!'

Inside the palace, Chernov's comrades were realising what danger he was in. In desperation, they sent out several respected leftists – Martov, Kamenev, Steklov, Woytinsky – to rescue him. But, shoving through the crush, Raskolnikov beside him, it was Trotsky who reached him first.

A trumpet blasted out and the crowd fell quiet. Trotsky made his way to the car into which someone had shoved Chernov. He harangued the febrile crowd as he came, demanding they listen to him. Trotsky climbed onto the bonnet.

'Comrade Kronstadters!' he shouted. 'Pride and glory of the revolution! You've come to declare your will and show the Soviet that the working class no longer wants to see the bourgeoisie in power. But why hurt your own cause by petty acts of violence against casual individuals? Individuals are not worthy of your attention.'

He faced down the furious heckles. He reached out his hand to an especially voluble sailor. 'Give me your hand, comrade,' he shouted. 'Your hand, brother!'

The man would not oblige, but his confusion was palpable.

'Those here in favour of violence,' Trotsky shouted at last, 'raise your hands.'

No hand was raised.

'Citizen Chernov,' Trotsky said, opening the car door, 'you are free to go.'

Bruised, terrorised, humiliated, Chernov scurried back inside the palace. That he very probably owed Trotsky his life did not stop him sitting down that night to write a slew of blistering attacks on the Bolsheviks.

About 6 p.m., a joint meeting of the Soviet Executive Committees convened. The moderates turned to the army for help. They sent a plea to the reactionary General Polovtsev for some of the loyal troops stationed in the suburbs – because the political debates had not swayed all soldiers in the area – to come and defend them. 'Now', Polovtsev would recall the irony, 'I was free to assume the role of saviour of the Soviet.'

Outside, tens of thousands of people still hollered, now for

Tsereteli himself. Zinoviev, a popular Bolshevik, came out to calm them with banter and bonhomie, and begged them to disperse. But he could not dissuade them all from their aims, and a resolute group of protestors burst suddenly into the Catherine Hall where the terrified Soviet committees were meeting.

In response to this invasion, some of the Soviet members, in Sukhanov's exquisite formulation, 'did not reveal a sufficient courage and self-restraint'. They cowered from those furiously insisting that they take power.

With striking aplomb, disconcerting the man into silence, Chkheidze handed one heckler an official appeal to go home.

'Please read it carefully,' he said, 'and don't interrupt our business.'

As well as the army, the Soviet appealed to the fleet. A little after 7 p.m., Dudorov, assistant to the naval minister, called for four destroyers to intimidate the Kronstadters. In a shocking escalation, he ordered that 'any ships attempting to depart from Kronstadt without specific orders are to be sunk by the submarine fleet'.

But the call was intercepted by the hard-left Baltic Fleet Central Committee, Tsentrobalt. It forced the commander, Verevsky, to respond: 'Cannot carry out your orders.'

On the Mars Field, Cossacks charged Kronstadt sailors.

The Soviet kept debating. Like the demonstrators, the Bolsheviks, Spiridonova's Left SRs and Martov's Menshevik–Internationalists insisted that the current arrangement could not be allowed to continue. Mainstream and moderate SRs and Mensheviks, on the other hand, remained adamant that in this country, with its capitalism still undeveloped, its bourgeois phase unfinished and its proportionately small workers' movement, a government without non-socialists would be a disaster. That coalition was indispensable at this stage.

In the Tauride Palace hall, workers' and soldiers' representatives pleaded for land to go to the peasants, for peace, for workers' control.

'We trust the Soviet, but not those whom the Soviet trusts,' said one delegate. 'Now that the Kadets have proclaimed their refusal to work with us,' said another, 'we ask you: who else will you barter with?'

Outside, shots and standoffs continued. Ambushes, sudden fusillades and the reek of smoke. Machine guns ripped horsemen from their mounts. A stampede of riderless horses, sprayed with men's blood, hurtled along the embankment, hooves echoing, leering in terror.

Early evening and the skies were still too light. Abruptly, the 176th Regiment arrived and entered the palace.

These followers of the Mezhraiontsy had received a call to 'defend the revolution', and had come from Krasnoe Selo. By chance, the first authoritative figure they met was the Menshevik Dan. He wore, as he often did, his military uniform, and seeing the armed newcomers he had the presence of mind to immediately order them to sentry duty. The 176th complied.

Later, Sukhanov would mock them for obeying an enemy, one of the very moderates they opposed. Trotsky, however, would insist that their move was strategic, allowing them to enforce a degree of order while knowing where their opponents were. Either way, it is a curio of the moment that hard-left advocates of 'all power to the soviets' were delegated by a soviet opponent to defend the Soviet currently arguing furiously against taking the power they wanted it to take.

Those debates over power ground on. At 8 p.m. on the Liteiny Bridge, Cossacks engaged the workers: this was not February. A hammering of shots, the cries of those wounded or dying, and blood seeped through the crack where the bridge would part and its halves rise. Across the water from Kshesinskaya, 2,000 armed Kronstadt sailors breached the entrance of the Peter and Paul Fortress and took control of the military complex. A spectacular, gratuitous act: they did not know what to do with it now they had it. And still the Soviet

Tsar Nicholas II and Tsarina Alexandra, February 1913.

Grigori Rasputin, 1916.

Vladimir Ilyich Ulyanov, better known as Lenin.

'Konstantin Petrovich Ivanov': a clean-shaven Lenin in disguise, August 1917.

Alexandra Kollontai, a provocative and brilliant Bolshevik leader.

Leon Trotsky, 'charismatic and abrasive, brilliant and persuasive and divisive and difficult'.

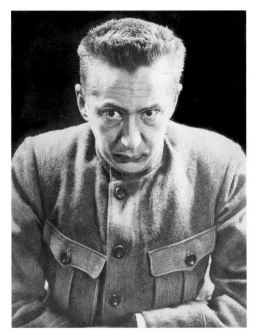

The flamboyant lawyer and politician Alexander Kerensky, 1917.

Maria Spiridonova, who, at age twenty, shot and killed a brutal security chief.

Menshevik leader Julius Martov, 'a rather charming type of bohemian … by predilection a haunter of cafés, indifferent to comfort, perpetually arguing and a bit of an eccentric'.

Demonstration in Petrograd, February 1917.

Revolutionary soldiers on the streets of Petrograd as news spreads of the tsar's abdication, March 1917.

'In March demonstrations in favour of the revolution shook Baku, Azerbaijan ... a patchwork of medieval and modern edifices, watched over by the steep ziggurats of oil derricks.'

An advanced outpost of Petrograd Soviet soldiers ready to face General Kornilov, August 1917.

Members of the Red Guard below a banner reading, 'To the health of the armed peoples, above all the workers'.

Cadets besieged in the Winter Palace on the eve of the October Revolution.

The armoured ship *Aurora*, after the revolution.

Yaroslav Sergeevich Nikolaev, *Lenin's Death Day* (1957), oil on Canvas, State Russian Museum, St Petersburg. 'The revolution of 1917 is a revolution of trains.'

continued to debate. Loyal troops at last started to reach Petrograd. Dead horses lay among scattered cartridges and broken glass.

By midnight, three positions were put before the Soviet. On the right, Avram Gots suggested pledging support to the rump Provisional Government until a Soviet Executive Committee plenum met. For Martov, to his left, 'the Russian bourgeoisie as a whole has definitely gone over to the attack against the peasants' and workers' democracy', 'history demands that we take power into our own hands' — and he called now for a new radical Provisional Government, this time with a majority of Soviet representatives. Lunacharsky, for the far left, demanded full Soviet power.

One by one, the delegates stood up to cast their votes. They announced for Gots; Dan of the Mensheviks; Kondratenko of the Trudoviks; Chaikovsky of the People's Socialist Party; the SR Saakian; and more, person after person, from group after group. The left fought to keep making their case, knowing now that they would lose.

Close to 1 a.m., as Tsereteli declaimed at the rostrum, there came the noise of of heavy footfalls. The deputies rose, pale again with fear.

Then Dan shouted in relief. 'Regiments loyal to the revolution have arrived', he called, 'to defend the Central Executive Committee!'

In came the Izmailovsky Guards, then the Preobrazhensky and Semenovsky Regiments. Their bands played the Marseillaise, and the Mensheviks and SRs sang along in delight. The Soviet had been saved, was safe to not take power.

The soldiers who had delivered them were stern, still dismayed by what they had recently been told, information which was not yet public: the shock news that Lenin was a spy.

The July Days rippled through the larger provincial cities, reflecting local volatilities, particularly where garrisons were threatened with redeployment to the front: in Saratov, Krasnoyarsk, Taganrog,

Nizhni Novgorod, Kiev, Astrakhan. In Nizhni Novgorod, an order for the muster of the 62nd Infantry Reserve Regiment on the evening of the 4th sparked a confrontation between loyalist and discontented soldiers, resulting in several deaths. On the 5th, the mutineers elected a Provisional Committee and for a short time took local power. In Ivanovo-Voznesensk, a militant working-class textile town, the soviet briefly asserted full authority.

For the most part, however, such events were not much more than hastily organised rallies. In the second city, for example, on hearing news of the Petrograd actions, the Moscow Bolsheviks issued a lukewarm call for a march to demand soviet power on 4 July. This was promptly banned by the Moscow Soviet, and the majority of workers obeyed. Many Bolsheviks would have been content, too, to let the matter rest, but, realising that their younger members, newly radicalised and enthusiastic, were likely to go ahead with some action anyway, they reluctantly joined them in a desultory, somewhat pathetic demonstration.

Between 2 a.m. and 3 a.m., in Petrograd, the Bolshevik CC issued what they described as a 'call' on workers and soldiers to terminate the street demonstrations: it was, more accurately, a post factum recognition of the inevitable, as the movement ebbed.

On the morning of the 5th, on its back page, *Pravda* unconvincingly explained the party's 'decision' to end the demonstrations – as if it were a decision, or the party's to make. They had proceeded thus because 'the object of the demonstration was achieved'; that is, 'the slogans of the vanguard of the proletariat and of the army were imposingly and worthily proclaimed'. Imposing, perhaps: but the Bolsheviks had dithered lengthily over the appropriateness of 'proclaiming' them in such a way.

In any case, the goals the slogans expressed had, to put it mildly, not been met.

★

Dawn on the 5th. The authorities opened the bridges. Their ends pointed skyward, cutting the rebels off.

Lenin had just left the *Pravda* printworks when loyalist soldiers arrived to arrest him. So they arrested the workers instead, ransacked the files and smashed the equipment, bellowing about spies, German agents, treachery.

The previous day, as Perverzev spread stories about Lenin's supposed treachery, a Bolshevik sympathiser in his ministry had sent word to the CC, which immediately requested that the Ispolkom stop the slander. Out of residual solidarity, out of concern for due process, or to avoid inflaming the situation in the city, Tsereteli and Chkheidze had telephoned the Petrograd newspapers. They enjoined them not to publish unverified claims.

Most acquiesced. But on the morning of the 5th, the morning the soldiers came, the front page of one sensationalist hard-right rag, *Zhivoe slovo* – the 'Living Word' – screamed: 'Lenin, [his comrades] Ganetsky, Kozlovsky: German Spies!'

Nothing could stop the rumours now.

Kerensky quickly distanced himself from the release, but this was coy: on the 4th, he had already written from the front to Lvov (who disapproved), stating that it was 'necessary to hasten the publication of the information in our hands'. The Byzantine details of the calumny were based on the say-so of one Lieutenant Yermolenko, and a merchant, Z. Burstein. The latter alleged that a German spy network in Stockholm, headed by the Marxist-theoretician-turned-German-patriot Parvus, maintained Bolshevik connections. Yermolenko, for his part, claimed to have been told of Lenin's role by the German General Staff, while he, Yermolenko, was a prisoner of war whom those Germans (according, possibly, to a convoluted chain of mistaken identity) had attempted to recruit – which, said he, he ultimately gave them the impression they had successfully done.

These claims were a tangle of mendacity, invention and tendentiousness. Yermolenko was a strange character, at best a fantasist, while even his own government handlers described Burstein as wholly untrustworthy. The dossier had been prepared by an embittered ex-Bolshevik, Alexinsky, with a reputation for shit-stirring and malice so great he had been denied entry to the Soviet. Few serious people, even on the right, believed any of this stuff for a moment, which explains why some of the less dishonourable or more cautious right were furious with *Zhivoe slovo* for publishing.

Nonetheless, in the immediate term the effects were devastating.

July 5 was a day of bleak reaction. The pendulum swung.

That day Petrograd was not safe for the left. A *Pravda* distributor was killed on the street. Cossacks and other loyalists exerted control through intimidation and thuggery. The far right were exultant.

The danger was not all from the right, though, even in what should have been left strongholds. One party activist, E. Tarasova, came into a Vyborg factory she knew well, and instantly the women workers she had been speaking to days earlier screamed abuse, calling her a German spy, and hurled nuts and bolts at her, savagely cutting her hands and face. A Menshevik, they explained, shamefaced, when the panic abated, had been agitating against the Bolsheviks.

Nor was it only Bolsheviks who had reason to be afraid that day; the left Menshevik Woytinsky called the mood a 'counterrevolutionary orgy', marked by the 'debauchery of the Black Hundreds'. Those sadistic vigilantes roamed the streets, smashing their way into houses on the hunt for 'traitors' and 'troublemakers'. And they were not without popular support. 'Public opinion', Woytinsky noted gloomily, 'demanded drastic measures.'

The Bolshevik left, like Raskolnikov, made ready to defend the Kshesinskaya Mansion. Some nursed illusions about returning to the offensive. But most of the leadership understood the gravity of their situation. That afternoon, Zinoviev forcefully demanded that the last demonstrators in the Peter and Paul Fortress surrender it. Any other course would be an absurd, doomed provocation.

The Bolsheviks began to disperse, for safety, and in preparation for a crackdown. Many of the top leadership headed into hiding, as they tried to come up with plans.

Three young activists, Liza Pylaeva, Nina Bogoslovskaya and Yelizaveta Koksharova slipped out of Peter and Paul disguised as nurses, carrying party funds and documents under bandages. They were swiftly intercepted by government forces who demanded to know what they were carrying in their baskets. Pylaeva grinned and said, 'Dynamite and revolvers!' The men chided her for the bad taste of her joke, and let her pass.

Now the Bolshevik CC voted 'not to reverse the decision to end the demonstrations' – as if, again, the decision had been theirs, as if a decision to reverse that 'decision' would have had any effect.

The July Days were over.

The Bolshevik leaders, rather nervously, sent a representative to the Soviet, to ascertain its position with regard to the party; the Soviet for its part sent Executive representatives to the Kshesinskaya Mansion. They promised that no further repressive measures would be taken against the party, and that demonstrators not accused of specific crimes would be released. The Bolsheviks agreed to call back the armoured cars of their supporters, surrender Peter and Paul (as Zinoviev had insisted, although the occupiers within continued to hem and haw) and send the sailors back to Kronstadt.

If the Soviet, notionally, committed itself to no more punitive measures, this was not the case for the Provisional Government.

At dawn the next day, General Polovtsev directed to the Kshesinskaya Mansion and to the Peter and Paul Fortress a huge attack force. Eight armoured cars, the Petrogradsky Regiment, sailors, cadets and the Aviation Academy were backed by terrifying heavy artillery. With them, too, was a front-line bicycle brigade: the idea of such soldiers was not then faintly comic, as now, but evocative of speed and modernity, and all major powers were experimenting with the bicycle, what one approving British brigade major called 'this, the youngest, excrescence' of the military. Before they set out, all the men of the attack force were galvanised with speeches: some of those there to exhort them, tellingly, were Soviet dignitaries.

At 7 a.m., the commander gave those within the mansion an hour to surrender. The MO was still in denial. Some members managed to get quickly away across the Sampsonievsky Bridge to Peter and Paul. There, they fondly imagined, they might make a stand. The 500 members remaining in Kshesinskaya did not resist. The firepower arrayed against them was awesomely disproportionate. When government soldiers entered to arrest them, they found seven members hurriedly burning party files. Soon thereafter, even the sailors who had made it to the Peter and Paul Fortress agreed, miserably, to surrender.

As a warning to the rest of the army, the authorities did not just punish but humiliated the Machine Gun Regiment, disarming and parading them publicly. Krupskaya witnessed the scene. 'As they led their horses by the bridle so much hatred burned in their eyes, there was so much more hatred in their slow march, that it was clear that a more stupid method could not have been devised' – if, that is, the aim of the government was social peace.

Even now, a few ultras from the Petersburg Committee, meeting in the deeps of the Vyborg district, wanted to continue this struggle. That afternoon, Latsis and a few of his comrades crept through the unfriendly city to the Reno factory. There, hiding in a watchman's hut, Lenin was waiting.

Latsis enthusiastically put the case to him for summoning a general strike.

Incredulous, furious, Lenin laid down some home truths. He insisted that they take stock of the sheer scale of the setbacks, that they must understand the nature of the conjuncture. He scolded Latsis like a naughty child. Finally, not trusting the Petersburg Committee to do it themselves, Lenin drafted a back-to-work call on their behalf.

That evening, at a small Vyborg apartment, Zinoviev, Kamenev, Stalin, Lenin and Podvoisky weighed up their predicament. The SRs and Mensheviks, Lenin declared, had made it clear that they would not accept power, even on a plate: they would choose to cede it to the bourgeoisie. The slogan 'All Power to the Soviets', therefore, was obsolete. It was time instead to demand, in peremptory if unwieldy fashion, 'All Power to the Proletariat Led by Its Revolutionary Party – the Bolsheviks'.

For now, though, the Bolsheviks were hardly in a position to demand anything. The more pressing question was safety: that night, the cabinet issued warrants for the arrests of all the 'organisers' of the troubles, including Lenin, Zinoviev, Kamenev, Kollontai, and Lunacharsky. To which list Trotsky, with typical twinkling arrogance, would soon demand to be added, a request the government granted.

As late as the evening of Friday 7 July, shots could still be heard in the city, even while trams rattled once more over the bridges and the lights of their reflections swayed in the Neva. Firing in Vyborg, a sudden volley near Vasilevsky Island, the staccato of some automatic weapon. Secret routes wound across the top of Petrograd, a roof-world above the courtyards, secret skyline walkways: 'Perhaps the scoundrels are shooting again from housetops,' wrote Harold Williams for the *Daily Chronicle*. He knew the percussions he heard were mopping-up operations. Reds and rebels being disarmed, or worse.

Some in the Bolsheviks, on the arrest list, operated in the open, daring the government to take them. Others gave themselves up. Initially, Lenin decided he would face a public trial. He was dissuaded from this course by various comrades – including his sister Maria – who felt that iron reaction in the capital would make his situation too dangerous. So he stayed in hiding. His decision was controversial: Kamenev and others worried it made him look guilty of the spying of which he was accused.

Lenin moved between comrades' houses. He holed up in the apartment of one Margarita Fofanova, then on the top floor of 17

Rozhdestvenskaya Street, with the Alliluyev family. He shaved off his iconic beard, put on a worker's tunic and an unlikely hat. He tried to fade into the crowd. On 9 July, still hunted by the police, he left Petrograd altogether.

It was the first of a series of heart-in-mouth escapes.

Late at night, Lenin and Zinoviev went to the Primorsky Station to meet their comrade Yemelyanov, a worker in an arms factory. Elbowing past the usual inebriated late travellers, ignoring the drunken songs, they made it onto the last train at 2 a.m. There they crouched on the steps of the rearmost coach, gripping the handles as the train clattered through the cool night. They were tense, poised to jump off in a moment, to launch themselves into the dark should anyone shout their names, should they be recognised. No matter how fast it sped, they decided, they would not risk staying aboard. They would rather leap. But they made it to Yemelyanov's home village of Razliv, just beyond the city, without mishap.

They stayed there a few days in his barn, but when police extended their searches to this area, the fugitives made their way through the undergrowth to a crude hut by Lake Razliv's deserted south-eastern shore. Zinoviev and Lenin disguised themelves as Finnish peasants, complete with a haystack by their rough lodgings. They waited out the days. There, with one tree stump for his table and another for his chair, Lenin kept out of sight, a martyr to the remorseless mosquitoes and the rain, and wrote.

The July events left residue. The crime rate of Petrograd was still rising. But, after the quasi-revolt of July, there came a spike in murders of a particular sort, a bleak social symptom. Murders born of political argument. The ill-tempered slanging matches of the day escalated abruptly into fights, even armed violence. After February, political debates had been fiery and exuberant. Now, they could be deadly.

Everywhere was confrontation, sometimes in sordid form. Strange threats. The pages of *Petrogradsky listok* carried a weird warning against the street justice and lynching parties, an ultimatum and a cruel negotiation from old-fashioned criminals themselves. They would no longer restrict themselves to robbery, said a spokesperson for this villainy, but would 'kill anybody we meet at the dark corner of streets'. Burglary would be a prelude to slaughter. 'Breaking into a house, we will not simply loot, but will murder everyone, even children, and won't stop our bloody revenge until acts of mob violence are stopped.'

It seemed as if the disaster of the July Days had set the Bolsheviks back years. Steklov was arrested. The authorities ransacked the house of Anna Elizarova, Lenin's sister. They took Kamenev on the 9th. By the late days of the month, Lunacharsky and Trotsky had joined many of the Bolshevik leaders, and other activists, in Kresty prison, where the guards stoked up the criminals against the 'German spies'.

Still the political prisoners made space and time and conditions to write, and to debate. Some moderate left papers – *Izvestia*, *Volia naroda*, *Golos soldata* – still refrained from comment on the spying allegations. Even the Kadet paper, *Rech*, cautiously affirmed that the Bolsheviks were innocent until proven guilty. This did not, of course, inhibit it from backing the demands of right Mensheviks and SRs for punitive measures against them. Such examples of restraint aside, Lenin was denounced across the Russian media. By 11 July, when he tried to refute the charges in a piece sent to Gorky's paper *Novaya zhizn*, the clamour was deafening.

'The counterrevolution is victorious,' wrote Latsis miserably on 12 July. 'The Soviets are without power. The junkers, running wild, have begun to raid the Mensheviks too.' The Left SRs, as well, were hounded by the police.

The Bolshevik Moscow Regional Committee reported resignations from the party, 'disarray in the ranks'. In Vyselki, Ukraine, a 'pogrom mood' prevailed, and the party 'was in flames', riven by splits and bled by defections. Recruitment stalled. The workers, one activist from Kolpinsky reported, 'turned against us'. In six districts, Bolsheviks were thrown out of factories by their workmates. On 16 July, in a punitive macabre ritual, a factory committee on

Vasilievsky Island forced representatives of their local Bolsheviks to attend the funeral of a Cossack killed during the unrest.

That the Mezhraiontsy at last entered the party felt like little compensation for the retrenchment. Even some local Bolshevik groups came out against their own leadership. The Executive Committee of the party in Tiflis and, of all places, in Vyborg pledged full support to the Soviet, and demanded that the Bolshevik leadership turn themselves in.

Amid the setbacks came a few triumphs. None were more important than the left-moving Latvia, where the Bolsheviks held the workers' soviets and landless peasants' soviets, and cleaved to an uncompromising line. There, the July Days had their echo in a confrontation in Riga between Latvian riflemen and one of the 'Death Battalions', shock troops of the regime, that had left several dead on both sides. The Fifth Latvian Social Democratic Conference took place immediately after, from 9 to 19 July, and the Bolsheviks consolidated their hold, exercising measures of control over society at large – food distribution, local administration, and so on. The Latvian party already acted like a government-in-waiting. In possessing such confidence, though, it was an outlier.

Most ominous across the country was a certain rise of ultra-right, antisemitic pogromists. A group called Holy Russia put out *Groza* – Thunderstorm – with repeated calls to violence. Street-corner agitators fulminated against the Jews.

From his hide, throughout these bad days, Lenin sent articles to his comrades, and repeatedly proclaimed his innocence of spying. He received contacts who made the trek to the lonely shore, Yemelyanov's son standing guard by the dark water, ready to make the bird-call sound that was an alarm if strangers appeared.

Lenin prepared for death at the hands of reaction. 'Strictly *entre nous*,' he wrote to Kamenev, 'if I am done in, please publish my notebook "Marxism and the State".'

He was not done in, and soon, in Finland, he would have a chance to develop that notebook on the state and revolution.

★

The street-fighting right may have been stronger immediately after the July Days, but the Provisional Government was not. On the contrary, the schisms at its heart were still intractable.

On 8 July, in the face of the gulf between himself and the cabinet socialists, Prime Minister Prince Lvov resigned. To replace him, he invited the only figure who seemed even remotely able to bridge that gap, a man of both the Duma and the Soviet – Kerensky.

Kerensky, of course, accepted. He began the unenviable process of putting together a new unity government.

In the demented early days of the Kerensky cult, the poet Marina Tsvetaeva recast the object of devotion as Napoleon:

> And someone, falling on the map,
> Does not sleep in his dreams.
> There came a Bonaparte
> In my country.

Now, Lenin too, months later, argued in *Rabochy i soldat* that Kerensky's rule was Bonapartism – but from him that was not a flattering description. He used the term much as Marx and Engels had, in a technical way, to describe 'the manoeuvring of state power, which leans on the military clique … for support, between two hostile classes and forces which more or less balance each other out'. For Lenin, Kerensky's degenerating Bonapartism was a balancing act between opposed social forces.

The catastrophe at the front could no longer be hidden. The day he became prime minister, Kerensky made the redoubtable General Kornilov commander of the south-western front, where Russian troops were disintegrating at the most dramatic rate. In this move he was strongly encouraged by the government representative to that front, the extraordinary Boris Savinkov.

Savinkov played an important political role in those turbulent months. He was a man who had undergone a dramatic political journey. Not only an SR but, in the years leading up to the 1905 revolution, a flamboyant and notorious activist within the SR's terrorist wing, its Battle Organisation, he had been involved in the killings of several tsarist officials. After 1905, he had become a writer of sensationalist novels. The advent of the war aroused in him a boundless chauvinism and militarism: in exile, he had joined the French Army, returning to Russia in April 1917, where he grew close to Kerensky. Though he believed in the judicious use of the commissars, the people's representatives, to mediate between officers and soldiers, in his fervidly authoritarian patriotism, Savinkov was also an advocate of utterly ruthless measures against ill discipline – up to and including, it seems, military dictatorship.

On his appointment, Kornilov, the iron disciplinarian, demanded the authority to execute fleeing soldiers. Even before receiving his less than deferential request, in fact, Kerensky had already authorised commanders to fire on retreating soldiers, and within days the government reinstituted capital punishment at the front, as demanded. Still, when the details of Kornilov's confrontational exchange with Kerensky were leaked to the press, Kornilov's reputation as a hard man of the right soared, among both enemies and friends.

On 16 July, Kerensky, accompanied by Savinkov and his close collaborator Maximilian Filonenko, the right SR commissar of the Eighth Army, met with the Russian high command at Stavka, in Mogilev, to take stock of the military situation. Kornilov was not present – tellingly, the chaos and disintegration of the troops in his area would not permit it – and he telegraphed in his own, rather mild, report. Most of those generals who did attend, however, including Alexeev, Commander-in-Chief Brusilov, and Denikin of the western front, were nothing like so restrained.

Denikin in particular poured vitriol on the revolution, blaming it for the army's collapse. He blasted the commissars to the stunned Kerensky, railed against Order Number 1, denounced the undermining of authority. The generals insisted that all such features of Dual Power be overturned.

On the train back to Petrograd, where he would preside with his usual histrionics at the funeral of Cossacks slain in the July Days, the shaken Kerensky decided that the gravity of the situation made it imperative to replace Brusilov with Kornilov as commander-in-chief. Within two days, he had taken the army away from a thoughtful, relatively open-minded career officer and delivered it to a hard-line, ambitious counterrevolutionary.

Emboldened by recent developments, disgusted at the state of the country, malcontents on the right pined for reaction, dreaming ever more loudly of a dictatorship.

On 18 July, Kerensky's government moved into the Winter Palace. In an unsubtle snub, it requested the Soviet leave the Tauride Palace to make way for the Fourth State Duma. This was not a request that could be declined.

On 19 July, the Congress of Trade and Industry attacked the government for having 'permitted the poisoning of the Russian people'. It demanded 'a radical break … with the dictatorship of the Soviet', and wondered openly if 'a dictatorial power is needed to save the motherland'. Such a clamour against the Soviet would only increase. Take power, the streets had demanded, and the Soviet had declined the invitation. Now it was being bled of such power as it had.

At the urging of the Kadets, Kerensky passed laws imposing tough restrictions on public meetings. The brief window of permissiveness towards Ukrainian and Finnish nationalism closed: Russia had been building up troops on Finnish soil since it declared its semi-independence, and now, on 21 July, its parliament was dissolved – which provoked an alliance of the Finnish Social Democrats (who had held a majority) with the Bolsheviks. 'The Russian Provisional Governement', raged the SD paper *Työmies*, 'together with Finland's reactionary bourgeoisie has stabbed parliament and the whole Finnish democracy in the back.'

Reaction came to Petrograd as, around the country, peasant revolts grew in violence and anarchy continued, especially over the hated war, the catastrophic offensive costing hundreds of thousands of lives. On 19 July, in Atarsk, a district capital in Saratov, a group of angry ensigns waiting for a train to the front smashed the station lanterns and went hunting their superiors, guns at the ready, until a popular ensign took charge, and ordered the officers' arrest. Rioting soldiers detained, threatened and even killed their officers.

Perhaps Kornilov's relatively mild telegram of the 16th had lulled Kerensky into believing he might find in the general a collaborator. Such hopes were destroyed quickly and comprehensively. By the 19th of the month, the new commander-in-chief bluntly demanded total independence of operational procedures, with reference only 'to conscience and to the people as a whole'. His people leaked this message to the press, that the public might marvel at his toughness.

Kerensky began to fear that he had created a monster. He had.

He was not alone in this growing sense of alarm. That month, shortly after Kornilov's ascension, an anonymous 'true friend and comrade' sent a terse, prophetic note to the Executive Committee of the Soviet: 'Comrades. Please drive out that fucking son of a bitch General Kornilov, or else he's going to take his machine guns and drive you out.'

For a time, Kerensky was distracted from this rightist jostling by his own efforts to create a government. It took several attempts, but on 25 July, Kerensky at last managed to inaugurate the second Coalition Government. It was made up now of nine socialist ministers, a slight majority, but all except Chernov came from their parties' right wings. In addition, and crucially, they entered cabinet as individuals, not as representatives of those parties, or of the Soviet.

In fact, the new government – including these ministers – did not recognise Soviet authority. Dual Power was done.

It was in this distinctly unfriendly climate that the Bolsheviks held their delayed Sixth Congress.

Late on 26 July, in a private hall in Vyborg, 150 Bolsheviks from across Russia came together. They assembled in a state of extreme tension and semi-illegality, rudderless, their leaders imprisoned or on the run. Two days after the start of their meeting, the government banned assemblies deemed harmful to security or the war, and the congress quietly relocated to a workers' club in the south-west suburbs.

Embattled, the Bolsheviks were grateful for whatever solidarity they could get. Their welcome to left Mensheviks who attended, like Larin and Martov, was rapturous, notwithstanding the rebukes the guests offered along with their greetings.

But as the days passed and the caucusing continued, furtive, curtailed, anxious as the party was, something began to grow clear. The apocalypse had not, in fact, occurred. The mood was tense, but brighter than it had been two weeks before. The July Days had hurt the Bolsheviks – but that hurt had not cut deep, nor did it last long.

Fear of attacks from the right, among even considerably more moderate socialists, meant that district soviets had started closing ranks against perceived counterrevolution, even protecting the Bolsheviks as their own, if resented, left flank. In April, the party had 80,000 members in seventy-eight local organisations: now – after the crisis of July and a short, demoralising haemorrhage of members – it still numbered 200,000, in 162 organisations. Petrograd contained 41,000, with similarly strong numbers in the Ural mining territory, though there were fewer (and politically more 'moderate') Bolsheviks in and around Moscow. But the Mensheviks, by contrast – the party of the Soviet, still a crucial institution – had 8,000 members.

On the last two days of July, after a protracted debate, as per Lenin's analysis and plea, the Bolsheviks dropped the slogan 'All Power to the Soviets'. They began to plot a new course. A course that was predicated not on the strength and potential of the Soviets, but on direct seizure of power by the workers and the party.

8

August: Exile and Conspiracy

In those late days of summer, as the right ruminated a cleansing, there flourished a millennial indulgence. Bands and all-night dances, stained silk dresses and cravats, flies circling warming cake and vomit and spilt drink. Long days, warm orgiastic nights. A sybariticism for the end of a world. In Kiev, said the Countess Spersansky, there were 'suppers with gypsy bands and chorus, bridge and even tangoes, poker and romances'. As in Kiev, so across the cities of Russia, among the dreaming rich.

On 3 August, the Sixth Russian Social Democratic Workers Party Congress – the Bolshevik Congress – unanimously passed a resolution in favour of a new slogan. It was a compromise between the impatient 'Leninists', who saw the revolution entering a new post-Soviet phase, and the moderates, who still thought that they might be able to work with the socialists to their right to defend the revolution. Nonetheless, the symbolic importance of the shift in phraseology was immense. The lesson shook out, the calls changed. July had done its work. No longer did the Bolsheviks call for 'All Power to the Soviets'. Instead they aspired to the 'Complete Liquidation of the Dictatorship of the Counterrevolutionary Bourgeoisie'.

★

The Soviet relocated as required. The Smolny Institute was built in the early 1800s, a grandiose neoclassical edifice in the Smolny district east of the city centre, by the Neva. A building of cavernous corridors, white floors, watery electric light. On the ground level was a great mess hall, between hallways lined with offices full of secretaries and deputies and fractions of the parties of the Soviet, their military organisations and committees and conclaves. Piles of newspapers, pamphlets, posters covered the tables. Machine guns protruded from windows. Soldiers and workers packed the passages, sleeping on chairs and benches, guarding gatherings, watched by empty gold frames from which imperial portraits had been cut.

Until just before the revolution, the institute had been a facility for the education of daughters of the nobility. An erstwhile guarantor of state power, the Soviet was demoted to squatting a finishing school. When the full Soviet met, it did so in what had been the ballroom.

On the 3rd, Kornilov came to meet Kerensky, and again made several demands of the man who was technically his boss. These included, in a hardening of his previous attitude, the strict curtailing of the soldiers' committees. Though they broadly accepted its substance, Kerensky, Savinkov and Filonenko would together rework the document Kornilov presented, so as to disguise its inflammatory contempt. The general's disgust at the government only increased when, as he prepared to brief the cabinet on the military situation, Kerensky quietly advised him not to be too specific with details. Some of the cabinet's Soviet members, he insinuated, particularly Chernov, might be security risks.

During their meeting, Kerensky asked Kornilov a curious question.

'Suppose I should withdraw,' he said, 'what will happen? You will hang in the air; the railways will stop; the telegraph will cease to function.'

Kornilov's reserved response – that Kerensky should remain in position – was less interesting than the question itself. The point behind its melancholy is opaque. Was Kerensky seeking reassurance that Kornilov would support him? Was he, perhaps, tentatively sounding out the possibility of a Kornilov dictatorship?

We are all legion, and Kerensky was more legion than most. His plaintive query may have expressed both horror at and hope in the idea of giving up, of surrendering to the tough-talking commander-in-chief. A political death drive.

Hatred for the war still waxed. From around the country came scores of reports of soldiers resisting transfer.

A propaganda battle intensified around Kornilov, reflecting the growing split between the hard right in the country, to which the Kadets were gravitating, and the dwindling power of the moderate socialists. On 4 August, *Izvestia* hinted at plans to replace Kornilov with General Cheremisov, a relative moderate who believed in working with soldiers' committees. To which, on the 6th, the Council of the Union of Cossack Troops responded that Kornilov was 'the sole general who can recreate the power of the army and bring the country out of its very difficult situation'. They in turn hinted at rebellion if Kornilov was removed.

The Union of Cavaliers of St George gave Kornilov their support. Prominent Moscow conservatives under Rodzianko sent him gushing telegrams, intoning that 'in this threatening hour of heavy trial all thinking Russia looks to you with hope and faith'. It was a civil war of words.

Kornilov demanded from Kerensky command of the Petrograd Military District. To the delight of a coup-hungry right, he ordered his chief of staff, Lukomsky, to concentrate troops near Petrograd – this would permit their speedy deployment to the capital.

The background to this manoeuvering was not only the catastrophic and worsening economic and social situation, but a conscious and deliberate ratcheting of tensions by sections of the punitive right. At a gathering of 300 industrial and financial magnates in early August, the opening speaker was Pavel Ryabushinsky, a powerful textile businessman. 'The Provisional Government possesses only the shadow of power,' he said. 'Actually a gang of political charlatans are in control ... The government is concentrating on taxes, imposing them primarily and cruelly upon the merchant and industrial class ... Would it not be better in the name of the salvation of the fatherland to appoint a guardian over the spendthrifts?'

Then came a sadism so startling it stunned the left. 'The bony hand of hunger and national destitution will seize by the throat the friends of the people.'

Those 'friends of the people' he dreamed into the grasp of predatory skeletal fingers were socialists.

It was not only from the right, however, that pressure piled on. Also on the 6th, in Kronstadt, 15,000 workers, soldiers and sailors protested at the arrest of the Bolshevik leaders, of Steklov and Kamenev and Kollontai and the rest. In Helsingfors, a similarly large gathering resolved for a transfer of power to the soviets. Of course that demand was now outdated as far as many Bolsheviks were concerned, but it represented a leftward shift for most workers. Pushed by the Bolsheviks and the militant Left SRs, the next day, the workers' section of the Petrograd Soviet criticised the arrest of leftist leaders, as well as the return of the military death penalty. They won the vote. Mensheviks and SRs began to complain of defections to their left – to their own maximalist sections, or beyond.

Such signs of left recovery were patchy and uneven: on 10 August, in Odessa elections, for example, the Bolsheviks won only three out of over 100 seats. But in Lugansk municipal elections in early August, the Bolsheviks won twenty-nine of seventy-five seats. In elections in Revel (now Tallinn) they took over 30 per cent of the vote, very nearly the same in Tver, a little later, and in Ivanovo-Vosnessensk their tally was double that. Over the territory of the empire, the trend was definite.

Huddled in his hut, on a day of heavy rain, Lenin was startled by the sound of cursing. A Cossack was approaching through the wet undergrowth.

The man begged shelter from the downpour. Lenin had little choice but to stand aside and let him in. As they sat together listening to the drumbeat of water, Lenin asked his visitor what brought him to this out-of-the-way spot.

A manhunt, the Cossack said. He was after someone by the name of Lenin. To bring him back dead or alive.

And what, Lenin asked cautiously, had this reprobate done?

The Cossack waved his hand, vague about the details. What he did know, he stressed, was that the fugitive was in some way 'muddled'; that he was dangerous; and that he was nearby.

When the skies lightened at last, the visitor thanked his temporary host and set out through the sodden grass to continue the search.

After that alarming incident, Lenin and the CC, with which he remained in secret communication, agreed that he should move to Finland.

On 8 August, Zinoviev and Lenin abandoned their hut in the company of Yemelyanov; Alexander Shotman, a Finnish 'Old Bolshevik'; and the flamboyant, extravagantly moustached activist Eino Rahja. The men set out through the lakeside swamp for a local station, on a long, wet, arduous trek punctuated by wrong turnings and ill feeling, hauling themselves out at last by the railway at the village of Dibuny. Their troubles were not over: there on the platform, a suspicious military cadet challenged and arrested Yemelyanov. But Shotman, Rahja, Zinoviev and Lenin swiftly made it onto an arriving train headed to Udelnaya, in Petrograd's outskirts.

From there, Zinoviev continued into the capital. Lenin's travels were not yet done.

The next day, train 293 for Finland arrived at Udelnaya Station. The driver was Guro Jalava, railwayman, conspirator, committed Marxist.

'I came to the edge of the platform,' he later recalled, 'whereat a man strode from among the trees and hoisted himself up into the cab. It was, of course, Lenin, although I hardly recognised him. He was to be my stoker.'

The photograph in the fake passport with which Lenin – 'Konstantin Petrovich Ivanov' – travelled has become famous. With a cap perched high on a curly wig, the contours of his beardless mouth unfamiliar, wryly upturned, his deep small eyes are all that is recognisable.

Lenin rolled up his sleeves. He set to work, so enthusiastically that the train spewed out generous plumes of smoke. His driver recalled how Lenin shovelled with gusto, feeding the engine, making it run fast, bearing him away on the ties and rails.

When he alighted at last, Lenin the stoker still had a circuitous clandestine journey ahead of him. It was not until 11 p.m. on 10 August that Lenin arrived at a small, homely apartment at 1 Hakaniemi Square, in the north of Helsingfors. This was the Rovio residence. With his wife away visiting family, Kustaa Rovio, an activist for the Social Democrats, had agreed to shelter the Russian Marxist.

A large, imposing man, Rovio's career had taken a staggeringly unlikely turn. A socialist of long standing, he was also now the head of the Helsingfors Police.

Quite how he came to square this role with his revolutionary commitment is unclear. Of the guest who had, a few years previously, advocated stockpiling 'bombs and stones, etc., or acids' to drop on his colleagues, police chief Rovio said: 'I have never met such a congenial and charming comrade.'

Lenin's sole demands – and on these he was adamant – were that Rovio should procure him the Russian newspapers every day, and arrange the secret delivery of letters back to his party comrades. This his host did even when, due to the imminent return of Mrs Rovio, Lenin relocated to the apartment of a socialist couple, the Blomqvists, in nearby Telekatu.

Taking her own hazardous routes, hiking on foot through a forest over the border, Krupskaya more than once visited her husband. Lenin himself strolled Helsingfors with remarkable freedom. 'It is necessary to be quick, Kerensky,' he declared with relish at the Blomqvists' kitchen table, reading of the government's hunt for him, 'in order to catch me.'

Above all, throughout August, as he had in July and as he would in September, Lenin wrote. Messages and letters and instructions to comrades, and another, longer work. The very first day he lodged with him, Rovio found Lenin asleep at a desk, his head in his arms, a closely written notebook before him. 'Consumed with curiosity,' Rovio reported, 'I began turning over the pages. It was the manu-script of his book *The State and Revolution*.'

This is an extraordinary, sinewy negotiation of remorseless anti-statism with the temporary necessity of 'the bourgeois state without the bourgeoisie', under the proletariat. The historic text, described by Lucio Colletti as 'Lenin's greatest contribution to polit-ical theory', was composed on a log by a mosquito-ridden lake, and then on a policeman's table. It would not yet be quite finished when circumstances changed, and Lenin made his way back to Russia. The text closes with a legendary truncation: 'It is more pleasant and useful to go through the experience of the revolution than to write about it.'

The same day that Lenin arrived at the Rovios' flat, on 10 August, Kornilov went again to meet Kerensky in Petrograd, at Savinkov's insistence. They were to discuss the general's new demands: now he wanted control of the railways and war industries. He asked, too, peremptorily, for the right to employ extraordinary repression as he considered necessary, including relocating slacking workers to the front.

Mistrust between prime minister and general was such that Kornilov arrived with a substantial and provocative bodyguard. This was a body of Turkmen fighters from the so-called Savage Division of volunteer soldiers from across the Caucasus – heavily mythicised figures, chosen to intimidate. As Kerensky watched in alarm from the Winter Palace, the red-robed warriors came jogging into view down the wide streets, surrounding Kornilov's car, brandishing scimitars and machine-guns. They took up positions around the palace door like enemies preparing for a parlay.

The meeting was icy. Kornilov had heard rumours that he might be replaced, and he menacingly advised Kerensky against any such step. When Kerensky would not commit to everything he wanted, Kornilov insisted on meeting with the cabinet to put his case; but Kerensky would only convene an informal group, excluding the Kadets, that agreed in principle to most of Kornilov's demands but were vague about the time frame, and continued to oppose the militarisation of railways and industries. The general left in a severe temper.

In fact, the desperate Kerensky was not altogether opposed even to those rejected measures, given the context of social collapse. He was, however, understandably fearful of the reaction such moves would provoke in the Soviet and beyond. His strategy of 'balance' now had him provoking the fury of those to his left and those to his right.

In a strained effort to reconcile widening social divisions, the Provisional Government scrambled to put together a symbolic, consultative gathering. Almost 2,500 delegates would attend the Moscow State Conference, representing trade unions, Dumas, commerce and the soviets. The event was to take place in the splendid neoclassical edifice of the second city's Bolshoi Theatre, between 12 and 14 August.

Through their membership of the Soviet and VTsIK, the Bolsheviks qualified for delegates. Initially they planned to make a scornful declaration followed by an ostentatious walkout, but Chkheidze got wind, and refused to permit any such thing. The party decided that they would stay away altogether.

The hard-left Bolshevik Moscow Regional Bureau called a one-day strike as the conference opened. The Moscow Soviet, where the mainstream SRs and Mensheviks had a small majority, opposed the move, if narrowly, but after debates and battles in the city's factories, in a sign of Bolshevik strength, most of the workers stayed out. Delegates descended to streets where streetcars did not run and restaurants were closed. The buffet of the theatre itself was shut: the strike forced the attendees of this showcase of national and cross-class unity to prepare their own food. And to do so in the dark: the gaslights were unlit.

It must be allowed, the Moscow Soviet's *Izvestia* wrote, 'that the Bolsheviks are not irresponsible groups but one of the elements of the organised revolutionary democracy behind whom stand the broad masses'.

Such grudging acknowledgement came amid an unusual degree of Menshevik–SR–Bolshevik cooperation. Not revolutionary collaboration, exactly: it might rather be described as grudging counter-counterrevolutionary collaboration. The moderate socialists were canny enough to understand that, whatever their arguments with those to their left, were the restless reactionaries to triumph in the country the Bolsheviks might be first in the firing line – and that might not even be a metaphor – but they themselves would not be spared.

The fact was that rumours about the intentions of Kornilov and the right had grown so deeply alarming that the Moscow Soviet felt obliged to form a Provisional Revolutionary Committee to defend the government and the Soviet, mobilising the vigilant grassroots. And to it, alongside two Mensheviks and two SRs, it appointed the prominent Bolsheviks Nogin and Muralov. In an astonishing acknowledgement of the limits of its persuasive power compared to theirs, it even gave the party – even so recently after the July Days – temporary access to the Moscow garrison barracks, to argue for this defence.

This was the context of political fear in which the conference set out to smooth tensions between right and left. In this it was not merely unsuccessful: it was grotesquely counterproductive.

The Moscow State Conference opened to a house literally, visibly divided. On the right of the hall, slightly numerically preponderant,

were the elite – industrialists, Kadets, business people, career polit-
icians, high-ranking soldiers. On the left were the moderate socialist
intelligentsia, Menshevik lawyers and journalists, trade union organisers, lower-ranking officers and privates. And there, sitting with
owlish precision exactly in the middle, was Kerensky.

'Let everyone who has already tried to use force of arms against
the power of the people know that such attempts will be crushed
with blood and iron,' he declaimed, and at that broadside against
the Bolsheviks, for the first and last time, the whole hall applauded.
'Let those who think the time is ripe to overthrow the revolutionary
government with bayonets', he continued, 'be even more careful.'
At this warning to Kornilov, it was only the left who clapped.

For two hours, Kerensky rambled tremulously, hammy and
overwrought, transporting himself. 'He appeared to want to scare
somebody and to create an impression of force and power,' Milyukov reported in contempt. 'He only engendered pity.'

A naive observer hopeful for social peace might see moments
to strike optimism, as when Tsereteli made a point of reaching out
to shake hands with the prominent industrialist Bublikov. But they
were few and unconvincing. When the Kadet Maklakov demanded
that the government 'take the daring steps necessary ... [because]
the judgement day is approaching', the right cheered and the left
sat mute. When Chkheidze read out VTsIK's platform, the left
applauded and the right scowled. One side clapped, the other sat like
stone. The other cheered, the one booed.

On the 12th, Kornilov arrived in Moscow, flanked again by his
Turkmen guards. He was met at the station by a throng of military cadets, a band, and representatives from one of the Womens'
Battalions of Death. These all-female volunteer army units had
been set up at Kerensky's request under the remarkable young
Novgorod soldier Maria Bochkareva, who had at the start of the
war inveigled royal permission to join the army, and distinguished
herself in bloody combat. Kornilov passed through the military
escort into a shower of petals scattered by an ecstatic upper-class
crowd.

In his welcome speech, the Kadet Rodichev entreated him: 'Save Russia, and a thankful people will crown you.' With heavy-handed symbolism, Kornilov's first stop was at the Iversky shrine, where the tsars had traditionally worshipped. Among the visitors he received that day, more than one debated with him the question of an armed overthrow of the government: the right-wing business group the Society for the Economic Rehabilitation of Russia, for example, represented by Putilov and Vishnegradsky, went so far as to offer funds specifically for an authoritarian regime.

The next day, the 13th, Kornilov came to the Bolshoi to speak.

As he prepared to mount the rostrum of the packed hall of the Moscow conference, Kerensky stopped him. He pleaded with the general to confine his remarks to military matters.

'I will give my speech', Kornilov responded, 'in my own way.'

Kornilov ascended. The right rose in ovation. 'Shouts ring out,' states the record. '"Cads!" "Get up!"' No one on the left benches obeyed.

To Kerensky's intense relief, Kornilov, never a confident speaker, gave a speech both inexpert and surprisingly mild. The continuing roars of rightist approval were for him qua figurehead, rather than for anything in particular that he said.

After Kornilov, speaker after speaker excoriated the revolution that had wracked Russia, and hankered loudly for the restoration of order. General Kaledin, the elected leader – ataman – of the Cossacks of the Don region, announced to the delight of the right that 'all soviets and committees must be abolished'. A young Cossack officer, Nagaev, quickly insisted that working Cossacks disagreed with Kaledin, eliciting corresponding ecstasy on the left.

As he spoke, someone on the right interrupted with shouts of 'German marks!' The accusation of treachery provoked bedlam. When the heckler would not identify himself, Kerensky finally declared that 'Lieutenant Nagaev and all the Russian people ... are quite satisfied with the silence of a coward.' It was a rare moment of good theatre left in the man once considered Russia's hope.

Kerensky's concluding speech, by contrast, was an almost

incomprehensible, pitiful mix of longueurs and schmaltz. 'Let my heart turn to stone, let all the chords of my faith in men fade away, let all the flowers of my dreams for man wither and die,' he wailed. 'I will cast away the keys to this heart that loves the people and I will think only of the state.'

From the audience, a few sentimentalists obligingly responded in kind – 'You cannot! Your heart will not permit it!' – but for the most part the spectacle was merely excruciating. Even one of Kerensky's diminishing number of loyal supporters, Stepun, uneasily admitted that 'one could hear not only the agony of his power, but also of his personality'.

Thus the slow death of the Provisional Government continued.

Troops radicalised or gave up hope or both in the grinding war. They wrote bitter, raging letters now to the country's leaders. One soldier, Kuchlavok, and his regiment sent *Izvestia* a long, near-glossolalic sermon of despair that their revolution had been in vain, a deflected apocalypse, catastrophe without renewal.

> Now another Saviour of the world must be born, to save the people from all the calamities in the making here on earth and to put an end to these bloody days, so that no beast of any kind living on the earth created not by princes and rulers but by God-given nature is wiped out, for God is an invisible being inhabiting whoever possesses a conscience and tells us to live in friendship, but no there are evil people who sow strife among us and poison us one against another pushing us to murder, who wish for others what they would not wish for themselves … They used to say that the war was foisted off on us by Nicholas. Nicholas has been overthrown, so who is foisting the war on us now?

The mass desertions, politicised and other, did not end – and were even announced in advance. With angry courteousness, a group of anonymous soldiers 'from various regiments' wrote to Kerensky with due notice: 'we are going to stay in the trenches at the front and repel the enemy, and maybe even attack, but only until the first days of baneful autumn'. If the war continued beyond that point, they warned, they would simply walk away.

Another group of soldiers sent the Soviet Executive Committee an extraordinary ingenuous query: 'All of us ... ask you as our comrades to explain to us who these Bolsheviks are ... Our provisional government has come out very much against the Bolsheviks. But we ... don't find any fault with them.' They had previously been opposed to the Bolsheviks, they explained, but were now gradually going over to them. But to make sure they understood this choice exactly, they asked the Soviet to send clearer explanations.

Yet more reports came in of peasants seizing land, with greater and uncompromising violence. In some regions they abjured and despised the *zemstvos*, the local organisations of the Provisional Government. 'Call our future governance what you will but don't use the word *zemstvo*' was the quote in one newspaper from the depressing travels of local government activists in south-eastern Russia. 'We have grown disgusted by this word.' In Kursk, during a trial for land confiscation, the peasants drove away the plaintiff – *and the court*. 'Anarchy reigns supreme,' read an official report on one village from the Tambovsk district. 'The peasants are storming the gardens and looting.'

Across many regions the push for independence was intensifying. Prices of essentials soared. Petrograd's food situation went abruptly from grave to desperate.

What centre remained could not hold. The Mensheviks held what they called a 'Unity Congress' in Petrograd: its name was a bad joke. Martov's internationalists had a third of the delegates, but the remaining two-thirds, following the leadership, had moved even further in favour of collaboration – what Tsereteli called 'cooperation with the living forces of the country'. The chasm was wider than ever, and the right maintained its formal authority.

Mid-August, and a wave of mysterious explosions rocked

munitions factories in Petrograd and Kazan. It was seemingly the work of pro-German saboteurs.

In Latvia, Riga tottered as the Germans approached. The city's chances of withstanding a serious German assault were nil: at the conference, Kornilov warned that without more effort to hold the Gulf of Riga, it would be lost, and the way to Petrograd open to the Germans. Even as he spoke, the Germans were preparing.

Would Petrograd follow Riga? came the whispers.

Indeed, would the government even fight for Petrograd?

Of eleven wealthy Muscovites he met one evening for dinner, ten told the great American journalist John Reed that if it came to it, they would rather have Wilhelm than the Bolsheviks. In the journal *Utro Rossii*, Rodzianko wrote with astonishing candour: 'I say to myself, "Let God take care of Petrograd." They fear that if Petrograd is lost the central revolutionary organisations will be destroyed … I rejoice if all these organisations are destroyed; for they will bring nothing but disaster upon Russia.'

'I want to take a middle road,' Kerensky despaired, 'but no one will help me.'

All rumours of incipient coups notwithstanding, after the Moscow conference, Kerensky was willing to accept the crushing curbs on political rights that Kornilov demanded, hoping they might stem the tide of anarchy. He did not relish the final break with the Soviet that this would inevitably mean, but he was a man who felt he had no choice.

Kornilov pressed his advantage. On 19 August, he telegraphed Kerensky to 'insistently assert the necessity' of giving him command of the Petrograd Military District, the city and areas surrounding. At this, though, Kerensky still drew the line.

On the banks of the river Mazā Jugla in Latvia, the legendary Latvian riflemen went into action, in what would come to be known as the Battle of Jugla. They strove with doomed courage to keep Riga from German hands. The next day, the First Don Cossacks and the Savage Divisions moved to Pskov and its environs, threateningly close to a polarising Petrograd.

In the Petrograd city Duma elections on the 20th, the Kadets received 114,000 votes, the Mensheviks a derisory 24,000. The SRs won, with 205,000 votes – but the Bolsheviks were, shockingly, within spitting distance, with 184,000.

'In comparison with the May elections', wrote Sukhanov, the SRs' total did not represent a victory 'but a substantial setback.' By contrast, he, no supporter of Lenin's party, was clear that 'the sole real victor … was the Bolsheviks, so recently trampled into the mud, accused of treason and venality, utterly routed … Why, one would have thought them annihilated for ever … Then where had they sprung up from again? What sort of strange, diabolical enchantment was this?'

The day after this strange, diabolical enchantment, after hours of German bombardment shook the fairy-tale facades of the Latvian capital, the Russian armies fled. Columns of Germans marched into the city. German submarines took the gulf and shelled the shoreline villages, blasting them from the cold sea.

Riga had fallen.

Watching from his Finnish exile, Lenin was incandescently furious with what he considered the collaborationism of Moscow Bolsheviks. Their sin? To participate in the Soviet's Provisional Revolutionary Committee alongside the Mensheviks and SRs.

Lenin was scornful of the counterrevolutionary scare with which the committee had justified itself. On 18 August he wrote 'Rumours of a Conspiracy', in which he implied that such fears were contrived by the moderates, as part of a campaign to fool the masses into supporting them. 'Not a single honest Bolshevik who had not taken leave of his senses completely would agree to any bloc' with the SRs or Mensheviks, he wrote, 'even in the event that a counter-revolutionary attack appeared genuine.' Which in any case this supposed one, he implied, was not.

Lenin was wrong.

★

If anything, the sheer confusion of the moment, scattered and unclear evidence suggests, was in part due to a failure of joined-up counterrevolution – there was *more than one conspiracy* simmering away on the right.

Various shadowy groups – the Union of Officers, the Republican Centre and Military League – were meeting to discuss plans for martial law. They decided that rallies slated by the Soviet for the 27th, to celebrate six months since February, could be used to justify imposing a regime at the barrels of Kornilovite guns. And if those rallies did not oblige with disorder, the conspirators would use agents provocateurs to ensure it was provided.

On 22 August, the army chief of staff summoned various officers to Mogilev, ostensibly for training. But on arrival they were briefed on the schemes, before being sent on to Petrograd. Exactly how apprised of these specifics Kornilov himself was is unclear: that he was preparing to move on his enemies on the left – and in the government – is not.

And it was not only the hard right considering martial law under Kornilov. In anguish, lugubriously, incoherently, bizarrely, grasping at a possible way out, so was Kerensky himself.

On 23 August, Savinkov, for Kerensky, went to the Stavka to see Kornilov. The meeting opened in an unpromising atmosphere of very bad blood.

Savinkov presented Kornilov with three requests. He asked for his support in the dismantling of the Union of Officers and the political department of the Stavka, both rumoured to be heavily implicated in coup-mongering; for the exemption of Petrograd itself from Kornilov's direct control; and then, amazingly, for a cavalry corps for Petrograd.

At this last, the startled Kornilov grew markedly more cordial. These mounted soldiers were intended, Savinkov confirmed, for 'the actual inauguration of martial law in Petrograd and for the defence of the provisional government against any attempt whatever'. As

General Alexeev would later attest, 'the participation of Kerensky [in planning martial law] is beyond question … The advance of the Third Cavalry Corps's division on Petrograd was made upon Kerensky's instructions … transmitted by Savinkov'.

Kerensky, it seemed, was offering to sanction the very counter-revolutionary operation that Kornilov was planning.

In so far as it can be reconstructed from the dense murk of the moment, it appears that, agitated at the possibility of Bolshevik uprising, Kerensky was split between opposition to martial law, and a belief in its necessity. Even in the necessity of a collective or individual dictatorship.

And for his part, Kornilov, too, was flexible: perfectly willing to overthrow Kerensky, he was also ready to accommodate him, under certain conditions. Now, reassured by Savinkov that the government had come round to his way of thinking, he was much more relaxed about accepting Kerensky's other proposals, as well as his opposition, 'for political reasons', to putting the hard-right General Krimov at the head of the cavalry corps. Thus Savinkov was reassured that Kornilov was not angling against Kerensky – to whom, when Savinkov probed, the general even, if not very vociferously, pledged loyalty.

It seemed as if compromise could be reached, an acceptable martial law thrashed out. But, unknown to Savinkov and Kornilov, the previous evening Kerensky had received a visitor. And thus had begun reaction's sinister comedy of skulduggery and errors.

Vladimir Nikolaevich Lvov – not to be confused with the ex-premier – was a dunderheaded Muscovite busybody, an ingenuous ruling-class Pooter. A liberal deputy in the Third and Fourth Dumas, Lvov was part of a network of Moscow industrialists who held that Russia needed a right-wing authoritarian 'national cabinet'. So far, so usual. What was less common was that he also retained a certain respect for

Kerensky. When, therefore, rumours of Stavka conspiracies reached his ears from a party thereto, he hoped he might be able to forestall a clash between Kerensky and Kornilov.

During his meeting with Kerensky, Lvov expounded various platitudes about the necessity of having more conservatives in government, and offered to sound out key political figures to that end. He allowed, portentously, that he represented 'certain important groups with significant strength'. Beyond that, later testimonies diverge.

Lvov would claim that Kerensky authorised him to be his proxy; Kerensky, rather more lukewarm, that he 'did not consider it possible to refrain from further discussions with Lvov, expecting from him a more exact explanation of what was on his mind'. By encouraging Lvov to report back from informal discussions, Kerensky thought he might gain insight into some of the plotting at which his visitor hinted. Hence he encouraged Lvov to sound out these mysterious circles.

It may be that Lvov, never the most perspicacious man, misunderstood Kerensky's encouragement; or that, puffed up with his mission, he convinced himself that he was on official business. Either way, as Kerensky got on with failing to shore up a collapsing state, Lvov bustled off to Stavka.

As he did so, the widespread terror of a coup grew, as did plans on the left to oppose it. On 24 August, the Petrograd Interdistrict Conference of Soviets (an organ led by the left Menshevik Gorin, strongly influenced by Bolsheviks) demanded the government declare Russia a democratic republic, and announced the formation of a 'Committee of Public Safety', mobilising armed squads of workers and the unemployed to defend the revolution. Vyborg Bolsheviks, disgruntled at their party's inadequate response to the threat of counterrevolution, scheduled an emergency meeting of the Petersburg Committee.

This was precisely the kind of thinking that Lenin denounced as scaremongering. And as the activists succumbed to it, Kornilov set an actual counterrevolutionary conspiracy in motion.

Kornilov sent instructions to Krimov to push on to Petrograd in response to a bruited 'Bolshevik uprising'.

It was as such intrigues swirled that Lvov arrived at Stavka, on the important mission he had invented in his head.

Introducing himself as Kerensky's emissary, Lvov met with Kornilov and one of his advisors, a tall, stout, greying man named Zavoiko – who was, though Lvov did not know this, an intriguer himself, of a more serious kind. A wealthy hard-right parapolitical hustler, Zavoiko had for months seen in Kornilov a potential dictator, and so made himself the general's indispensable vizier.

Lvov asked Kornilov for his thoughts on the composition of a new government. Kornilov answered cautiously, but, coming after the request for cavalry, he felt hopeful that Lvov's question was further evidence that the government was disposed to compromise, and was coming over to his views.

In the wake of that earlier meeting with Savinkov, the right-wingers at Mogilev had begun open discussions about who would take what ministry in their authoritarian government. Now, Kornilov and Zavoiko laid out for Lvov some of that vision – their desiderata. Petrograd must be placed under martial law. No controversy there. The question was, martial law under whom?

Lvov suggested three possibilities: Kerensky could be dictator; there could be a directorate, a dictatorial small cabinet, including Kornilov and, presumably, Kerensky; or Kornilov himself could be dictator.

Judiciously, Kornilov expressed his preference for the third option. After all, it might be simpler if all civil and military authority in the country belonged to the commander-in-chief – 'whoever', he modestly added, 'he might be'.

Kornilov mooted the possibility of positions for Kerensky and Savinkov in this government, and asked Lvov to urge them for their own safety to repair to Mogilev within two days. Lvov remained blithely untroubled throughout the rest of the discussion, suggesting

216

various other figures for a cabinet. But after the meeting had ended and Lvov prepared to board his train back to Petrograd, perhaps misjudging his visitor's loyalties, perhaps not caring, Zavoiko, with swaggering arrogance, made a shocking, casual pronouncement.

'Kerensky is needed as a name for the soldiers for ten days or so,' he said, 'after which he will be eliminated.'

Lvov sat stunned in his carriage as the train pulled away. He was finally, dimly aware that Kerensky's aspirations and Kornilov's might not, shall we say, perfectly overlap.

Kornilov placed the Third Corps – the cavalry requested by Savinkov! – on alert. He had Krimov draft an order for distribution upon his entry to Petrograd, announcing the imposition of martial law, a curfew and the banning of strikes and meetings. Disobedience, the leaflet read, would be harshly met: 'the troops will not fire into the air'. Yet more soldiers made for Petrograd, in preparation for its forthcoming military occupation and policing.

As previously arranged, Kornilov telegrammed Savinkov, telling him the forces would be in place by the evening of the 28th. 'I request that Petrograd be proclaimed under martial law on 29 August': thus, courteously, Kornilov prepared to bring the revolution to an end.

The hard-right press warned of leftist massacres on the 27th. Provocateurs provoked: socialists received multiple reports of 'strangers in soldiers' tunics' trying to whip up insurrection. Kerensky's intended collaboration with Kornilov did not preclude the continuance of other, chaotic right-wing putschist plans.

The air stank of counterrevolution. On 26 August, the Petrograd Trade Union Soviet and Central Soviet of Factory-Shop Committees jointly endorsed the Interdistrict Conference's call for a Committee of Public Safety.

This was the cauldron into which Lvov returned. He hastened to the Winter Palace.

★

Savinkov had just reported to Kerensky on his own cordial meeting with Kornilov when Lvov arrived. Reassured by Savinkov's account, Kerensky asked Lvov what he had learnt. And then he listened in growing, bewildered horror.

Lvov relayed to Kerensky as *demands* those *preferences* Kornilov had expressed from among the options Lvov had put to him – on behalf, Kornilov had believed, of Kerensky himself. Kornilov wanted Kerensky to come to Mogilev, Lvov said, but warned that the invitation was dangerous, as he had heard from Zavoiko's own mouth. Kerensky, he insisted, must flee.

Kerensky laughed in nervous disbelief.

'This', Lvov said, face like flint, 'is no time for jokes.'

Kerensky struggled to make sense of what he was hearing. He had Lvov put Kornilov's 'demands' in writing. Martial law; all authority including civil to devolve to the commander-in-chief; all ministers, including Kerensky, to resign. What Kornilov had thought was a discussion of possibilities now read as the declaration of a putsch.

Reeling, Kerensky asked Lvov to meet him at the Ministry of War at 8 p.m., to speak directly with Kornilov: he wanted to be absolutely certain of what was afoot. But there was to be a final absurdity. Lvov was late for the appointment. At 8:30, therefore, so agitated he could not wait, Kerensky wired Kornilov and simply pretended that Lvov was with him. And the farce unfolded in clicks and crackles, recording every back-and-forth in the ribbon of text.

Kerensky: 'Good day, General. V. N. Lvov and Kerensky on the line. We ask you to confirm that Kerensky is to act according to the communication made to him by Vladimir Nikolaevich.'

Kornilov: 'Good day, Alexander Fedorovich, good day, Vladimir Nikolaevich. To confirm again the outline of the present situation I believe the country and the army are in, which I asked V. N. to convey to you, I declare again that the events of the past few days and those I can see coming make it imperative to reach a definite decision in the shortest possible time.'

Kerensky now impersonated Lvov. 'I, Vladimir Nikolaevich, ask whether it is necessary to act on that definite decision which you asked me to communicate privately to Alexander Fedorovich. Without your personal confirmation, Alexander Fedorovich hesitates to give me his full confidence.'

Kornilov: 'Yes, I confirm that I asked you to convey to Alexander Fedorovich my urgent request that he come to Mogilev.'

Kerensky, hollow-chested, had Kornilov verify that Savinkov, too, should come. 'Believe me,' Kornilov added, 'only my recognition of the responsibility of the moment makes me so persistent in my request.'

'Shall we come only in case of demonstrations, of which there are rumours, or in any case?' Kerensky asked.

Kornilov: 'In any case.'

The connection broke, ending the most epochal talking-at-cross-purposes in history.

At his headquarters, Kornilov exhaled mightily in relief. Kerensky, he thought, would now come to Mogilev, and submit to – even join – a government under him.

Kerensky, meanwhile, believed 'the definite decision' which Kornilov had just validated was not just that he, Kerensky, should come to him, but that Kornilov would take dictatorial powers. That Kerensky had been given an ultimatum. That he was being dispensed with.

Had Lvov not warned him to run for his life?

When Lvov at last showed up, Kerensky had the startled man arrested.

His own recent plans for martial law had dragged Kerensky so far right he did not know if he could still now turn to the Soviet for support, nor how the Petrograd masses would respond to any of his appeals. At a hasty cabinet meeting, he read out the transcript 'proving' Kornilov's 'treachery'. He demanded the astonished ministers grant him unlimited authority against the coming danger. The Kadets, deeply imbricated with the Kornilovite milieu, objected, but the majority gave Kerensky a free hand. They resigned as he requested, remaining only in caretaker capacities.

Thus, at 4 a.m. on 27 August, the Second Coalition ended.

Once more, Kerensky telegrammed Kornilov. 'I order you immediately to turn over your office to General Lukomsky,' he dictated, and the keys tapped out, 'who is to take over temporarily the duties of commander-in-chief, until the arrival of the new commander-in-chief. You are instructed to come immediately to Petrograd.'

That done, he retired to his rooms, right next door to where Lvov was being held. Kerensky tried to calm his own nerves by bellowing arias. The sound of his voice went straight through the wall, waking his confused informant and keeping him awake all night.

Sunday 27 August, the day of Soviet celebration, dawned warm and clear and tense. 'Sinister people are circulating rumours of a rising set for today and allegedly organised by our party,' warned the Bolsheviks' *Rabochy*. 'The CC implores workers and soldiers not to yield to provocations … and not to take part in any action.' The party's fears were still more of threats from within, from provocateurs, than of those from without.

And the conspirators waited for their moment. That morning, and for the next two days, Colonel L. P. Dyusimeter and P. N. Finisov of the Republican Centre, and Colonel V. I. Sidorin, their liaison with the Stavka, bar-hopped around the drinking dens of Petrograd, waiting for news of Krimov, ready to unleash their coup.

A little after 8 a.m. on Sunday, Kornilov received Kerensky's telegram. At first he was stupefied. Swiftly, he was apoplectic.

General Lukomsky, no less blindsided, refused the position Kerensky had thrust on him. 'It is too late to halt an operation started with your approval,' he wired back, the bewilderment in the last three words palpable. 'For the sake of Russia's salvation you must go with Kornilov, not against him … Kornilov's dismissal would bring horrors the likes of which Russia has never seen.'

Kerensky put Savinkov in charge of military preparations for defence against the coup, while Kornilov directed the Third Corps under Krimov to occupy the city. Kerensky sent word urging them to stop, assuring the men that there was no insurrection to 'overcome' – the supposed pretext for their arrival. They did not pause.

Garbled rumours of a rift between Kornilov and Kerensky began to spread through Petrograd. Those rumours, of course, also implied a pre-rift agreement.

In the mid-afternoon, Soviet leaders and their parties gathered in emergency session. They were not even certain what it was that they needed to discuss or debate. The situation was tense but incomprehensible.

It was only in the early evening that matters became clearer, when Kerensky released a proclamation. Through Lvov, he announced, Kornilov had demanded civil and military power to inaugurate a counterrevolutionary regime. In the face of this grave threat, the government had mandated Kerensky to take countermeasures. For that reason, the announcement made clear, martial law was now declared.

Kornilov swiftly responded to Kerensky's statement, insisting – truthfully – that Lvov was not his representative.

'Our great motherland is dying,' he stated. 'Under the pressure of the Bolshevik majority in the Soviets, the Provisional Government acts in complete harmony with … the German General Staff … I want nothing for myself, except the preservation of a Great Russia, and I vow to bring the people by means of victory … to a Constituent Assembly, where they themselves will decide their fate.'

Generals Klembovsky, Baluev, Shcherbatov, Denikin and others all pledged their allegiance to Kornilov. The Union of Officers enthusiastically telegrammed army and naval headquarters around the country, proclaiming the end of the Provisional Government and urging 'tough and unflinching' support for Kornilov.

Kerensky ineffectually declared battle; Kornilov declared war.

Instantly a plethora of ad hoc committees sprang up to mobilise citizens against the coup, to procure weapons, coordinate supplies, communications, services. Vikzhel, the Menshevik-controlled All-Russian Executive Committee of Railway Workers, formed a bureau for struggle against Kornilov, working with the Interdistrict Conference. Word was dispatched to Kronstadt. The left gathered its forces. At Smolny, party fractions scrambled.

By sour irony, that very night in the Narva District, the Bolshevik Petersburg Committee met for that session scheduled three days earlier – in response to the Vyborg Bolsheviks' concern at the party's inadequate attention to the counterrevolutionary threat. The leadership had almost certainly been intending to pooh-pooh such anxieties: now as the thirty-six party officials met, Kornilov's troops descended on Petrograd. Rarely can doom-mongers have felt so vindicated.

And the Vyborg rank and file were angry not only with the leadership's tardiness in assessing the baleful situation, but also with the ambiguous tactical resolutions of the recent Sixth Congress. One, 'On the Political Situation', encouraged cooperating with *all* forces combatting counterrevolution – while 'On Unification' declared the Mensheviks to be permanent deserters from the proletarian camp, which would preclude cooperation with them. How, then, to proceed?

The meeting was fractious. Andrei Bubnov, a career militant recently arrived from Moscow to join the CC, warned his comrades to trust neither Mensheviks nor SRs. During the Moscow State Conference, he told them, 'First the government turned to us for help and then we were spat upon.' He was against collaboration in any self-defence organisations, insisting that the Bolsheviks work alone, to steer the masses against Kornilov and Kerensky both. Against him, Kalinin, from what was still, *contra* Lenin, the leadership's mainstream, insisted that if Kornilov really were on the verge of overthrowing Kerensky, it would be absurd not to take the position that the Bolsheviks would have to intervene on Kerensky's side.

Hostility exploded. Radical speakers slammed party authorities for lack of leadership, for 'defencism', for acting as a 'coolant' on the masses, for operating 'in a fog' during the July Days, and since.

The meeting degenerated into a welter of grievances, resentments and generalised attacks. Rage distracted from the urgency of the moment, until at last someone shouted: 'Let's get down to concrete defence measures!'

Everyone was clear that it was crucial to mobilise as widely as possible against Kornilov. The Bolsheviks established a communications network, drafted leaflets calling workers and soldiers to arms. Members were allocated to coordinate with mass organisations. And everyone, including Bubnov, agreed that the party must maintain contact with the Soviet leadership's defence organ – 'for purposes', it was vaguely glossed, 'of information'.

For Bubnov, then, 'informational' exchange with the Soviet was indispensable, even while 'there must be no interaction with the Soviet majority'. This was not a 'dialectical synthesis' so much as a holding fudge demanded by the scale of the crisis. Kerensky and Kornilov were equally bad, but at that moment, Kornilov was more equally bad.

At 11:30 p.m., the Soviet Executive Committee met to discuss their relations with government, given the emerging scandal of Kerensky and Kornilov's recent alliance and its collapse, and given that Kerensky was now calling for a Directory, a small cabinet with authoritarian powers. More urgently, they debated how to preserve the revolution.

For the moderates, Kerensky, even now, and however critically, had to be defended.

'The only person who can form a government at this time is Comrade Kerensky,' said the Menshevik Vainshtein. If Kerensky and the government were to fall, 'the revolutionary cause will be lost'.

The Bolsheviks took the hardest line: that the Provisional Government *in toto* could not be trusted. They wanted the instigation of democracy in the army, the transfer of land to peasants, the eight-hour day, democratic control of industry and finance, and the devolution of power to revolutionary workers, peasants and soldiers. However. Having made their points, the Bolsheviks in the Soviet Executive Committee, more conciliatory than Lenin or their Vyborg comrades, did not tie up proceedings with a resolution. They kept their oppositionism trenchant but abstract.

Astonishingly, they even abstained on a resolution that, while opposing the Directory he wanted, granted Kerensky power not only to maintain the existing form of government but also to fill cabinet vacancies with carefully chosen Kadets. More astonishingly still, they voted *with* Mensheviks and SRs to convene (yet) another 'state conference' – though this time made up exclusively of 'democratic elements', the left – to discuss the government question, and act as overseer until the convocation of a Constituent Assembly.

But when its representatives told Kerensky of this Soviet decision, he remained adamant that he must create a six-man Directory. It was deadlock, and the Soviet's move.

'All directories spawn counterrevolution,' protested Martov in the Soviet, to vigorous agreement. Lunacharsky, too, was magnificent in opposition. He branded both Kornilov and the Provisional Government counterrevolutionary, and demanded the transfer of power to a government of workers, peasants and soldiers – which here meant the soviets. Thus Lunacharsky abruptly reintroduced the content, if not quite the form, of the slogan 'All Power to the Soviets'. The very slogan Lenin had decreed obsolete.

But the night brought to the exhausted delegates word that general after general was declaring for Kornilov. Pressed on the government question by what felt increasingly like necessity, the meeting moved slowly rightward.

At last the Executive Committee adopted a resolution from Tsereteli supporting Kerensky, and leaving to him government's form. This was to rubber-stamp his Directory.

The Bolsheviks in the chamber vehemently contested the resolution. But even so, in dramatic evidence of their moderation, by their party standards, they agreed that if that government were seriously committed to fighting the counterrevolution, they would agree to 'form a military alliance with it'.

The enemy approached. The Soviet issued emergency orders to provincial soviets, to railway workers and soldiers to the effect that the Stavka must be defied, counterrevolutionary communications disrupted. They called for the Soviet's orders – and the government's – to be immediately obeyed.

The collaboration of that night was not all from the Bolsheviks present with those on their right: it flowed the other way, too. When Weinstein, a right Menshevik, proposed a dedicated group to organise military defence, everyone there agreed the Bolsheviks must be integral to it.

On 28 August, Prince Trubetskoy of the foreign ministry telegrammed Tereshchenko from Mogilev. 'The entire commanding personnel, the overwhelming majority of the officers and the best fighting units ... will follow Kornilov,' he predicted. 'The entire Cossack host, the majority of the military schools, and the best combat units ... Added to this ... is the superiority of the military organisation over the weakness of the government organs.'

In Petrograd, mobilisation against the counterrevolutionaries accelerated, but the news was unremittingly bleak. Kornilov's troops had reached Luga, the city heard, and the revolutionary garrison had surrendered. Nine troop trains had hauled passed Orodezh. Reaction was on its way.

The response from the Soviet and many on the left, Bolsheviks not excluded, was panicked. But, in large numbers, Petrograd's workers and soldiers reacted differently. Trubetskoy's glum claim, that 'the majority of the popular and urban masses have grown indifferent to the existing order and will submit to any cracking of the whip', was startlingly wrong.

Soldiers mobilised in their thousands against the coming coup. In factories, alarms and whistles blared to summon the workers together. They took stock, reinforced security, organised themselves into fighting detachments.

Some organisations had foreseen the danger. The Petrograd Interdistrict Committee of Soviets, for example, had been warning of such a threat for some time, and it was primed to take prompt action. Vikzhel directed that 'suspicious telegrams' be held up and suspect troop movement tracked. By the afternoon of the 28th, the group suggested by Weinstein, the Committee for Struggle Against the Counterrevolution, was operational.

As agreed, the committee comprised representatives of Mensheviks, SRs, Bolsheviks and other democratic organisations. In Sukhanov's words,

> the masses, in so far as they were organised, were organised by the Bolsheviks and followed them ... Without [them], the committee was impotent ... it could only have passed the time with appeals and idle speeches ... With the Bolsheviks, the committee had at its disposal the full power of the organised workers and soldiers ... And despite their being in the minority, it was quite clear that ... control was in the hands of the Bolsheviks.

The committee liaised with the self-organised, makeshift defence groups that were springing up. One crucial task – and for the Bolsheviks, a condition of participation – was the arming of workers' militias. A transformation of 40,000 people practically overnight. Toolers, metalworkers, people of all trades becoming an army. The chambers of industrial plants resonated with the sound of inexpert marching, the music of a new militia.

'The factory looked like a camp,' Rakilov, one of these Red Guards, as they were with increasing frequency known, would remember. 'When you came in, you could see the fitters at the bench, but they had their packs hanging by them, and their guns were leaning against the bench.'

Forty thousand people swiftly organised into these new roles. They took time to pose for photographs with their units. They steadied their weapons for the cameras with variable skill, their faces set, fretful, excited, determined. Guard after proud guard rigged out not just in work clothes or makeshift militaria but in their very best, as if for church, a wedding, a funeral. They were dressed up for an occasion in those stiff suits, their ties straight and tight, bowlers or homburgs on their heads, kneeling with rifles at the ready. The occasion was self-defence.

The Bolsheviks negotiated their tactical contradictions. They collaborated with moderates, but in such a way that these armed workers were at the vanguard of the defence.

In Petrograd itself, most military school cadets backed Kornilov, but that by no means meant all were willing to fight for him, while the Cossacks remained neutral, refusing to fight for either side. All other units in the city sent detachments to construct defences at its vulnerable points.

In the strained military atmosphere, it was dangerous to show open support for Kornilov. In the streets of the Vyborg district, enraged soldiers murdered several officers who refused to acknowledge the authority of a revolutionary commissar. In Helsingfors, the crew of the battleship *Petropavlovsk* voted to execute officers who would not pledge their allegiance to 'democratic organisations'.

The Schlusselburg gunpowder works sent a bargeload of grenades to the capital, for distribution by factory committees. Estonian and Finnish soviets sent word of their solidarity. Throughout Petrograd, soviet posters urged discipline, excoriating the scourge of drunkenness. The city Duma formed a commission to aid with food supplies. And most importantly, it selected deputies to go to Luga, for the purpose of agitating among Kornilov's troops.

In the south of Petrograd, armed workers erected barricades. They strung barbed wire across the roads, dug trenches in the city's approaches. The suburbs became military camps.

Initiative was beginning to slip from the right. They could feel it. They pushed back.

In the afternoon of the 28th, Milyukov offered himself as a go-between, in the hopes that he might persuade Kerensky to stand down. The high-ranking Kadet Kishkin pressured Kerensky to resign in favour of Alexeev – who supported Kornilov. A majority of Kerensky's (acting) ministers were quickly in favour of this proposal, and even foreign representatives were advising him to consider 'negotiation'.

The Soviet, however, categorically opposed any such move. In view of the sheer scale of revolutionary defence to which the Soviet had swiftly made itself key, and uneasily aware of the likely resistance of workers and soldiers if he went against this opposition, Kerensky had to reject the pressure to negotiate.

On the 28th, Dyusimeter and Finisov quietly set out for Luga. They left Sidorin behind them, with funds from Putilov and the Society for the Economic Rehabilitation of Russia to finance a coup when they sent word. His job would be to concoct a 'Bolshevik riot', to justify military repression.

But setbacks for the right began to come faster. That evening, the Ussuriysky Mounted Division was blocked on its approach to the city: it reached Yamburg only to discover that the Vikzhel had got its message through: railway workers had ruined the tracks. They were blocked, wrenched up and bent out of line, splayed. Elements of the Savage Division did get as far as Vyritsa, only thirty-seven miles from the capital. But there that train, too, met torn-up rails. The tracks of the revolution jutted like broken bone.

Kornilov's troops were cut off – but they were not alone.

Here to meet them where they found themselves stranded were scores of emissaries. They came from the Committee for Struggle, from district soviets, from factories, garrisons, Tsentroflot, from the Naval Committee, the Second Baltic Fleet Crew. And locals had come, too. All stamping across the scrub and through the trees towards that wheezing train. They came with agitation in mind. They came to beg the Savage Division to resist being used by counterrevolution.

By revolutionary fortune, the Executive Committee of the Union of Muslim Soviets was visiting Petrograd when the crisis began. It sent its own delegation to meet the engine – one of whom was a grandson of Imam Shamil. Shamil was a legendary nineteenth-century liberation hero of the Caucasus – including to the men of the Savage Division. Now a man of that celebrated blood was imploring them to stand with the revolution they had been sent to bury.

The soldiers of the Savage Division were, in fact, unaware of the purpose of their transfer. They were not predisposed to support Kornilov, and the more they heard from those pleading with them, the less they were minded to. They listened and argued and considered what they were told as darkness came, and on into the night. Their train and its surrounds became a debating chamber, a gathering of urgent discussions. Their officers despaired.

In Petrograd, alarmed by reports that officers of certain units were aiding Kornilov with their own ca'cannies, sluggish obedience and inadequate resolve, the Committee for Struggle sent commissars to oversee the mobilisation. The city hummed with Red Guards. Three thousand armed sailors arrived from Kronstadt to lend assistance. The Central Soviet of Factory-Shop Committees coordinated preparations. The Union of Metalworkers – by far the most powerful union in Russia – put its money and expertise at the Committee for Struggle's disposal.

Kerensky's appointees to the effort, Savinkov and Filonenko, strove to keep watch on the Bolsheviks at least as assiduously as to forestall Kornilov. The notion that these two were in charge of Petrogad's defences was an obvious fiction. At best, they were onlookers to Soviet and grassroots work.

The Bolsheviks were indispensable to the measures. So much so that when several of their members escaped from detention in the Second District Militia headquarters, the Committee for Struggle agreed, extraordinarily, that 'in order to participate in the common struggle' they should remain free.

Concretely, the party's approach was to push for the maximum possible bottom-up mobilisation against Kornilov, without supporting the Provisional Government. The journalist Chamberlin describes them as defending the government with 'tongue in cheek'.

And, amid the self-organisation and mass meetings, a familiar demand returned. 'In view of the emerging bourgeois counter-revolutionary movement,' insisted a group of pipe factory workers, 'all power must be transferred to the soviet of workers', soldiers' and peasants' deputies.' On the 29th, thousands of Putilov workers announced for rule by 'representatives of the revolutionary classes'. Workers at the Novo-Admiralteysky shipbuilding plant demanded power 'be put into the hands of the workers, soldiers and poorer peasantry, and be responsible to the soviets of workers', soldiers' and peasants deputies'.

'All Power to the Soviets' had definitively returned.

'No disturbances expected,' Kerensky wired to Krimov, desperate to keep him away. 'There is no need for your corps.'

As if, by that point, Kerensky controlled Krimov. But no more did Krimov control his own troops. The Ussuriysky Cossack Mounted Division, still stalled at Yamburg (now known as Kingisepp), was surrounded by crowds from the Narva and Yamburg soviets, military units, mass organisations and local factories, plus a delegation led by Tsereteli. A reading of Kerensky's proclamation about Kornilov was enough to dampen the Cossacks' resolve.

Krimov himself, with the First Don Cossacks, was blocked, hemmed in, besieged, by men of the 20,000-strong garrison at Luga. Street orators circled the train endlessly, yelling entreaties through the windows, to the Cossacks' bewilderment and Krimov's rage. Kornilov ordered him to push on the last miles to Petrograd, but the Luga garrison would not allow it – and by that time, the Cossacks were not minded to argue. The incensed Krimov could only watch his men shuffle away to various spontaneous mass meetings, their mettle dwindling before his eyes.

Late on the 29th, in Petrograd, the telegram of his co-conspirators

Dyusimeter and Finisov at last reached Sidorin. A chilling prod: 'Act at once according to instructions.' They were requesting that helpful riot.

But it was too late, as even its supporters on the right had been forced to acknowledge. General Alexeev, seeing that the cause of the coup was hopeless, threatened to commit suicide if the plan to engineer a provocation went ahead.

By 30 August, the Kornilov Revolt had collapsed.

'Without firing a single shot we were victorious,' Kerensky wrote, ten years later. The 'we' was breathtakingly tendentious.

Lenin received all Russian news after a delay. He was late to the news of the threat, and late to the news that it had been averted. On the 30th, as the CC met in Petrograd, a city now breathing out, he wrote to them in haste.

What Lenin sent was not an explicit *mea culpa* for claiming that counterrevolution was 'a carefully thought-out ploy on the part of the Mensheviks and SRs'. Yet the letter perhaps contained an implicit one, in its expression of sheer astonishment at this 'most unexpected ... and downright unbelievably sharp turn in events'. Of course, any such change must entail a shift. 'Like every sharp turn,' he wrote, 'it [the circumstance] calls for a revision and change of tactics.'

In Zurich earlier that year, trying to convert the Romanian poet Valeriu Marcu to revolutionary defeatism, Lenin had coaxed him with what would become a famous phrase. 'One must always', he said, 'try to be as radical as reality itself.' And what is a radicalism that does not surprise?

Reality, radical, now stunned him.

It has sometimes been insinuated that during the Kornilov Crisis, the Bolsheviks pursued their energetic, effective non-collaborative cooperation with the government under Lenin's guidance. This is false: by the time his instructions began to arrive, the party had been in the Committee for Struggle for days, and the revolt was largely played out. The course he outlined, however, did amount to a pleasing post factum legitimation.

He did not spell out what he would consider 'permissible' cooperation with the Mensheviks and SRs he had so recently denounced as beyond the pale, but he did imply its necessity. And 'we shall fight Kornilov, of course, just as Kerensky's troops do, but we do not support Kerensky', he said, which was, broadly, just how things had been. The very day he wrote, the Moscow Bolshevik *Sotsial-demokrat* said: 'The revolutionary proletariat cannot tolerate either the dictatorship of Kornilov or of Kerensky.'

'We expose his weakness,' Lenin wrote, by pointing out Kerensky's vacillation and by making maximalist demands – the transfer of estates to peasants, workers' control, the arming of workers. That last, of course, had already been met. The approving scribble Lenin appended to his letter before sending it was understandable: 'Having read six issues of *Rabochy* after this was written, I must say our views fully coincide.'

On the 30th, Kornilov's crack Savage Division raised a red flag. The Ussuriysky Cossacks pledged loyalty to the Provisional Government. General Denikin was incarcerated by his own troops. Commanders from other fronts began to announce for the government, against the rightist conspiracy. At Luga, where Krimov received spurious alerts from Finisov and Dyusimeter that 'Bolshevik disorders' would break out any moment, the Don Cossacks had become so radicalised that they muttered about arresting him.

That afternoon, an envoy from the government arrived. The man promised Krimov safety, and invited him to meet Kerensky in the capital.

In his ineffectual way, Kerensky wanted to clean house. But, even though it had saved Petrograd, the left frightened him almost as much as the right. For example, while he sacked Savinkov for his proximity to various plotters, he replaced him with Palchinsky, whose politics were extremely similar – and one of whose first

232

actions was to close down the Bolshevik *Rabochy* and Gorky's *Novaya zhizn*. As if to underline the point, as chief of staff Kerensky appointed General Alexeev, a man virtually identical in his views to Kornilov.

The ship sinking, rats began to scurry, shocked, shocked! by any suggestion that they might have supported Kornilov. Rodzianko declared grandly that 'to start internecine warfare and argument now is a crime against the motherland'. All he knew of the conspiracy, he blustered, was what he read in the papers.

In his cell, the preposterous Vladimir Lvov got word that the tide had turned. He sent Kerensky his hearty congratulations, delighting that he had 'delivered a friend from Kornilov's clutches'.

That evening, when Krimov arrived, it was to a quiet city.

On the morning of 31 August, Krimov and Kerensky met for a heated discussion in the Winter Palace. Precisely what was said is unknown.

It is likely that Kerensky accused Krimov of mutiny, which Krimov would have unconvincingly denied. Like Kornilov, Krimov was furious at what seemed Kerensky's duplicity, his inexplicable turnabout. At last too enervated to continue, Krimov agreed to a further interview and repaired to a friend's apartment.

'The last card for saving the motherland has been beaten,' he said to his host. 'Life is no longer worth living.'

Krimov excused himself to a private room. There he wrote a note to Kornilov, took out his pistol and shot himself in the heart.

The contents of his last letter remain unknown.

Kerensky ordered a commission of inquiry into the attempted coup. But still he tried to ingratiate himself with a right who despised him, limiting the investigation's remit to individuals, rather than institutions. He proceeded with his plans to set up an authoritarian coalition of right socialists and liberals, strengthening the power of the Kadets.

But on the streets of Petrograd, it was the radical workers and sol-diers who had defeated the conspiracy, and they were buoyed with confidence. The failure of the Kornilov Revolt pulled the political lever left again. Soldiers of the Petrograd Garrison proclaimed that 'any coalition will be fought by all loyal sons of the people as they fought Kornilov'. Now they demanded a government of workers and poor peasants. The Second Machine Gun Regiment insisted that 'the only way out of the present situation lies in transferring power into the hands of the working people'.

Previously neutral units were beginning to turn, as were workers in plants under the sway of moderates. A plethora of motions – Bol-shevik, Left SR, Menshevik-International, unaffiliated – insisted on power to the soviets, left unity, a crackdown on counterrevolu-tion, an exclusively socialist government to end the war. Martov's comrade Larin reached the limit of exasparation with the pro-coalition Mensheviks, and came over to the Bolsheviks, along with several hundred workers.

Late in the afternoon of the 31st, the All-Russian Executive Com-mittee of the Soviet debated the government, and its relation to it. Evoking the power and unity the Soviet had shown against Kornilov, its ability to save the city, Kamenev put forward a motion.

In Bolshevik terms, this proposal, like Kamenev himself, was decidedly moderate – but it represented a fundamental leftward break with Soviet practice. A repudiation of compromise. It called for a national government of representatives of the working class and poor peasantry only. The confiscation of manorial land without compensation, and its transfer to the peasants. Workers' supervision of industry. A universal democratic peace. Albeit Kamenev airily announced that he was not 'concerned … with the purely technical aspects of forming a government', his motion was interpreted as a call for all power to the soviets.

At 7:30 p.m. the Executive Committees adjourned without a vote. Shortly after, the Petrograd Soviet itself met in its place. The mass of delegates talked for a long time under the harsh glare of the lamps, as the hands of the clocks reached slowly skyward. They discussed Kamenev's proposal as August ended and September began, and they continued to discuss it as the world turned towards a new day.

There seemed to be a new, shared will for a government of the left. A pathway to socialist unity. To power.

9

September: Compromise and Its Discontents

At 5 a.m. on 1 September, after a long, weary debate on Kamenev's motion and on their relationship to the government in general, the Petrograd Soviet voted.

The SRs suggested the Executive Committees appoint a cabinet responsible to a 'Provisional Revolutionary Government', but still insisted that it include some bourgeois groups – though no Kadets. In these post-Kornilov hours, the Kadets were despised for their complicity in the conspiracies.

The SR proposal was rejected. Instead, the meeting voted in favour of Kamenev's.

Soldiers outnumbered workers in the Soviet two to one, but many were still on duty, so only a relatively small fraction of the membership was present for the tally. And Kamenev's proposal was 'moderate' compared to the 'Leninism' of the Sixth Party Congress. All the same, this was a profoundly charged moment.

In March, Bolshevik opposition to the Provisional Government had lost by a humiliating 19 votes to 400. In April, arguing against participation in the cabinet had got them 100 votes against 2,000. But now, even after the debacle of the July Days, months of crisis in government, economy and war, and the dramatic counterrevolutionary attempt, had utterly changed the lie of the political land. Now, with its members supported by left Mensheviks and Left SRs – who were by that point the majority of the SRs in the capital – the Petrograd Soviet for the first time adopted a Bolshevik resolution: 279 for, 115 against, and 51 abstentions.

The vote seemed to signal an opportunity. Perhaps the Bolsheviks and other socialists could find common ground.

Such collaborative aspirations extended to unlikely quarters. In his Finnish hide, Lenin sat down to write his document 'On Compromises'.

At the Sixth Congress, he had described the soviets as advancing 'like sheep to the abattoir' behind their leaders. He had foreclosed any possibility of working with Mensheviks and SRs, insisted on the absolute necessity of a forceful seizure of power. But 'now, and only now,' he wrote, in another dizzying shift of perspective, 'perhaps during only a few days or a week or two', it appeared there was a chance for a socialist soviet government to be set up 'in a perfectly peaceful way'.

Struck by the mass opposition to the Kadets, and by the soviets' impressive mobilisation against Kornilov, Lenin proposed that his party 'return' to the pre-July demand, 'All Power to the Soviets' – which call had, in any case, returned unbidden. 'We ... may offer a voluntary compromise,' he suggested, with the moderate socialists.

Lenin proposed that the SRs and Mensheviks could form an exclusively socialist government, responsible to local soviets. The Bolsheviks would remain outside that government – 'unless a dicta-torship of the proletariat and poor peasants has been realised' – but they would not agitate for the seizure of power. Instead, assuming the convocation of a Constituent Assembly and freedom of propa-ganda, they would operate as a 'loyal opposition', striving to win influence within the soviets.

'Perhaps this is already impossible?' Lenin wrote of this appeal, in particular, to the rank and file of the Mensheviks and SRs. 'Perhaps. But if there is even one chance in a hundred, the attempt at realising this opportunity is still worthwhile.'

Late that evening of the 1st, the All-Russian Executive Committees resumed session. And as if to rubbish Lenin's tantalising, as-yet-unseen thoughts, leading Mensheviks and SRs lined up to repudiate the passing of Kamenev's motion by the Petrograd Soviet. They argued instead for support for Kerensky – notwithstanding his announcement that day that full power lay with a so-called Council of Five, the Directory on which he had insisted.

Kamenev taunted his opponents. He mocked them remorselessly for standing by while Kerensky 'reduced [them] to nothing'. 'I would hope', he said, 'that you will repel this blow as you repelled Kornilov's attack.' Martov, still adamantly against any Directory, proposed an all-socialist ministry. But the majority would not have it. Instead, in what could have been a bitter parody of wheel-spinning bureaucracy, they proposed yet another conference, a 'Democratic State Conference' this time, for all 'democratic elements'.

Its purpose? Almost unbelievably, it was – to discuss the government.

In the early hours of 2 September, the committee rejected the Bolshevik and Menshevik–Internationalist proposals. Instead they offered their support to Kerensky.

The next day Lenin got word of the decision, just as he prepared to send 'On Compromises'. No wonder he added to the manuscript a quick and melancholy postscript.

'I say to myself: perhaps it is already too late to offer a compromise. Perhaps the few days in which a peaceful development was still possible have passed too ... All that remains is to send these notes to the editor with the request to have them entitled: "Belated Thoughts". Perhaps even belated thoughts are sometimes not without interest.'

Kerensky's only sop to the Soviet was the exclusion from his dictatorial Directory of any Kadets. Alexeev took over as chief of staff, and Kornilov was transferred with thirty other conspirators to the

Bykhov Monastery, where sympathetic jailers let his bodyguards stay with him, and families visited twice daily.

Striving to smother radical agitation, Kerensky directed military commanders, commissars and army organisations to end political activity among the troops. The order had precisely no effect. Kerensky's negotiations with Kornilov were by then common knowledge, and they dried up whatever dregs of his authority remained. Only the moderate socialists still looked to him. For the right, he had betrayed Russia's best hope; for the left, especially the soldiers, Kerensky had been negotiating with Kornilov a return to the hated regime of officers' power.

Kerensky remained head of the government not through strength but despite weakness, propped up by widespread tensions elsewhere. If this was still, as Lenin described it, a balancing act, it was a negative one – a Bonapartism of the despised.

And yet, doggedly, in line with a certain stageism underlying their politics and their insistence on coalition, the moderate socialists still determined that power should remain Kerensky's. Alliance with liberalism was non-negotiable. Even when opposing Kerensky's concrete orders, they maintained that those orders were his to give.

On 4 September Kerensky demanded the dissolution of all revolutionary committees that had arisen during the crisis, including the Committee for Struggle Against the Counterrevolution. That committee immediately met – in itself an act of civil disobedience – and bullishly expressed confidence that, given the continuing counter-revolutionary threat, such bodies would continue to operate.

Recalcitrance from the grassroots like this, as well as the growing and dramatic splits between left and right wings of the Mensheviks and SRs, kept Lenin hopeful for possibilities for compromise, his recent postscript notwithstanding. Between 6 and 9 September, in 'The Tasks of the Revolution', 'The Russian Revolution and Civil War' and 'One of the Fundamental Questions of the Revolution', he maintained that the soviets could take power peacefully. He even granted to his political opponents a degree of respect for their recent endeavours, declaring that an alliance of Bolsheviks, Mensheviks and SRs in a soviet regime would make civil war impossible.

These articles provoked consternation among his party comrades, particularly those on the Moscow Regional Bureau and Petersburg Committee. One might have thought them inured to surprise at Lenin's switches, but here they were, astonished by this turn from the man they had recently defended from the left against Bolshevik moderates. Now, Lenin's 'On Compromises' was rejected for publication by *Rabochy put'* as too conciliatory.

And there were good reasons to be sceptical that his new aspiration for cooperation would bear fruit, even beside the Soviet All-Russian Committees' support for Kerensky. On 3 September, the make-up of the newly planned Democratic Conference was announced, and it boded ill for the left. Of the 1,198 delegates, the proportion of seats for urban workers and soldiers was low compared to those for more conservative rural soviets, *zemstvos* and cooperatives.

Even so, the Bolsheviks sent out caucusing instructions to its delegates. Lenin's approach seemed now, after all, compatible with that of the party right, those like Kamenev who thought the country unripe for socialist revolution, as well as with those more radical, for whom soviet power could be a transitional form away from capitalism. And all the while, up from the grassroots, there still came great pressure and hope for cross-party socialist unity. It seemed worth a shot to try for it.

The country was polarising not only between right and left, but between the politicised and the disengaged. Hence, perhaps counterintuitively, as social tensions increased, the numbers voting in elections for the countless local bodies were declining. In Moscow in June, for example, 640,000 ballots were cast in municipal elections: now, three months later, there were only 380,000. And those who did vote gravitated to harder positions: the Kadet share grew from 17.2 to 31.5 per cent; the Bolsheviks soared from 11.7 to 49.5 per cent.

And the moderates plummeted. The Mensheviks went from 12.2 to 4.2 per cent, and SRs from 58.9 to 14.7 per cent.

The Left SRs gained control of the party's organisations and committees in Revel, Pskov, Helsingfors, Samara and Tashkent, among others, including Petrograd itself. They demanded a national Congress of Soviets and an exclusively socialist government. The Russian SR leadership seemed paralysed in the face of its surging left flank, which it had tried to high-handedly ignore. It now 'expelled' the Petrograd organisation, among others, for its deviation – a meaningless non-sanction, leaving all resources in place with the radicals. The SR CC staked everything on the Constituent Assembly elections, scheduled (then) for November.

In Baku, where Bolshevik orators had been shouted down at street meetings a few weeks before, the party's motions were now sweeping factory committees and gatherings. 'The Bolshevisation noticeable in all of Russia has appeared in the widest dimensions in our oil empire,' wrote the local stalwart Shaumian of his region. 'And long before the *Kornilovshchina* [Kornilov Affair]. The former masters of the situation, the Mensheviks, are not able to show themselves in the workers' districts. Along with the Bolsheviks the SR-Internationalists [the left] have begun to get stronger ... and have formed a bloc with the Bolsheviks.'

Across the empire, the Mensheviks were splintering. Some went to the right, as in Baku; at the other extreme, the Mensheviks in Tiflis, Georgia, took a hard-left position for a united socialist government that would include the Bolsheviks.

On the 5th, it was the turn of the Moscow Soviet to vote in favour of Kamenev's 31 August resolution. A soviet congress in Krasnoyarsk, Siberia, gained a Bolshevik majority. On the 6th, as Lenin's 'On Compromises' was published, power in Ekaterinburg in the Urals passed into the hands of the soviets, and workers refused to recognise the Provisional Government. In protest at Kerensky's Directory, nineteen Baltic Fleet committees recommended all ships fly red flags.

And whether or not dissent took socialist forms, the national aspirations of Russia's minorities were amplifying. In Tashkent, Uzbekistan, tensions between Russian inhabitants and Muslim Uzbeks flared, until on 10 September local soldiers formed a revolutionary committee, expelling government representatives and taking control of the city. From the 8th to the 15th, the Ukrainian Rada provocatively convened a Congress of the Nationalities, bringing together Ukrainians, Jews, Poles, Lithuanians, Tatars, Turks, Bessarabian Romanians, Latvians, Georgians, Estonians, Kazakhs, Cossacks and representatives of various radical parties. The Congress, in an escalation from the language of 'cultural autonomy', agreed that Russia must be 'a federative-democratic republic', each component part to decide how it would link to others. Except in the case of Poland, and to a lesser extent Finland, the orientation (let alone formal demand) was not for full independence. But dynamics towards independence in some form were at least implicit – and, later, would come very much to the fore.

The presidium of the Petrograd Soviet, composed of right Mensheviks and SRs, dismissed Kamenev's victory of 1 September as just a side effect of how depleted the Soviet had been that night. On 9 September, they threatened to resign if the decision were not overturned.

The Bolsheviks were fearful they would not win the motion this time around. In an attempt to appeal to waverers and gain influence, they suggested a reform of the presidium along fair, proportional lines, to include previously unrepresented groups – including the Bolsheviks. 'If coalition with the Kadets was acceptable,' they argued in the chamber, 'surely they can engage in coalition politics with the Bolsheviks in this organ.'

To this manoeuvre, Trotsky added a masterstroke.

Long ago, in the very earliest days of the Petrograd Soviet, he recalled, Kerensky himself, of course, had been on the presidium. So, asked Trotsky, did that presidium still consider Kerensky, he of the dictatorial Directory, a member?

The question put the moderates in an invidious position. Kerensky was now reviled as a counterrevolutionary – but their political commitment to collaboration forbade the moderate Mensheviks and SRs to repudiate him.

The presidium allowed that he was, indeed, one of them.

Not since Banquo had so unwelcome a ghost been at the table. The insult of Kerensky's membership tipped the balance for the wider membership. The Petrograd Soviet sided, 519 to 414, with 67 abstentions, with the Bolsheviks and against their presidium, its toxic absent member included. The compromised presidium resigned en masse, in protest.

This is not to say that the Bolsheviks now commanded overwhelming support in this venue. They could still not be sure of passing all their motions. Nevertheless, this politicised procedural manoeuvre was a triumph. Lenin would later condemn it as excessively conciliatory: a harsh, unconvincing reproach, given its success and effects.

In September, the upward trajectory of the peasant war did not slow. In growing numbers, villagers sacked more estates, more violently, often with fire, often side by side with soldiers and deserters. In Penza, Saratov, Kazan, and especially Tambov, estates burned. Village soviets arose. Wrecking and theft blossomed into full-blown jacqueries.

Sometimes with these came notorious murders, like that of the landowner Prince Viazemskii the previous month, a killing that shocked liberal opinion because of the man's charitable works. The situation grew bad enough for the Council of the Tambov Union of Private Landowners to issue a plea for help, signing it as 'The Union of Unfortunate Landowners'.

In the first half of September, an official in Kozlovsk County put together a list of attacks on local estates. He documented fifty-four incidents, including 'Condition of portions of the estate'. A spreadsheet of rural fury and destruction. 'Wrecked'. 'Wrecked and partly burned'. 'Wrecked and burned'. 'Wrecked'.

In the cities, a strike wave brought out not only skilled but white-collar and unskilled workers, hospital workers, clerks. Repeatedly the Red Guards now confronted government militias, and not always bloodlessly. Bosses locked out workers; starving proletarian communities raged from house to house in bands, hunting for both food speculators and food.

'Anarchy essentially ruled over Petrograd,' said K. I. Globachev. A former chief of the Okhrana, he had himself spent the days between February and August in the dark castle of Kresty jail, in punishment for that role. His observations, though, were fair. 'Criminals multiplied to an unimaginable extent. Every day robberies and murders were committed not only at night, but also in broad daylight.'

The prisons could not hold the prisoners: due to the political upheavals, or the inadequacy of the guards, countless inmates simply walked out of jail to freedom. Globachev himself, fearful of how a secret policeman of the old regime would fare on the post-February streets, remained by choice behind Kresty's walls.

In Ostrogozhsk, a town in Voronezh, looters targeted an alcohol store over three violent days that culminated in a vast conflagration. When troops finally suppressed this apocalyptic nihilo-drunkenness, fifty-seven people were dead, twenty-six of them burned alive.

The paper of the Right SRs, *Volia naroda*, editorialised about the growing anarchy with a terse, jittery, bullet-pointed list of 'virtually, a period of civil war'.

> A mutiny in Orel ...
>
> In Rostov the town hall is dynamited.
>
> In Tambov Governorate there are agrarian pogroms ...
>
> Gangs of robbers on the roads in Pskov ...
>
> Along the Volga, near Kamyshin, soldiers loot trains.

How much worse, the paper wondered, could things get? It blamed Bolshevism.

Soviets across Russia were shifting to the left. In Astrakhan, a meeting of soviets and other socialists voted 276 to 175 against Menshevik/SR appeals for unity – *including* with groups that had been involved with Kornilov. Delegates instead backed the Bolshevik call to transfer power to workers and poor peasants.

In mid-September, military intelligence reported 'open hostility and animosity ... on the part of the soldiers; the most insignificant event may provoke unrest. Soldiers say ... all the officers are followers of General Kornilov ... [and] should be destroyed'. The war minister reported to the SRs 'an increase of attacks on officers by soldiers, shootings, and throwing of grenades through the windows of officers' meetings'. He explained the soldiers' fury thus: 'On the heels of declaring Kornilov a rebel, the army received instructions from the government to continue to execute his operative orders. Nobody wanted to believe that an order in such contradiction to the preceding instruction could be true.'

It was. Such was Kerensky's crumbling government.

The festival feeling of March and April was replaced by the sense of a closing, an ending, and not in peace but in catastrophe, the mud and fire of war.

The renovated language of the early days seemed drowned out by bestial gibbering. 'Where are they now, our deeds and our sacrifices?' begged the writer Alexey Remizov of this apocalyptic world. He could find no answers. Only visions. 'Smell of smoke and the howling of apes.'

On 14 September, the Democratic Conference opened in Petrograd's famous Alexandrinsky Theatre. The hall was vivid with red banners, as if to express a unity of left purpose that was very much lacking. On the stage beyond the presidium's table was the set of a play: behind the speakers were artificial trees, and doors to nowhere.

The hopes of radicals for the conference, never high, sank as attendees declared their affiliations. Some 532 SRs were present, only seventy-one of the party's militant left wing; 530 Mensheviks, fifty-six Internationalist; fifty-five Popular Socialists; seventeen unaffiliated; and 134 Bolsheviks. The conference was heavily skewed in the moderates' favour. Nonetheless, the Bolsheviks were committed to trying to use the gathering to push for compromise, socialist government.

In their party caucus, Trotsky aspired to the transfer of power to the soviets; whereas Kamenev, unconvinced of the readiness of Russia for transformation and hoping to gain a wider base for workers' rule, argued instead for the transfer of state power, 'not to the Soviet', but to a socialist coalition. The differences between these two positions bespoke distinct conceptions of history. But for the party delegates in that moment they were minor strategic nuances. Either way, the point was that Bolsheviks were fully engaged with the conference, poised to put the case for cooperation with the moderate left parties, for coalition and the peaceful development of the revolution – just as Lenin himself had argued since the start of the month.

So it was like a thunderbolt when, on the conference's second day, the Bolshevik leadership received two new letters from their leader-in-hiding.

Now, hard as a stone, he upended all his recent conciliatory suggestions.

'The Bolsheviks, having obtained a majority in the soviets of workers' and soldiers' deputies in both capitals,' began the first communication, 'can and *must* take state power into their own hands.' Lenin pilloried the Conference as '*the compromising upper strata of the petty bourgeoisie*'. He demanded Bolsheviks declare the necessity of 'immediate transfer of all power to *revolutionary democrats, headed by the revolutionary proletariat*', and then walk out.

Lenin's comrades were utterly aghast.

Paradoxically, it was the continuation of the leftward shift of Russia itself, the trend that had raised in Lenin hopes of cooperation, that now changed his mind. Because with that tendency had come those triumphs for Bolsheviks in the two main cities' soviets, and Lenin grew fretful about what would happen if the party did *not* act on its own. He feared revolutionary energies might dissipate, or the country slide on into anarchy – or that brutal counterrevolution might arise.

Unrest was shaking the German army and society. Lenin felt sure the whole of Europe was growing ripe for revolution, towards which a full-scale Russian revolution would be a powerful shove. And he was very anxious – for good reason, and in this he was not alone – lest the government surrender Petrograd, the red capital, to the Germans. If they did so, Bolshevik chances, he said, would be 'a hundred times less favourable'.

The party had been right, he repeated, not to move in July, without the masses behind it. But now it had them.

Here again was one of those switchbacks that so discombobulated his comrades. It was not mere caprice, however, but the results of minute attention to shifts in politics, and exaggerated responses to these. Now, he insisted, with the masses behind it, the party must move.

Late on 15 September, a group of Bolshevik grandees left the Alexandrinsky and made for their HQ. There, in utmost secrecy, they discussed Lenin's terrifying letters.

There was not a scintilla of support for his demands. He was utterly isolated. And, further, it was imperative to his comrades that his voice be muted, his message not get to Petrograd workers, or Petrograd or Moscow Bolshevik committees. Not because they would think Lenin wrong: because they might think him right. If that happened, Lomov would later explain, 'many would doubt the correctness of the position adopted by the whole CC'.

The leadership delegated members to the MO and Petersburg Committee to make sure no calls for action reached workplaces or barracks. The CC readied themselves for conference business, as previously agreed.

Lenin's new position was, literally, unspeakable. The CC voted to burn all but a single copy of each letter. As if they were pages from some dreadful grimoire. As if they would have liked to bury the ashes and sow the ground with salt.

Lenin's scepticism about the potential of the starkly divided conference was vindicated. Throughout it, most Mensheviks and SRs remained as adamantly committed as ever to coalition with the bourgeoisie – which meant giving the despised and tottering Kerensky his head.

On the 16th, blithely dissimulating, the Bolshevik leadership published Lenin's words – of two weeks before. They put out his amelioratory essay 'The Russian Revolution and Civil War'.

Its author's fury can be imagined: as far as he was concerned, that piece was now a fossil. On the 18th, the party's formal conference statement on the government modelled itself on another of their leader's antediluvian relics, 'On Compromises'. Yes, the Bolsheviks did mobilise a demonstration outside the theatre, demanding a socialist government, but this rather dutiful intervention was far from the militant, armed, insurrectionary 'surrounding' of Alexandrinsky for which Lenin had just called.

Unable to tolerate what was going on, in agonies at his distance from the action, Lenin disobeyed a direct CC instruction. He decided to set out for the Finnish city of Vyborg (sharing its name with the district of the Russian capital), eighty miles from Petrograd. From there he would plot his way back into the heart of things.

He needed a disguise. Kustaa Rovio escorted him to a Helsingfors wigmaker, who threatened to scupper the pressing plan by insisting it would take a fortnight to personalise something suitable. The shopkeeper was flabbergasted to see Lenin impatiently fingering a ready-made grey hairpiece. Most buyers were attempting to rejuvenate themselves: this would have the opposite effect. But Lenin rebuffed all the man's attempts to dissuade him. For a long time after that day, the wigmaker would tell the story of the youngish client who had wanted to look old.

In Vyborg, Lenin stayed a few weeks at 15 Alexanderinkatu, in the brick-making area of the city. He spent his days reading newspapers and writing, lodged in the shared dwelling of the socialist Latukka and Koikonen families. A solicitous and undemanding guest, the scourge of the established order quickly made himself popular. When at last – after more than one ferocious argument with the CC's emissary, Shotman – he insisted on returning to Petrograd, the Latukkas and Koikonens were sad to see him go.

On the 19th, after four days of arguments about the future government and a gruelling five-hour roll call, the Democratic Conference at last voted on the principle of coalition with the bourgeoisie.

It was no surprise that the overrepresented moderates had it: the vote went 766 to 688 for coalition, with 38 abstentions. However, straight after this passed, delegates had to discuss two competing amendments.

The first insisted that those Kadets and others complicit in the Kornilov Affair be excluded from coalition; the second that the *entirety* of the Kadet party, as counterrevolutionaries, be excluded *tout court*.

The Bolsheviks, along with Martov, sensed an opportunity. They spoke for *both* amendments, no matter that they were not complementary.

There was tense, confused debate. But those who were deemed to have collaborated with Kornilov had come to be so roundly despised that when the votes came, both amendments passed. This meant the altered proposal had to be voted on anew. As doubly amended, it declared in favour of coalition with the bourgeoisie, but now on the basis that this should be without the participation of Kornilovites, including implicated Kadets; *and*, incoherently, that it should be without any Kadets at all.

The latter condition was unacceptable to the right moderates, who could not envisage any coalition without Kadets, and they therefore voted against. As, of course, did the left, because (though many had voted for at least one, if not both) these amendments were essentially irrelevant to them: they remained implacably opposed to any such coalition at all with the representatives of property. This absurd, temporary alliance of right and left in the conference ensured that the motion was overwhelmingly rejected.

No conclusion had been reached. Nothing was settled.

The man with whom the moderates urged coalition, Kerensky, remained pitifully weak, and growing weaker. He struggled, lashed out to shore up his authority. On 18 September he pronounced the dissolution of the Central Committee of the Baltic Fleet. The sailors responded simply that his order was 'considered inoperative'.

The Democratic Conference, too, strained for relevance. After an exhausting all-day presidium session to deal with the unhelpful results of the vote on the 19th, a new presidium vote on coalition produced a split of fifty in favour and sixty against.

Almost unbelievably, with Beckettian comedy, faithful to some autotelic cycle of committee-generative committees, Tsereteli proposed establishing yet another body. This one, he said, would decide the make-up of a future cabinet, based on the Soviet's political programme agreed on 14 August. The Bolsheviks (alone) had opposed this programme – but even their leadership, even now, still straining for the collaboration that Lenin had declared impossible, agreed to the formation of this 'Democratic Council', or Preparliament.

Which the presidium promptly voted must include propertied elements.

The previous day, Conference had approved coalition, but rejected coalition with Kadets. Now they rejected coalition, while mooting political cooperation with the bourgeoisie, including Kadets. The proceedings were outdoing their own absurdity.

The mechanisms, members and powers of the Preparliament

were complicated and provisional, but that door did remain open to working with the right. A self-selecting team of moderates – since the left firmly opposed any such involvement of the bourgeoisie – were granted authority to meet with the government to decide a way forward.

And yet, despite all this, the Bolshevik CC decided on the 21st not to walk out of the Democratic Conference. They did vote among themselves against participating in the Preparliament, but so narrowly – by nine votes to eight – that they felt they must take the debate further, and convened an emergency meeting with delegates to discuss the issue.

Trotsky spoke for boycott, Rykov against. When after a stormy caucus the vote came, it was seventy-five to fifty in favour of taking part in the Preparliament.

Small wonder many Bolsheviks, particularly of the left, were sceptical of this decision. The very next day, as if to goad them, the unelected Preparliament commenced negotiations with Kerensky and his cabinet – and with representatives of the Kadets.

But the officials of the bourgeoisie with whom it negotiated would not accept the Soviet's moderate 14 August programme. Nor would they agree to the Preparliament having any formal powers, insisting it should be merely consultative. In the face of this intransigence, Trotsky put to the newly inaugurated Preparliament a repudiation of their negotiations with the cabinet. But on the 23rd, this was easily defeated, and the negotiations themselves, albeit narrowly, were endorsed.

It was increasingly clear to Bolsheviks that other arenas of struggle might prove more congenial. They successfully demanded that the Soviet Central Executive Committee convene a nationwide Congress of Soviets in Petrograd, the next month. With what was surely relief, the party subordinated preparliamentary work to the tasks of building that October Congress, and of mobilising for the transfer of power to the soviets.

Meanwhile, with the inevitability of sunrise, Tsereteli's team backed down on their own diluted platform, to make it more palatable to the despised Kadets on whom they would not turn their backs. One hundred and fifty representatives of property would, they agreed, be added to the 367 'democratic' Preparliament delegates – who would, they also miserably allowed, have no power over the government.

And as this dilution, this self-abasement, continued, that bony hand of hunger was tightening its grip.

The American writer Louise Bryant had recently arrived in the capital. Walking in the cold of the early morning, she was horrified to see the food queues. Every day before dawn, people shivering in wretched clothes in the shadowy streets of Red Petrograd. They lined up for hours, long before the sun rose, as the wind scoured the boulevards. For milk, for tobacco, for food.

His comrades' attempts to conceal Lenin's intransigence were becoming increasingly blatant. From the city of Vyborg he sent rebuke after scathing rebuke, all of which were promptly bowdlerised.

As the Democratic Conference ended he dispatched to *Rabochy put'* an essay entitled 'Heroes of Fraud and the Mistakes of the Bolsheviks', insisting that the Bolsheviks should have walked out, subjecting his party, and Zinoviev in particular, to remorseless criticism. The piece appeared on the 24th, as Preparliament negotiated – but now it was called 'Heroes of Fraud', and all attacks on the Bolsheviks had been excised.

Lenin's fury grew awesome.

The next day, sulkily enabled by the Preparliament, Kerensky named his third coalition cabinet. Technically, again, it comprised a majority of socialists, but these moderate leftists held no key posts. And flatly breaking the Democratic Conference's resolution, the Preparliament signed off on a cabinet that included the hated Tereshchenko, as well as four Kadets.

That was the day the Petrograd Soviet's new, more representative presidium convened, after the walkout of its predecessors on the 9th. It was made up of one Menshevik, two SRs, and, in a historic shift that gave the party an absolute majority, four Bolsheviks.

One of the four was greeted with loud cheers and applause. Twelve years after he held a commanding role in the Soviet's earlier, 1905 iteration, Leon Trotsky took his seat.

Trotsky immediately tabled a resolution stating that Petrograd's workers and soldiers would not support the new, weak, reviled government. That instead, the solution lay with the forthcoming All-Russian Congress of Soviets.

Overwhelmingly, his motion passed.

And still Lenin's comrades censored his writing. Between 22 and 24 September, his 'From a Publicist's Diary' derided the party's participation in the Preparliament. The *Rabochy put'* board suppressed it – Trotsky among them, despite the piece praising him for his pro-boycott stance. On the 26th, with breathtaking cheek, they published instead part of 'The Tasks of the Revolution' – another pro-compromise throwback from that bygone epoch of three weeks previous.

His rage at last drove Lenin to conspiracy.

On the 27th, he wrote to Ivar Smilga, the ultra-left Bolshevik chair of the Regional Executive Committee of the Army, Fleet and Workers in Finland. Lenin did not so much flout as shatter the vaunted 'discipline' of a revolutionary party. What he attempted was no less than to create an alternative pro-insurrectionary axis within his organisation – an axis in which Finland was key.

'It seems to me that we can have completely at our disposal only the troops in Finland and the Baltic Fleet, and only they can play a serious military role,' he wrote to Smilga. 'Give all your attention to the military preparation of the troops in Finland plus the fleet for the impending overthrow of Kerensky. Create a secret committee of absolutely trustworthy military men.'

These preparations took place amid increasing anxiety about the potential forthcoming fall of Petrograd – especially when, on 28 September, the Germans landed on the Estonian island of Saaremaa, near Riga. This was the start of Operation Albion, to gain control of the West Estonian archipelago, outflank Russian defences and leave Petrograd open for the taking.

Across Russia, fear was growing that the right, and the government, would simply surrender the city, this thorn in their side. That they would allow Red Petrograd to fall.

On 29 September, Lenin sent the CC 'The Crisis Is Ripe'. It was a declaration of political war. This time, to circumvent the usual gagging treatment, he also circulated the document to the Petrograd and Moscow committees.

In the piece, Lenin repeated his strong conviction that Europe-wide revolution was at hand. He charged that unless the Bolsheviks seized power immediately, they would be 'miserable traitors to the proletarian cause'. As far as he was concerned, waiting for the planned Second Soviet Congress was not just a waste of time, but a real risk to the revolution. 'It is possible to take power now,' he insisted, 'whereas on 20–29 October you will not be given the chance.'

Then came the bombshell.

In view of the fact that the CC has even left unanswered the persistent demands I have been making for such a policy ever since the beginning of the Democratic Conference, in view of the fact that the central organ is *deleting* from my articles all references to such glaring errors on the part of the Bolsheviks ... I am compelled to regard this as a subtle hint that I should keep my mouth shut, and as a proposal for me to retire.

I am compelled to *tender my resignation from the Central Committee*, which I hereby do, reserving for myself freedom to campaign among the *rank and file* of the party and at the Party Congress.

Even as this message arrived, Zinoviev was busy putting the leadership's case in *Rabochy put'* – a strategy directly at odds with Lenin's.

'Start getting ready for the Congress of Soviets,' Zinoviev wrote. 'Don't become involved in any kind of separate direct action!'

Zinoviev: 'Let's concentrate all our energies on preparations for the Congress of Soviets.'

Lenin: 'It is my profound conviction that if we "wait" for the Congress of Soviets, and let the present moment pass, it will *ruin* the revolution.'

10

Red October

In October, in the forests, leaves were coming down in drifts, clogging the train tracks. The trees shook from the thud of guns. Kerensky remained Russia's only hope: of this he was still certain. He gathered the rags of his messianism about him, believing himself chosen by something or other for something or other.

By the constant threat of reshuffles, he kept his last, etiolated Provisional Government in line. Kerensky was corroded by malicious gossip. The cult of him, a memory to embarrass its erstwhile devotees. He was Jewish, bigots whispered. He was not a real man, homophobes insinuated, calling him by feminine forms. And with the demise of the last shreds of faith in him, came social and military panic.

On the first day of the month, amid the spiralling crime in Petrograd came a fresh horror. A man and his three young children were found savagely murdered in their Lesnoi apartment. Another atrocity among so many. But these victims' home was in the very same building as the headquarters of the local branch of the city militia, the security patrols organised by the city duma.

How could anyone feel safe? Was it not bad enough that parts of the city were now controlled by criminals, no-go zones for the authorities? By the Olympia amusement park on Zabalkanskii Prospect; Golodai, near Vasilievsky Island; Volkovo in the Narva district. Was it not enough that the city had ceded territory to outlaws and bandits, without them now mocking the very idea of retribution? How could anyone believe that the authorities had authority when this monstrosity could occur right above the militia's heads?

Disgusted crowds gathered outside the headquarters. They threw stones. They broke down the door, and smashed the place apart.

As power evaporated, some convulsions took predictable, ugly forms. On 2 October in Smolensk, the town of Roslavl received, as the *Smolensk Bulletin* put it, 'the following cup of poison to drink: a pogrom'. A mob of Black Hundreds chanting 'Beat the Yids!' attacked and murdered several people they accused of 'speculation'– a charge provoked by finding galoshes in a Jewish-owned store the clerks of which had claimed they had none. The rampage continued throughout the night and the next day. The newspapers and authorities tried to link the Bolsheviks to the violence. This was a growing theme in the liberal press, despite its patent political absurdity, and despite the recorded efforts of Bolshevik soldiers in the town to stop the carnage.

On 3 October, the Russian General Staff evacuated Revel, the last bastion between the front and the capital. The next day, accordingly, the government sought advice on the evacuation of the executive and key industries – but not of the Soviet – to Moscow. News of the discussions leaked out. There was a storm: the bourgeoisie were indeed planning to abandon the city built for them two centuries before. The city of bones. The Ispolkom forbade any such move without its approval, and the unstable government shelved the idea.

In this ambience of perfidy, weakness and violence, Lenin took his campaign for insurrection to the wider party.

There is no record of the CC's reaction to Lenin's resignation threat. Perhaps it provoked pleading negotiations. Whatever the particulars, it was not raised again, and he did not step down.

On 1 October, he sent another letter, this time to the Central, Moscow and Petersburg committees, and to Bolsheviks in the

Petrograd and Moscow soviets. Citing peasant and labour unrest, mutinies in the German navy, and the growing Bolshevik influence after local elections in Moscow, he once more emphasised that delaying insurgent action until the Second Congress of Soviets was 'positively criminal'. The Bolsheviks must 'take power at once', and appeal 'to Workers, Peasants and Soldiers' for 'All Power to the Soviets'. But on this question of timing, he remained isolated: that same day, a meeting of Bolsheviks from towns outlying Petrograd opposed any action prior to the Congress.

The CC could not hide his communications forever. On the 3rd, a letter at last reached the militant Moscow Regional Bureau, in which Lenin incited them to pressure the CC to prepare for insurrection. Several of his essays found their way to the Petersburg Committee. The members were divided as to Lenin's demands, but united in outrage at the CC's obfuscations. On the 5th, the Petersburg Committee met to discuss their reactions to what they had read.

The debate was long and it was rancorous. Latsis loudly questioned the revolutionary credentials of those with the temerity to go against Lenin. In the end a proposal to decide on insurrectionary preparations was shelved. However, the Executive Commission delegated three members – including Latsis – to evaluate Bolshevik military strength and prepare district committees for possible action. They did not inform the CC.

As awareness of Lenin's positions spread through the party, despite the CC's efforts to corral it, social upheaval was provoking a certain coterminous leftward shift on the CC itself. While the Petersburg Committee met in dissident conclave, at Smolny the CC at last voted to boycott the toothless Preparliament when it reconvened on the 7th. The decision was unanimous but for the ever-cautious Kamenev, who immediately called for patience from the Bolshevik Preparliamentarians, until a serious dispute might justify a walkout. He narrowly lost the argument to Trotsky's call for immediate action.

The next day, Petrograd commander General Polkovnikov

instructed city troops to prepare for transfer to the front. He had known this would unleash fury, and it did.

On the evening of the 7th, in the Mariinsky Palace, its remaining imperial crests decorously obscured with red draperies, before the eyes of the press and diplomatic corps, the Preparliament reopened. Kerensky gave another histrionic address, this one themed on law and order. There followed remarks from the Grandmother of the Revolution, Breshko-Breshkovskaya; then from Nikolai Avksentiev, the chair; and then at last Trotsky intervened. He stood to make an emergency announcement.

Blisteringly, he denounced the government and the Preparliament as tools of counterrevolution. The audience erupted. Trotsky raised his voice over their clamour. 'Petrograd is in danger!' he shouted. 'All power to the soviets! All land to the people!' To jeers and catcalls, the fifty-three Bolshevik delegates rose together and left the hall.

Their act was a sensation. An epidemic of rumours immediately followed: the Bolsheviks, people said, were planning an uprising.

It was at some uncertain moment during these accelerating days, early in October, that Lenin slipped back into Petrograd.

Krupskaya escorted him to Lesnoi. There he stayed again with his former landlady Margarita Fofanova. From her house he preached his gospel of urgency to an urgent city.

On 9 October, mass anger at the plan to relocate the troops spilled into the Soviet. In the Executive Committee, the Menshevik Mark Broido put forward a compromise: the soldiers would prepare for transfer, but a committee should also be created to draw up plans for the defence of Petrograd that would win popular confidence. This, he thought, could reduce the anxieties about government treachery and address the fears for the capital, while smoothing a path of collaboration between government and Soviet.

His proposal blindsided the Bolsheviks.

Trotsky, recovering, quickly put forward a counterproposal,

repudiating Kerensky and his government, accusing the bourgeoisie of preparing to surrender Petrograd, demanding immediate peace and soviet power, *and* summoning the garrison to prepare for battle. What he called for was a new iteration of the Committee for Struggle Against the Counterrevolution, for the defence of Red Petrograd from internal as much as from external enemies, 'attacks being openly prepared by military and civil Kornilovites', as he put it. This was rather different from defencism on behalf of Mother Russia.

Even now, with the Bolshevik majority on the Executive Committee, it was not Trotsky's but Broido's resolution that – narrowly – passed: anxiety about the war effort still precluded sanctioning the creation of a parallel military structure. But that evening, the two motions were put to a packed, uproarious session of the Soviet plenum. Now, backed by a huge majority of factory and barracks representatives, Trotsky's torquing of Broido's suggestion prevailed. Thus was born the Military Revolutionary Committee – Milrevcom, or the MRC.

Trotsky would later characterise this vote in favour of the MRC as a 'dry', a 'silent' revolution, indispensable to the full revolution to come.

The threat of Bolshevik insurrection was now openly discussed on all sides. Indeed, certain of their enemies invited it. 'I would be prepared to offer prayers to produce this uprising,' said Kerensky. 'They will be utterly crushed.' By contrast, many of the Bolsheviks themselves were more hesitant. The day after the Soviet meeting, a citywide party conference expressed clear reservations about an uprising before the Congress of Soviets.

For its part, the CC had no formal position on such an action. Yet.

As Sukhanov left his home for the Soviet on the morning of the 10th, his wife Galina Flakserman eyed nasty skies and made him promise not to try to return that night, but to stay at his office, as was his custom when the weather was so bad. That evening, as he settled down accordingly to sleep at Smolny, across the city figure after bundled-up figure slipped out of the grey drizzle and into his flat.

'Oh, the novel jokes of the merry muse of History!' wrote Sukhanov later, bitterly. Unlike her diarist husband, who was previously an independent and had recently joined the Menshevik left, Galina Flakserman was a long-time Bolshevik activist, on the staff of *Izvestia*. Unbeknownst to him, she had quietly informed her comrades that comings and goings at her roomy, many-entranced apartment would be unlikely to draw attention. Thus, with her husband out of the way, the Bolshevik CC came visiting.

At least twelve of the twenty-one-strong committee were there, including Kollontai, Trotsky, Uritsky, Stalin, Varvara Iakovleva, Kamenev and Zinoviev. They gathered in the dining room, quickly dealing with routine business. There entered a clean-shaven, bespectacled, grey-haired man, 'every bit like a Lutheran minister', Alexandra Kollontai remembered.

The CC stared at the newcomer. Absent-mindedly, he doffed his wig like a hat, to reveal a familiar bald pate. Lenin had arrived. The serious debates could begin.

Lenin held forth. He was impassioned. As the hours wore on he drove home his now-familiar points. The time had come, he insisted again, for insurrection. The party's 'indifference toward the question of an uprising' was a dereliction.

It was not a monologue. Everyone took their turn to speak.

Late at night, a knock at the door sent hearts lurching, plunging them all into fear. But it was only Flakserman's brother, Yuri. Another Bolshevik, privy to the meeting, he had come to help with the samovar. He busied himself with the huge communal kettle, making tea.

Kamenev and Zinoviev returned to that historic debate, assiduously explaining why they thought Lenin was wrong. They evoked the weight of the petty bourgeoisie, who were not – not yet, perhaps – on their side. They suggested that Lenin overestimated the Bolsheviks' power in Petrograd, let alone elsewhere. They were adamant that he was incorrect about the imminence of international revolution. They argued for 'a defensive posture', for patience. 'Through the army we have a revolver pointed at the temple of the bourgeoisie,' they said. Better to ensure the convening of a Constituent Assembly, and to continue to consolidate their strength meanwhile.

Their comrades called the consistently circumspect pair the 'Heavenly Twins', sometimes affectionately, sometimes in exasperation. They were not alone in the party hierarchy in their conservatism. But that night, those of similar bent – Nogin, Rykov and others – were absent.

Which is not to say that Lenin's position was accepted in all particulars by his other comrades. Trotsky, for one, felt less pressed by time than did Lenin, set greater store by the soviets, saw the forthcoming Congress as a potential legitimator of any action. But the key question of the night was this: were, or were not, the Bolsheviks mobilising for insurrection as soon as possible?

On paper torn from a child's notebook, Lenin scribbled a resolution.

The CC acknowledges the international situation as it affects the Russian revolution … as well as the military situation … and the fact that the proletarian party has gained majorities in the soviets – all this, coupled with the peasant insurrection and the swing of popular confidence to our party, and finally, the obvious preparations for a second *Kornilovshchina* … makes armed insurrection the order of the day … Recognising that an armed uprising is inevitable and the time fully ripe, the CC instructs all party organisations to be guided accordingly and to consider and decide all practical questions from this viewpoint.

At last, after prolonged and impassioned back-and-forth, they voted. By ten to two – Zinoviev and Kamenev, of course – the resolution passed. It was hazy in its details, but a Rubicon had been crossed. Insurrection was now the 'order of the day'.

The tension eased. Yuri Flakserman brought cheese, sausage and bread, and the famished revolutionaries fell to. Good-naturedly they teased the Heavenly Twins: hesitating to overthrow the bourgeoisie was so very Kamenev.

The time frame for the event was hazy, too. Lenin wanted insurrection the next day: Kalinin, on the other hand, for example, while praising 'one of the best resolutions the CC has ever passed', thought – in what could surely have been the position of Zinoviev and Kamenev – that 'perhaps in a year' it might be time.

On the 11th, the militant Northern Region Congress of Soviets gathered in the capital: fifty-one Bolsheviks, twenty-four Left SRs, four Maximalists (a revolutionary SR offshoot), one Menshevik–Internationalist, and ten SRs. All the delegates present, including those SRs, supported a socialist government. That morning, an exhausted Kollontai reported the CC's vote to the Bolshevik participants. She left, as one recalled, 'the impression that the CC's signal to come out would be received at any minute'. 'The plan', Latsis would remember, 'was that it [the Northern Region Congress] would declare itself the government, and that would be the start'.

But Kamenev and Zinoviev were still lobbying against action. All they had to do was turn twelve Bolsheviks and/or Maximalists, and the CC would have no majority for immediate insurrection against Kerensky. The gathering was loud and radical, charging political prisoners in Kresty jail not to hunger strike but to keep their strength up 'because the hour of your liberation is close at hand'. Nonetheless, to Lenin's intense frustration, it closed on the 13th not with revolution, but with an appeal to the masses stressing the importance of the forthcoming Second Soviet Congress.

Workers and soldiers still looked to the soviets. On 12 October, the Egersky Guards declared the Soviet 'the voice of the genuine leaders of the workers and poorer peasantry'.

That day, a closed session of the Ispolkom voted on whether to empower Trotsky's MRC to militarily defend Red Petrograd from the government. The Mensheviks assailed the motion, but they were outvoted. Trotsky's hasty riposte to Broido had created a 'front organisation', a party-controlled body with a non-party, soviet remit.

The rumours of Bolshevik uprising grew more specific. 'There is definite evidence', reported *Gazeta-kopeika*, 'that the Bolsheviks are energetically preparing for a coming-out on October 20.' 'The vile and bloody events of July 3–5', warned the rightist *Zhivoe slovo*, 'were only a rehearsal.'

Kerensky's cabinet remained bullish. 'If the Bolsheviks act,' one minister told the press, 'we will carry out a surgical operation and the abscess will be extracted once and for all.'

'We must ask the comrade Bolsheviks candidly,' said Dan with acid courtesy at a plenary of the All-Russian Executive Committees on the 14th, 'what is the purpose of their politics?' Were they 'calling upon the revolutionary proletariat to come out[?] I demand a yes-or-no answer'.

From the floor, for the Bolsheviks, Riazanov responded. 'We demand peace and land.'

That was neither yes nor no, nor was it reassuring.

15 October. At the corner of Sadovaya and Apraksina, where in July shots from above had left demonstrators dead and scattering, a crowd blocked the tramcars. They shouted for *samosudy*, a street trial for two shoplifters, a man in a soldier's uniform, a woman in smart clothes. The mob fought through the city militia into the department store where the thieves cowered. A heaving scrum hauled the man outside while his sobbing accomplice made for a telephone booth. The crowd overwhelmed an officer trying to protect her, wrenched open the door and pulled her out into a rain of blows.

'What are we waiting for?' someone shouted. He drew a pistol and shot the man dead. There was a silence. Then someone shot the woman too, while the militia looked helplessly on.

Sunday in Petrograd. This was how justice worked now.

★

The following day, a full session of the Soviet discussed the MRC – Milrevcom.

Eager not to present it as a Bolshevik body – which, though not formally, it effectively was – the party nominated to propose the resolution establishing it the young Pavel Lazimir, the chair of the soldiers' section of the Soviet, a Left SR. Broido furiously warned that the MRC was not intended to defend the city, but to seize power. Justifying its focus on counterrevolution, and thus on military preparation, Trotsky called attention to the persistent threat from the right. The case was not hard to make: he quoted a notorious recent interview during which Rodzianko thundered, 'To Hell with Petrograd!'

On the 17th, at Pskov, generals met a Soviet delegation to argue for the redeployment of troops, bringing with them representatives from the front. The revolutionaries were concerned about the bitter resentment of those front-line soldiers: to them, the unwillingness of the rear garrison to relocate seemed an unconscionable lack of solidarity. The Soviet anxiously affirmed the heroism of that garrison, and still refused to promise any support for the generals' call. As far as the General Staff were concerned, the encounter had been pointless.

That was the day that Milrevcom, the soviet organ of militarised suspicion of the suspicious government, was inaugurated. But the Bolshevik CC did not yet give it their full attention: they were distracted by in-party uncertainties.

On the 15th, the Petersburg Committee had assembled thirty-five Bolshevik representatives from across the city to prepare for the uprising. But the meeting was derailed by doubts, a caution that came from unlikely quarters.

For the CC, Bubnov made the case for a 'coming-out'. This time, one of those who argued against him was Nevsky.

Nevsky, the erstwhile ultra, representative of the party's trouble-making, radical Military Organisation, now reported that the MO 'has just become rightist'. He enumerated the difficulties he perceived with the CC plan, including what he considered to be the totally inadequate preparation. He was deeply sceptical that the party could take the whole country.

With the door to uncertainty opened, the committee read a long memorandum of concern circulated by Kamenev and Zinoviev. Its impact was palpable. Some districts and representatives remained optimistic – Latsis, as ever, was positively boosterish – but many grew chary. They were unsure whether the Red Guard, though bonded together 'with a band of iron', as one journalist put it, by 'hunger and hatred of wage slavery', was politically advanced enough for the task.

Few disputed that the masses would mobilise again against any counterrevolution, nor their support for the Soviet or the Bolshevik call for power thereto, but that would not necessarily translate into following the party into insurrection. The economic crisis had beaten the people down, some said, leaving them reluctant to go on the offensive for the Bolsheviks.

In the end, eight representatives thought the masses were ready to fight. Six considered them uncertain, and advocated delay. Five said the moment was wholly inopportune.

Bubnov was horrified. He demanded the talk turn to practical preparatory matters. The assembly did approve certain groundlaying measures – a conference of party agitators, building links with communications workers, weapons training – but it made no concrete plans for uprising.

The rebuffed CC hastily reconvened.

Wet snow over dark streets, Petrograd's northern Lesnoi district. A frantic Saint Bernard dog bayed at shadows slipping through the dark, each shape outlined briefly by the weather, then gone. With each howl, another figure passed, until at last more than a score of Bolshevik leaders were inside the building of the district Duma. As they stripped off their disguises, an agitated young woman greeted them.

It was the 16th. Ekaterina Alexeeva, employed as a cleaner of this building, was a member of the local Bolsheviks. The party chair, Kalinin, had given her a mission. He had enjoined her to prepare this secret meeting. When the poor dog outside grew too frenzied, Alexeeva sneaked out and tried to calm it. It would be a long night.

The Bolsheviks had come via a chain of passwords, in disguise, to a venue undisclosed until the last instant. Now they gathered, sat on the floor in a room with too few chairs.

Lenin was one of the last to arrive. He took off his wig, sat down in the corner, and launched into another passionate, desperate defence of his strategy. They had tried compromise. The masses' mood was not unready but protean, he said. They were *waiting*. They had 'given the Bolsheviks their trust, and demand from them not words but deeds'.

All who were there agreed that this was one of Lenin's finest rhetorical hours. Nonetheless, he could not banish all hesitation.

For the MO, those unlikely sceptics, Krylenko remained cautious. Volodarsky ventured that while 'nobody is tearing into the streets … everybody would respond to a call by the Soviet'. From the Rozhdestvensk district came 'doubts … on whether they [the workers] will rise'. From the Okhten district: 'Things are bad.' 'Matters are not so good in Krasnoe Selo. In Kronstadt, morale has fallen.' And Zinoviev saw 'fundamental doubts about whether the success of an uprising is assured'.

The familiar arguments wore on. Finally, as the slush continued outside, the Bolsheviks took it to a vote.

What Lenin wanted was a formal endorsement of the previous decision, though one leaving open the form and precise timing of insurrection, deferring to the CC and to the heads of the Petrograd Soviet and All-Russian Executive Committee. Zinoviev, by contrast, called for flatly *prohibiting* the organising of an uprising before the Second Congress, scheduled for the 20th, when the Bolshevik fraction could be consulted.

For Zinoviev: six votes for, fifteen against, three abstentions. For Lenin: four abstentions, two opposed, and nineteen in favour.

Where the missing vote went is a mystery of history. In any case, revolution it was, by a large margin. Though the schedule was still up for debate, for the second time in a week the Bolsheviks had voted for insurrection.

An anguished Kamenev played a last card. This decision, he said, would destroy the Bolsheviks. Accordingly, he tendered his resignation from the CC.

Deep in the small hours, the meeting was done and the Bolsheviks slipped away, leaving Alexeeva to clean up an almighty mess.

Kamenev and his dismayed allies begged to express their dissent in *Rabochy put'*. They were denied. Without a party outlet, but with Zinoviev's support, Kamenev went elsewhere.

Gorky's paper, *Novaya zhizn*, floated politically somewhere between the left of the Mensheviks and the Bolsheviks themselves. More pessimistic than the latter, its line was firmly against 'precipitous' insurrection. It was in *Novaya zhizn* that Kamenev published a stunning attack.

'At the present,' he wrote, 'the instigation of an armed uprising before and independent of the Soviet Congress would be an impermissible and even fatal step for the proletariat and the revolution.'

Though he strongly insinuated it, Kamenev stopped short of openly declaring that an insurrection was planned. But, especially from a militant of long standing, the publication of such doubts, let alone in a non-Bolshevik journal, was a profoundly shocking, and damaging, transgression of party discipline.

Lenin unleashed biblical wrath.

He could barely believe this treachery from Kamenev, with Zinoviev behind him. These were his old associates. In the barrage of Lenin's letters to the party that Kamenev's piece provoked, there is sharp and real pain. 'It is not easy for me to write in this way about former close comrades,' he wrote, amid a cataract of rage at the 'blacklegs', 'strikebreakers', committers of 'betrayal', a 'crime', purveyors of 'slanderous lies'. He insisted they be expelled.

But despite Lenin's authority and insistence, on the day of Kamenev's sensational attack, though fifteen of the eighteen delegates of Petrograd military units convening at Smolny denounced the government, fully half would still not commit to armed action. And those who were ready to come out would only do so, they made clear, for the Soviet. At a meeting of 200 Bolshevik activists called precisely to discuss seizing power, moderates like Larin and Riazanov attacked the CC's plans as premature. They were backed by Chudnovsky, a comrade who had come straight from the south-western front. Over there, he warned, the Bolsheviks had no stronghold. Any insurrection now, he said, would be doomed.

Amid the palpable and escalating tension, Soviet leaders nervously rescheduled the Second Congress for the 25th. The moderates hoped to use the time to mobilise wider social forces on their side. But this gave a fillip to Lenin, too: now he had an extra five days to prepare to pre-empt congress with insurrection.

He needed those days. The party was deeply divided.

The MO was suspicious of the parvenu MRC, and jealous of its power. The respect the members retained for leaders of the party right, and the discomfort that Lenin's scorched-earth harangues could provoke, boiled over: to one of Lenin's denunciations of the Heavenly Twins, the Bolshevik editors appended criticism of his 'sharp tone'. At a CC meeting on the 20th, Stalin objected to Kamenev's resignation. When Kamenev and Zinoviev were forbidden from openly attacking the CC, Stalin announced his own resignation from the editorial board, in protest.

The CC accepted neither his resignation, nor Lenin's demand for Kamenev and Zinoviev's expulsion. Kamenev's earlier resignation from the CC also seems, at some point, to have gone by the wayside.

'Our whole position', said Stalin, with uncharacteristic perspicacity, 'is contradictory.' The Bolsheviks were divided even in their agreements.

★

On the 19th, the MRC encountered a severe setback. The units at the Peter and Paul Fortress passed a resolution opposing coming out. These were soldiers who would be crucial in any uprising.

Milrevcom tried to regroup. On its first mobilising meeting, on Friday 20 October, it focused attention on the defence of the Soviet from potential attack. The coming Sunday was to be 'Petrograd Soviet Day', and the socialists had plans for various celebratory concerts and meetings. But that day was also the 105th anniversary of the liberation of Moscow from Napoleon, and the Soviet of the Union of Cossack Military Forces had scheduled its own religious procession. The left feared that the hard right might use this march to instigate a clash. Milrevcom sent representatives to city combat units to warn of such provocations, and scheduled a session of the Garrison Conference for the following morning.

Their Peter and Paul problem aside, mostly the MRC was energised. It was building momentum among the troops and winning over sceptics and 'party-only' strategists in the Bolsheviks with its successes. Now the CC asserted that 'all Bolshevik organisations can become part of the revolutionary centre organised by the Soviet'. But naysayers, both to its role and to the CC strategy, remained.

Lenin summoned the MO's Podvoisky, Nevsky and Antonov to a nondescript apartment in the Vyborg district. He was determined, Nevsky recalled, to 'eradicate the last vestiges of stubbornness' about the feasibility of an uprising. In fact, some of the anxieties the MO men raised seemed to strike home with him. But when they argued for a delay of ten to fifteen days, he was beside himself with impatience. And in addition, now that he had been won over by it, Lenin told the MO it must work within the MRC.

On the morning of the 21st, Trotsky opened the MRC's garrison conference. He urged soldiers and workers to support the MRC and the soviets in the struggle for power. The garrison passed a resolution calling on the forthcoming Congress of Soviets to 'take power'.

'A whole series of people spoke out in regard to the necessity of immediately transferring power to the soviets,' reported *Golos soldata*, a sceptical SR–Menshevik paper. There was reassurance, too, about what might occur on Sunday. 'The representative of the Fourth Don Cossack Regiment informed the assembly that his regimental committee had decided against participation in the next day's religious procession. The representative of the Fourteenth Don Cossack Regiment caused a sensation when he declared that his regiment not only would not support counterrevolutionary moves ... but would fight the counterrevolution with all its strength.' To rapturous applause, the speaker bent down to shake hands with his 'comrade Cossack'.

Buoyed, Milrevcom decided to confront the government.

At midnight on the 21st, a group of MRC representatives arrived at General Staff to meet General Polkovnikov. 'Henceforth', one Sadovsky told him, 'orders not signed by us are invalid.'

The garrison, Polkovnikov countered, was his responsibility, and one commissar from the Central Executive Committee was enough. 'We won't recognise your commissars,' he said. Battle was joined.

The delegation returned to MRC headquarters to meet with Antonov, Sverdlov and Trotsky. There, together, they formulated a key document of the October revolution.

'At a meeting on 21 October the revolutionary garrison united around the MRC,' it read.

> Despite this, on the night of October 21–22, the headquarters of the Petrograd Military District refused to recognise the MRC ... In so doing, the headquarters breaks with the revolutionary garrison and the Petrograd Soviet of Workers' and Soldiers' Deputies ... The HQ becomes a direct weapon of counterrevolutionary forces ... The protection of revolutionary order from counterrevolutionary attacks rests with the revolutionary soldiers directed by the MRC. No directives to the garrison not signed by the MRC should be considered valid ... The revolution is in danger. Long live the revolutionary garrison.

In the small hours of Sunday 22nd, in ad hoc session at Smolny, the garrison conference voted to endorse Trotsky's explosive declaration. Simultaneously, Polkovnikov initiated his moves against the MRC. He carefully invited representatives of garrison committees and officials of the Petrograd and All-Russian Executive Committees to a meeting.

Polkovnikov was shrewd. In response to their endorsement of the MRC declaration, he also invited the soldiers at Smolny to meet.

Petrograd Soviet Day. At various mass meetings throughout the capital, the greatest Bolshevik orators – Trotsky, Raskolnikov, Kollontai, Volodarsky – whipped up the crowds. Even Kamenev, surprisingly, was prominent, taking the opportunity of his own speeches to downplay the prospects of any insurrection before the Second Congress.

At the opera venue called the House of the People, Trotsky warned that Petrograd remained at imminent risk from the bourgeoisie. It was, he said, up to workers and soldiers to defend the city. According to Sukhanov, that perennial wry bystander, wryly standing by, this fostered 'a mood bordering on ecstasy'.

In such an atmosphere of cheers and shouts and clenched fists and militia determination and applause, Polkovnikov made his next move. His position was weak, and he knew it. Still seeking compromise, he now invited the MRC itself to meet with him the following day.

Nor was he the only general fervently strategising. That evening, the Petrograd Military District chief of staff, Jaques Bagratuni, requested the quick deployment from the northern front of an infantry and a cavalry brigade, as well as an artillery battery, to the city. Woytinsky, at the front, responded that soldiers were suspicious. They would need to know why before agreeing.

Kerensky, meanwhile, still grossly overestimated his hand. That very night, he proposed to his cabinet that Milrevcom be liquidated by force. Polkovnikov tried to persuade him to wait, hoping to get

Milrevcom to rescind their declaration of power. But the government went ahead and issued an ultimatum.

Either, it declared, the MRC would reverse its declaration of the 22nd, or the authorities would reverse it for them.

23 October. Milrevcom had almost finished appointing its commissars – mostly, surprising no one, Bolshevik Military Organisation activists. Now it was time to ramp up confrontation with the government. The committee circulated a decree granting itself veto power over military orders.

At midday, MRC representatives arrived back at Peter and Paul: they had requested a public meeting at the fortress where they had so recently been rebuffed. Much later, Antonov would claim that he had argued for sending pro-Bolshevik troops to take the fortress by force, but that Trotsky was convinced the soldiers there could be won over. Accordingly, Milrevcom organised a quite extraordinary debate.

The fort commander spoke for the existing chain of command, joined in his efforts by high-profile Right SRs and Mensheviks. The MRC was represented mostly by Bolsheviks. For hours, the intense arguments unfolded, raging back and forth before the mass gathering of soldiers.

As a drained Chudnovsky strove to make his best case for the MRC, he heard a surge of applause spread through the huge crowd. He blinked down at the growing commotion. He smiled.

'I yield my place', he shouted, 'to Comrade Trotsky!'

To the rising tide of euphoria, Trotsky mounted the platform. It was his turn to add his voice.

The meeting continued as the day grew dark. The crowds relocated, made their way to the great wooden building at 11 Kamennoostrovsky Prospect. The Modern Circus, a dimly lit amphitheatre where the Bolshevik women's journal *Rabotnitsa* held frequent gatherings, was a favourite forum for the revolutionaries. It had been the setting of many of the young Trotsky's greatest speeches in 1905. Later he would write a lyrical eulogy to those 1905 events, a description that might serve to conjure up that October night twelve years later.

> Every square inch was filled, every human body compressed to its limit ... The balconies threatened to fall under the excessive weight of human bodies ... The air, intense with breathing and waiting, fairly exploded with shouts and with the passionate yells peculiar to the Modern Circus ... No speaker, no matter how exhausted, could resist the electric tension of that impassioned human throng ... Such was the Modern Circus. It had its own contours, fiery, tender, and frenzied.

And it was there, at 8 p.m., that the soldiers finally, dramatically, voted.

Everyone for the MRC moved to the left: those opposed, to the right. There was a protracted shuffling and shoving. When it was done, there rose a huge and sustained cheer. On the right were only a few officers, and some intellectuals from one of those strange bicycle regiments. The majority, by far, stood for the MRC.

The Peter and Paul units, which had declared against the MRC only three days before, had joined them. The symbolism was immense. And with it came more concrete advantages. Most of Petrograd's weapon stores were now in MRC hands. And the cannon of the fortress looked out over the Winter Palace itself.

Delegates had started to arrive for the Congress of Soviets. Bolsheviks and Left SRs would certainly have a majority, and they would be able to demand power transfer to the soviets, a truly socialist government. At a meeting of the Petrograd Soviet plenum that night, the flamboyant Antonov reported all the MRC's moves, describing them as defensive, all for the sake of the Congress itself. As such, they received overwhelming support from the delegates.

Milrevcom's triumphs were indeed spectacular. It was therefore quite astonishing when, late that same night, it caved in to the

Military District's ultimatum. It withdrew its recent declaration – its veto power.

What precipitated this remarkable climbdown is not clear. What seems likely is that Menshevik moderates Bogdanov and Gots announced that if the committee did not capitulate, the Central Executive Committee of the Soviet would break off relations. It was in the Soviet's name that Milrevcom drew its support and its legitimacy: how would such a breakdown look?

Whatever threat it was that came, it was apparently not only the Left SRs, but also Bolshevik moderates like Riazanov who insisted the MRC cancel its claim to military authority, precipitating its own existential crisis.

At 2:30 a.m., a strange army came through the cold city night. It was cobbled from whatever forces were to hand, on which the right could count. Two or three detachments of Junkers; some cadets from officers' training schools; a few warriors from a Women's Death Battalion; a battery of horse artillery from Pavlovsk; various Cossacks; a bicycle unit with their thick-wheeled machines; and a rifle regiment of war-wounded veterans. They headed through the quiet city to defend the Winter Palace.

The MRC had blinked. Kerensky struck.

As he prayed for the imminent arrival of loyalist troops from the front, Kerensky ordered Bagratuni to deploy those few he had. In the small hours of 24 October, the assault on the Bolsheviks began.

In the early winter darkness, a detachment of militia and cadets arrived at the Trud press, where *Rabochy put'* was printed. They forced their way in and destroyed several thousand copies of the paper. They smashed equipment, sealed the entrance, and set a guard outside. In a fatuous nod at even-handedness, Kerensky also ordered the simultaneous shutdown of two hard-right journals, *Zhivoe slovo* and *Novaya Rus'*. No one, though, could mistake the target of this attack.

After a long day of meetings with newly arrived party delegates, several leading Bolshevik were deep asleep in the party's Priboi publishing house, snoring on their cots amid the piles of books. A phone began to ring and would not stop. They groaned. One Lomov, at last, stumbled over and picked up.

Trotsky's sharp voice, summoning them. 'Kerensky is on the offensive!'

At Smolny, Lazimir, Trotsky, Sverdlov, Antonov and others scrambled to formulate MRC alerts for regimental committees and new commissars. 'Directive Number One. The Petrograd Soviet is in direct danger ... You are hereby directed to bring your regiment to battle readiness ... Any procrastination or interference in executing this order will be considered a betrayal of the revolution.'

No one now knew if the Soviet Congress would even take place, now. Some in the MRC and the Petersburg Committee began, like Lenin, to agitate for immediate insurrection. But, even with their presses attacked and with loyalist forces on the move, the rump CC at Smolny, including Trotsky and Kamenev, considered pursuing negotiations between the MRC and the Military District. They seemed not yet to realise that Kerensky's actions had rendered such a course irrelevant.

The CC was still framing the actions it supported as wholly defensive, at least until the Soviet Congress. But now it endorsed Trotsky's decision to send guards to the Trud press, because 'the Soviet of Workers' and Soldiers' Deputies cannot tolerate suppression of the free word'.

To reopen the press would be less defence than counterattack. As at the front, so with insurrection: the distinction between 'defensive' and 'offensive' can blur.

At 9 a.m., Dashkevich of the Bolshevik MO and CC pulled up to the printers with a company of machine-gun-toting Litovsky guards. Effortlessly and bloodlessly they overwhelmed the loyalist militia, and broke the government seals. 'The comrade soldiers', one reporter drily noted, 'made no similar effort to liberate *Zhivoe slovo*.' An edition of *Pravda* was rushed out, pushing the mainstream CC line by urging pressure on the forthcoming Congress of Soviets to replace Kerensky's regime.

On the streets, armed workers and soldiers began congregating, trying to get a sense of the tides of events. The left were not the only side in motion.

Kerensky made his quick way to the Mariinsky Palace. There, in a bid to rally the Preparliament, that veteran melodramatist gave a speech that was rambling, incoherent and overwrought even by his own generous standards. The left, he wailed, was playing into German hands. He begged for support for his most Provisional of Governments. He pleaded for powers to suppress the Bolsheviks. The right applauded, while the Menshevik–Internationalists and Left SRs shifted in embarrassment at the spectacle he made of himself.

From there, Kerensky entrusted himself to the care of those meagre loyalist forces at the Winter Palace. He was certain that the Preparliament would now support him. The man was 'completely oblivious', the Left SR Kamkov would recall, 'to the fact that there was nobody to put down the uprising regardless of what sanctions he was granted'.

As he holed up, Trotsky was explaining to the Bolshevik delegates that the party was not in favour of insurrection before the congress itself, but that it would allow the government's own rot to undermine it. 'It would be a mistake', he said amid applause, 'to arrest the government … This is defence, comrades. This is defence.' Such was still the catechism.

That afternoon came a sudden ominous development: the army General Staff ordered the bridges of the city drawn. They yawned slowly open as their pulleys cranked, not to allow passage beneath but to prevent it above, marooning those growing gatherings of the people on their sides of the water. Only Palace Bridge remained passable, with government forces in control of it.

'I remembered the July Days,' Ilin-Zhenevsky of the Bolshevik MO later wrote. 'The drawing of the bridges appeared to me as the first step in another attempt to destroy us. Was it possible the Provisional Government would triumph over us again?'

Schools sent students home, and government departments their employees. Word of the bridge closures spread. Shops and banks pulled their shutters down. The tramlines curtailed their services.

But at 4 p.m., just as the cycle regiment at the Winter Palace abruptly abandoned their posts, loyalist artillery cadets arrived at one of those vital bridges, the Liteiny, and found themselves facing a large, furious crowd. This time, people had decided, the bridges would not be allowed to fall to the enemy. The outnumbered cadets could only surrender.

The Women's Death Battalion were ordered to the Troitsky Bridge, to hold it. But when they arrived, they realised that they stood squarely in the sights of the machine guns of the Peter and Paul Fortress. They balked.

Unbidden, Ilin-Zhenevsky directed garrison soldiers to secure the Grenadiers and Samsonovsky bridges. One group returned dragging heavy machinery behind them, and were followed by a shouting mechanic.

'We have lowered the bridge,' they told a curious Ilin-Zhenevsky, 'and to make sure that it stays down, we've brought part of the mechanism.' Ilin-Zhenevsky reassured the bridge technician that the revolutionaries would take good care of the bulky parts, and stashed them in the regimental committee room.

Not everything went the crowds' way. On Nikolaevsky Bridge, cadets took on committed but ill-disciplined Red Guards in their civilian clothes, and drove them off to take the crossing. On the Palace Bridge, cadets and women from the Death Battalion managed to hold their ground. Still, by early evening, the crowds held two of Petrograd's four main bridges. Enough.

At the insistence of the Left SRs, Milrevcom informed the press that 'contrary to all rumours and reports', it was not out to seize power, 'but exclusively for defence'. As its members repeated that line, on MRC orders, commissar Stanislav Pestkovsky came to the city's telegraph office. Its guards were of the Keksgolmsky Regiment, long since pledged to loyalty to the MRC. With them onside, without a shot fired, and though not one of the three thousand employees within was a Bolshevik, the city's communications passed into Milrevcom hands.

Evening in a city in strange equipoise. Armed revolutionaries were gathered on the bridges, grimly holding them from government forces, while groups of respectable citizens promenaded as usual on Nevsky Prospect, where most of the restaurants and cinemas were open. Upheaval was traced over a regular city dusk.

At Margarita Fofanova's apartment, in the outskirts, Lenin grew twitchy. Despite the relatively smooth progress of the fight so far, his comrades still would not declare for an uprising. Their defensive posture held sway.

'The situation is critical in the extreme,' he scrawled to them.

> To delay the uprising would be fatal ... With all my might I urge comrades to realise that everything now hangs by a thread; that we are confronted by problems which are not to be solved by conferences or congresses (even congresses of soviets), but exclusively ... by the struggle of the armed people ... We must at all costs, this very evening, this very night, arrest the government ... We must not wait! We may lose everything! ... The government is tottering. It must be given the death blow at all costs.

And who should take power? 'That is not important at present. Let the MRC do it, or "some other institution"'.

Lenin asked Fofanova to deliver the note to Krupskaya, 'and no one else'.

In Helsingfors, a radio operator handed a telegram to Dybenko, a young Bolshevik navy militant. 'Send the regulations'. An agreed code. His comrades in the capital were instructing him to dispatch sailors and ships to Petrograd.

The hard left were not the only ones preparing. That night, even waverers were coming to understand that wavering could not continue. The feeble Preparliament reconvened again to discuss Kerensky's pleas for support.

'Let's not play hide and seek with each other.' The Left SR Boris Kamkov was peremptory. 'Is there anybody at all who would trust this government?'

Martov stood to join the criticism. Somewhere in the hall, a wit of the right shouted, 'Here is the minister of foreign affairs in the future cabinet!'

'I'm nearsighted,' Martov shot back, 'and cannot tell if this is said by the minister of foreign affairs in Kornilov's cabinet.'

The preparliamentarians traded barbs with desperate panache as structures of authority shuddered into splinters.

That Kamkov and Martov demanded, yet again, an immediate peace, a socialist government, land and army reform, was a surprise to no one. But the day's upheavals, its lurches towards finality, were pushing moderates leftward, too.

Even Fyodor Dan, unexpectedly, after months of seeking coalition with the right, now insisted on 'the clear enunciation by the government ... of a platform in which the people will see their just interests supported by the government and the Council of the Republic and not the Bolsheviks'. What this meant was framing 'the questions of peace and land and the democratisation of the army ... in such a way that not a single worker or soldier will have the slightest doubt that our government is moving along this course with firm and resolute steps'.

The Kadets in the Preparliament, of course, proposed a resolution of support for the Provisional Government. Hard-line Cossacks put forth their own, viciously attacking that government from the right. But Dan articulated a newly mainstream SR/Menshevik resolution. Their calls were for the inauguration of a 'Committee of Public Safety' to work with the Provisional Government in restoring order – and for a radical programme for land and peace. The first, conciliatory-sounding, provision notwithstanding, this was a vote of left no confidence in Kerensky.

The chamber echoed as the debate over the three motions began.

At last, at 8:30 p.m., against opposition of 102 and with 26 crucial abstentions, Dan's 'left' resolution passed, with 123 votes.

A new era. Dan and Gots were now armed with a sliver-thin but newly radical mandate. Immediately they lit out through the cold evening to meet with the cabinet at the Winter Palace. This, they were sure, was the chance. They would demand the Provisional Government proclaim the cessation of hostilities. They would insist on peace negotiations, the transfer of manorial land, the convocation of the Constituent Assembly. Everything could now change.

Alas.

It was just as Preparliament voted that the Helsingfors Bolshevik Leonid Stark, with only twelve armed sailors, took the Petrograd Telegraph Agency, a news wire. One of his first actions was to plug the flow of information. News of the Preparliament's resolution went nowhere.

Though what difference that made is moot. Arriving at the Winter Palace, Dan and Gots were unnerved to find Kerensky at the point of derangement. One moment he morosely announced his intention to resign; the next he dismissed the Mensheviks, delusionally insisting that the government could cope alone.

The rebellion was, still, poised between defence and offensive. As late as 9 p.m., on the Troitsky Bridge, Osvald Denis, MRC commissar of the Pavlovsky Regiment, noticed increased movement among the loyalist forces. He wasted no time. He ordered barricades erected to block the way to the palace, and the arrest of government officials. But, very quickly, he received urgent word from Milrevcom. These measures were unauthorised, they told him. They ordered him to dismantle his checkpoints.

Incredulous, Denis ignored their command.

Lenin, meanwhile, could contain himself no longer. Directly contravening CC instructions – not for the first time – he did up his coat and placed a note on his hostess's table.

'I have gone', it read, 'where you did not want me to go.'

★

In wig, battered cap and ragged clothes, bandages swathed around his face in crude disguise, Lenin set out, together with his Finnish comrade Eino Rahja.

The two men crossed Vyborg in a swaying, near-empty tram. When, through chance remarks, the conductor revealed that she was a leftist, Lenin compulsively began to question her about – and lecture her on – the political situation.

They alighted near the Finland Station and continued on foot through the dangerous streets. At the bottom of Shpalernaya Street, Lenin and Rahja encountered a fired-up loyalist mounted patrol. Rahja held his breath.

But the cadets saw only a nervous injured drunk. They waved Lenin, the world's most famous revolutionary, on his way. So it was that shortly before midnight, Lenin and Rahja reached the Smolny Institute.

At street corners, patrols kept watch. Machine-gunners hunched ready over weapons at the building's entrance. That night the old finishing school was on a war footing. Vehicles came and went in a hubbub. Bonfires lit up the walls, the wary hard-eyed soldiers and the Red Guards.

Neither Rahja nor Lenin, of course, had an entry pass. The guards were adamant they could not come in. It seemed as if after their heart-in-mouth journey, the officious defences of their own side might stymie them.

But a crowd was gathering behind them, also demanding entrance. Its numbers grew, until abruptly under the riotous pressure of so many the sentries could only stand aside, helpless, and Lenin let the rush of people push him, take him with them through the perimeter, across the yard and on through the doors into the institute, and as 24 October became the 25th, he made his way at last along the corridors of Smolny to Room 36.

Where the Bolshevik caucus stared, stunned, as a shabby apparition interrupted them, unwinding bandages from his face, haranguing them to take power.

★

The All-Russian Executive Committee of the Soviet eagerly pushed Dan's newly left suggestions, the agenda that Kerensky had just rejected. These looked to be the best chance for stability. Left and even centrist Mensheviks were now scrambling to endorse the Committee of Public Safety, and to reaffirm the Preparliament's demands. Those late hours, the left-wingers had momentum. Easily the majority of their own party caucus, the Left SRs resolved to liaise with the Menshevik–Internationalists, to coordinate efforts towards an exclusively socialist coalition.

They were not the only ones moving fast. Irrespective of Lenin's exhortations and his furtive night journey, the logic of confrontation pushed Milrevcom ineluctibly towards a more overtly aggressive posture: the offensive it had done its best to avoid. Lenin's presence at Smolny was nonetheless momentous, accelerating the trends.

It was past midnight. Around two hours after Lenin's arrival at the institute, that resourceful commissar Denis, whose recent barricade-building had been so ill-received by his comrades, received new word from the MRC. Now they told him to reinforce the cordon they had previously ordered he destroy – a command he had declined to obey – and to exert control over movement in and out of the grounds of the Winter Palace. The final transition, from de facto to overt insurrection, had begun.

MRC commissar Michael Faerman took over the electric station and, on that harsh and freezing October night, disconnected government buildings. Commissar Karl Kadlubovsky occupied the main city post office. A company of the Sixth Engineer Battalion occupied Nikolaevsky Station. Their moonlit manoeuvres were watched by a statue, a scene from an uncanny story. 'The hulks of house looked like medieval castles – giant shadows followed the engineers,' one participant remembered. 'At this sight, the next-to-last emperor appeared to rein in his horse in horror.'

3 a.m. Kerensky, who only a few hours earlier had claimed to be ready to face down any challenge, tore back, distraught, to General

Staff headquarters, to hear a litany of strategic points falling. Loyalist morale pitched. Worse, though, quickly came.

At 3:30 a.m., a dark presence cut the shadowed Neva. Masts and wires and three looming smokestacks, great jutting guns. Out of the gloom came the armoured ship *Aurora*, making for the city's heart.

The cruiser had long been undergoing repairs in a Neva shipyard. The men of its crew were staunchly radical – when trouble flared, they had disobeyed orders from the government, panicked at their proximity, to set out for sea – and now it was at MRC command that they came. The *Aurora* took the treacherous river under an expert eye: when its captain refused to have anything to do with the enterprise, the men locked him in his cabin and set out anyway. But he could not bear the risk to his great ship. He begged them to let him out, so he could navigate. It was he who guided them to anchor in the blackness by Nikolaevsky Bridge.

The *Aurora*'s searchlights cut the night. The cadets on the bridge, the last under government control, panicked in the glare. They fled.

When a few shock troops arrived to recapture it, 200 sailors and workers were defending the bridge.

From Finland, armed groups set out by train and ship to join their comrades. More reds for Red Petrograd. In Room 36 of Smolny, Lenin gathered with Trotsky and Stalin, Smilga and Berzin – and Kamenev and Zinoviev. Their recent betrayal was hardly the most important thing on which to focus any more.

People bustled and came and went, bringing reports and instructions. The Bolsheviks leaned over maps, traced lines of attack. Lenin insisted that the Winter Palace must be taken and the Provisional Government arrested. This was now, without any question, an insurrection.

Lenin proposed to his comrades a – wholly Bolshevik – government to present to the Soviet Congress, when it opened later that day. But what should they call the appointees? 'Minister', he said, was 'a vile, hackneyed word'.

'What about people's commissars?' said Trotsky.

'Yes, that's very good,' Lenin said. 'It smells terribly of revolution.' The seed of the revolutionary government, the Council of People's Commissars, Sovnarkom, was sown.

Lenin suggested Trotsky for commissar of the interior. But Trotsky foresaw that enemies on the right would attack him – as a Jew.

'Of what importance are such trifles?' Lenin snapped.

'There are still a good many fools left,' Trotsky replied.

'Surely we don't keep step with fools?'

'Sometimes', said Trotsky, 'one has to make some allowance for stupidity. Why create additional complications at the outset?'

Dizzy with what was unfolding, the men drifted into strange, intense, playful, bureaucratic-utopian banter. The weight of their recent disagreements lightened. Lenin now *teased* Kamenev. The same Kamenev who, days before, he had denounced as a traitor, and who, hours before, had lugubriously opined that if they did take power, the Bolsheviks would not hold it for more than two weeks.

'Never mind,' Lenin told him. 'When, in two years' time, we're still in power, you'll be saying we can't survive any longer than two years.'

Dawn of the 25th approached. A desperate Kerensky issued an appeal to the Cossacks 'in the name of freedom, honour and the glory of our native land ... to act to aid the Soviet Central Executive Committee, the revolutionary democracy, and the Provisional Government, and to save the perishing Russian State'.

But the Cossacks wanted to know if the infantry was coming out. When the government's answer was equivocal, all but a small number of ultra-loyalists responded that they were disinclined to act alone, 'serving as live targets'.

Repeatedly, easily, at points throughout the city, Milrevcom disarmed loyalist guards and just told them to go home. And for the most part, they did. Insurgents occupied the Engineers' Palace by the simple expedient of walking in. 'They entered and took their

seats, while those who were sitting there got up and left,' one remi-
niscence has it. At 6 a.m., forty revolutionary sailors approached the
Petrograd State Bank. Its guards, from the Semenovsky Regiment,
had pledged neutrality: they would defend the bank from looters
and criminals, but would not take sides between reaction and revolution. Nor would they intervene. They stood aside, therefore, and
let the MRC take over.

Within an hour, as watery winter light washed over the city,
a detachment from the Keksgolmsky Regiment, commanded by
Zakharov, an unusual military school cadet come over to the revolution, set out to the main telephone exchange. Zakharov had worked
there, and he knew its security. When he arrived, he had no diffi-
culty directing his troops to isolate and disarm the sullen, powerless
cadets on duty there. The revolutionaries disconnected the government lines.

They missed two. With these, the cabinet ministers holed up and
huddled over two receivers amid the white-and-gilt filigrees, pilas-
ters and chandeliers of the Malachite Room of the Winter Palace,
and maintained contact with their meagre forces. They issued pointless instructions, bickering in low voices while Kerensky stared at
nothing.

Mid-morning. In Kronstadt, as they had before, armed sailors
boarded whatever they could find that was seaworthy. From Helsingfors they set forth in five destroyers and a patrol boat, all festooned
with revolutionary banners. Across Petrograd, revolutionaries were
once more emptying the jails.

At Smolny, a scruffy figure barged into the Bolshevik operations
room. The activists stared, disconcerted at the newcomer, until at
last Vladimir Bonch-Bruevich cried out and ran forward with his
arms open. 'Vladimir Ilyich, our father! I did not recognise you,
dear one!'

Lenin sat down to draft a proclamation. He was twitching
with anxiety about time, desperate for the final overthrow of the

government to be complete when Second Congress opened. He well knew the power of the fait accompli.

> To the Citizens of Russia. The Provisional Government has been overthrown. State power has passed into the hands of the organ of the Petrograd Soviet of Workers' and Soldiers' Deputies, the Military Revolutionary Committee, which stands at the head of the Petrograd proletariat and garrison.
>
> The cause for which the people have struggled – the immediate proposal of a democratic peace, the elimination of landlord estates, workers' control over production, the creation of a soviet government – the triumph of this cause has been assured.
>
> Long live the workers', soldiers' and peasants' revolution!

Quite convinced by now of Milrevcom's usefulness, Lenin did not sign for the Bolsheviks, but in the name of that 'non-party' body.

The proclamation was printed up quickly in the bold text blocks to which Cyrillic lends itself. As fast as copies could be distributed they were plastered as posters across countless walls. Operators keyed its words down telegraph wires.

In fact it was not a truth but an aspiration.

In the Winter Palace, Kerensky used his last channels of communication to arrange to join troops heading for the capital. To actually reach them, however, would not be at all easy. He might get away, but the MRC controlled the stations.

He needed help. The General Staff conducted a long and increasingly frantic search, and at last found a suitable car. Pleading, they managed to secure the use of another from the American embassy – a vehicle with handy diplomatic plates.

About 11 a.m. on the 25th, just as Lenin's prefigurative proclamation began to circulate, the two vehicles sped past MRC roadblocks that were more enthusiastic than efficient.

A broken Kerensky escaped the city with a tiny entourage, to go looking for loyal soldiers.

★

It seemed to many citizens, the upheaval notwithstanding, almost like a normal day in Petrograd. A certain amount of racket and kerfuffle was impossible to ignore, certainly, but relatively few people were involved in the actual fighting, and only at key points. As those combatants went about their insurrectionary or counterrevolutionary work, reconfiguring the world, most trams were running, most shops stayed open.

At midday, armed revolutionary soldiers and sailors arrived at the Mariinsky Palace. The Preparliamentarians anxiously discussing the unfolding drama were about to become actors in it.

An MRC commissar stormed in. He ordered the Preparliament's chair, Avksentiev, to clear the palace. Soldiers and sailors waving weapons shoved their way inside, scattering terrified deputies. In a daze, Avksentiev quickly gathered together as many of the steering committee as he could. They knew resistance was pointless, but departed under protest as formal as they could manage to make it, committed to reconvening as soon as possible.

As they stepped out into stinging cold, the building's new guards checked their papers, but did not detain them. The pitiful Preparliament was not the prize that, to Lenin's maddened exasparation, still eluded them.

That prize, now Kerenskyless, was in the Winter Palace. There, their world collapsing, the sullen embers of the Provisional Government still glowed.

At noon in the grand Malachite Room, the textile magnate and Kadet Konovalov convened the cabinet.

'I don't know why this session was called,' muttered the naval minister, Admiral Verderevsky. 'We have no tangible military force and consequently are incapable of taking any action whatever.' Perhaps, he posited, they should have convened with the Preparliament – and even as he spoke, news came that it had been dismissed.

The ministers received reports and issued appeals to their

dwindling interlocutors. Those not afflicted by Verderevsky's mournful realism spun out fantasies. With the last shreds of their power gusting away, they dreamed up a new authority.

With all the seriousness in the world, like burnt-out matches telling grim stories of the conflagration they will soon start, the ashes of Russia's Provisional Government debated which of them to make dictator.

This time the Kronstadt forces reached Petrograd's waters in a former pleasure yacht, two minelayers, a training vessel, an antique battleship and a phalanx of tiny barges. Another madcap flotilla.

Close by where the cabinet was fantasising of dictatorship, revolutionary sailors captured the Admiralty and arrested the naval high command. The Pavlovsky Regiment set up pickets on bridges. The Keksgolmsky Regiment took control north of the Moika river.

Noon, the original time slated for the seizure of the Winter Palace, had come and gone. The deadline was pushed forward by three hours, which scheduled the arrest of the government for after the 2 p.m. opening of the Congress of Soviets – exactly what Lenin wanted to avoid. So that opening was postponed.

But the hall of Smolny was now teeming with delegates from the Petrograd and provincial soviets. They demanded news. They could not be put off forever.

At 2:35 p.m., therefore, Trotsky opened an emergency session of the Petrograd Soviet.

'On behalf of the Military Revolutionary Committee,' he exclaimed, 'I declare that the Provisional Government no longer exists.'

His words aroused a storm of joy. Key institutions were in MRC hands, Trotsky went on over the commotion. The Winter Palace would fall 'momentarily'. Another huge cheer came: Lenin was entering the hall.

'Long live Comrade Lenin,' Trotsky cried, 'back with us again!'

Lenin's first public appearance since July was brief and exultant.

He offered no details, but announced 'the beginning of a new period', and exhorted: 'Long live the world socialist revolution!'

Most of those present responded with delight. But there was dissent.

'You are anticipating the will of the Second Congres of Soviets,' someone shouted.

'The will of the Second Congress of Soviets has already been predetermined by the fact of the workers' and soldiers' uprising,' Trotsky called back. 'Now we have only to develop this triumph.'

But amid proclamations from Volodarsky, Zinoviev and Lunacharsky, a small number of moderates, mostly Mensheviks, withdrew from the Soviet's executive organs. They warned of terrible consequences from this conspiracy.

The revolutionaries made slapstick errors. Baltic sailors arrived late to their postings. Some were marooned in a field beyond the Finnish city of Vyborg, thanks to a loyalist stationmaster who supplied an unreliable train.

At 3 p.m., the rescheduled assault on the Provisional Government was delayed yet again. Lenin raged at the MRC. He was, Podvoisky recalled, 'like a lion in a cage … He was ready to shoot us'.

At the Winter Palace itself, as morale among the remaining 3,000 or so hungry loyalist troops collapsed, the cabinet secluded within continued to imagine a future history. Dan and Gots of the Preparliament had ruled Kadets out of their proposed government; so now, in an epically insignificant snub to the Mensheviks, the cabinet determined that the new leader would be of that party: the former minister of welfare, Nikolai Mikhailovich Kishkin.

Just after 4 p.m., he was formally invested with power. Thus began the brief reign of Kishkin the dictator, all-powerful ruler of a clutch of palace rooms and a few outlying buildings.

Dictator Kishkin rushed to the military headquarters to take command. His first action was to dismiss the chief of staff, Polkovnikov, and replace him with Bagratuni. This provoked the first crack in his absolute authority: miraculously resistant to awe at Kishkin's power, Polkovnikov's associates resigned en masse in protest at his scapegoating.

Some made it through the perforated MRC defence and went glumly home. Some sat staring out of the windows.

6 p.m. Cold rain came down with the dark. Another MRC deadline to attack the palace passed. Red Guards watched in mild consternation as cadets in the Palace Square erected their own barricades. Periodically, some excitable revolutionary or other would let off a shot, only to be rebuked by comrades. Lenin sent note after furious note to the MRC leaders, demanding they get on with it.

At 6:15 p.m., a sizeable group of cadets decided they had no appetite for pointless sacrifice, particularly of themselves. They slipped out of the Winter Palace, taking their large-bore rifles with them. The ministers withdrew to Kerensky's private rooms for supper. Borscht, fish, artichokes.

At Peter and Paul, Blagonravov, the MRC commissar, decided the time really had come for the attack. He sent two cyclists to the General Staff with an ultimatum: his cannon, the guns of the *Aurora* and those of its sister ship the *Amur* would fire in twenty minutes unless the government surrendered.

Blagonravov was bluffing. He had discovered that the big weapons trained on the palace from the fortress walls were unusable, too filthy to fire. The smaller replacements dragged hurriedly into position he then realised were not loaded. And he had no suitable ammunition.

The generals went quickly to the cabinet to relay the MRC message. The last telegrapher in the General Staff tapped out to Pskov that the building was lost. 'I am leaving work', he added, 'and getting out of here.'

Someone in the palace wondered what would happen to it if the *Aurora* fired. 'It will be turned', said Verderevsky heavily, 'into a heap of ruins.'

Dictator Kishkin hurried to beg a few quaking cadets to stay. The cabinet, considering it their duty not to withdraw until the last possible moment, put out their own last telegram.

'To all, all, all! The Petrograd Soviet' – not the Bolsheviks, tellingly – 'has declared the Provisional Government overthrown, and demands that power be yielded to it under threat of shelling ... We have decided not to surrender and to put ourselves under the protection of the people'.

At 8 p.m., it was the turn of 200 Cossacks to walk away from their posts. Bagratuni resigned and he, too, got out. In the palace, the remaining loyalist forces waited for death, smoking morosely under the tapestries.

One flank was barely guarded. Anyone determined and lucky could sneak past the guards into the half-defended corridors. A succession of revolutionaries like Dashkevich and journalists like John Reed came and went, for the sake of curiosity, fraternisation, reportage. Chudnovsky was *invited* in, by cadets desperate to leave but fearful, and negotiating for their safety.

The ministers vacated the Malachite Room for a less vulnerable office – which contained a telephone, its line miraculously still connected. The men dialled the city Duma and implored Petrograd's mayor, Grigorii Shreider, down the line for help.

The Duma met immediately in emergency session, and sent mediators to the *Aurora*, Smolny and the Winter Palace. But the MRC barred them from the ship, and the besiegers of the palace rebuffed them. Nor was their white flag clear enough: some of the last defenders within, on whose behalf they had come, fired at them. At Smolny, Kamenev received them courteously and offered them safe passage to the palace, but the escorted group had no more luck than those who went direct.

It was at around this time that Kerensky managed to reach the front.

Blagonravov had been trying to prepare, and realised with relief that the six-inch guns of Peter and Paul were in firing condition after all. But his ridiculous travails were not over. The revolutionaries had agreed that the final assault on the Winter Palace would begin when his men raised a lighted red lantern on the fortress flagpole – and no one, it had transpired, had such a lantern.

Hunting for one throughout the dark grounds of Peter and Paul, Blagonravov promptly fell into a mud-pit. When, dirty and sodden, he finally found a suitable light and hared back to raise it, he discovered, nearly out of his mind with frustration, that 'it proved extremely difficult to fix it on the flagpole'. It was not until 9:40 p.m., almost ten hours after the original deadline, that he overcame these obstacles and was at last able to signal the *Aurora* to fire.

The ship's first shot was a blank. Its blast was sound without fury, but a sound much louder than that of live ammunition. A cataclysmic boom shook Petrograd.

On the banks of the river, curious onlookers dived in terror to the ground, covering their ears. Deafened and quivering from the report, scores of the last defenders in the palace lost heart and abandoned their posts, leaving only a hard core too committed, brave, paralysed, exhausted, stupid, or afraid to flee.

The minister Semion Maslov of the Right SRs screamed down the phone line to a Duma representative, who relayed his words to the hushed house. 'The democracy sent us into the Provisional Government: we didn't want the appointments, but we went. Yet now … when we are being shot, we are not supported … Of course we will die. But my final words will be: "Contempt and damnation to the democracy which knew how to appoint us but was unable to defend us."'

After almost eight hours of stalling, the soviet delegates could be put off no longer. An hour after that first shot, in the grand colonnaded Assembly Hall of Smolny, the Second Congress of Soviets opened.

The room was heavy with the fug of cigarettes, despite repeated shouts, many cheerfully taken up by the smokers themselves, that smoking was not allowed. The delegates, Sukhanov recorded with a shudder, mostly bore 'the grey features of the Bolshevik provinces'.

They looked, to his refined and intellectual eye, 'morose' and 'primitive' and 'dark', 'crude and ignorant'.

Of 670 delegates, 300 were Bolsheviks. A hundred and ninety-three were SRs, more than half of them of the party's left; sixty-eight Mensheviks, and fourteen Menshevik–Internationalists. The rest were unaffiliated, or members of tiny groups. The size of the Bolshevik presence illustrated that support for the party was soaring among those who voted in the representatives – and was also bolstered by somewhat lax organisational arrangements that had given them more than their proportional share. Even so, without the Left SRs, they had no majority.

It was not, however, a Bolshevik who rang the opening bell, but a Menshevik. The Bolsheviks played on Dan's vanity by offering him this role. But he instantly quashed any hopes of cross-party camaraderie or congeniality.

'The Central Executive Committee considers our customary opening political address superfluous,' he announced. 'Even now, our comrades who are selflessly fulfilling the obligations we placed on them are under fire at the Winter Palace.'

Dan and the other moderates who had led the Soviet since March vacated their seats to be replaced by the new, proportionally allotted presidium. To uproarious approval, fourteen Bolsheviks – including Kollontai, Lunacharsky, Trotsky, Zinoviev – and seven Left SRs, including the great Maria Spiridonova, ascended the platform. The Mensheviks, in dudgeon, abjured their three seats. One place was held for the Menshevik–Internationalists: in a move simultaneously dignified and pathetic, Martov's group declined to take it, but reserved the right to do so later.

As the new revolutionary leadership sat and prepared for business, the room suddenly reverberated with another cannon boom. Everybody froze.

This time the shot came from the Peter and Paul Fortress. Unlike the *Aurora*'s, its round was not a blank.

★

The oily flash of detonations reflected in the Neva. Shells soared up, arcing in the night and screaming as they descended towards their target. Many, in mercy or incompetence, combusted loud, spectacular and harmless in the air. Many more plunged with crashing splashes deep into the water.

From their own emplacements, the Red Guards fired too. Their bullets peppered the Winter Palace walls. The vestiges of government within cowered under the table as glass rained down around them.

At Smolny, as the ominous echoes of the onslaught sounded, Martov raised his tremulous voice. He insisted on a peaceful solution. He called hoarsely for a ceasefire. For negotiations to begin on a cross-party, united, socialist government.

There came a great tumult of applause from the audience. From the presidium itself, Mstislavsky of the Left SRs offered Martov full-throated support. As, and vocally, did most of those present – including many grassroots Bolsheviks.

For the party leadership, Lunacharsky rose. And then, sensationally, he announced that 'the Bolshevik fraction has absolutely nothing against the proposal made by Martov'.

The delegates voted on Martov's call. Support was unanimous.

Bessie Beatty, correspondent for the *San Francisco Bulletin*, was in the room. She understood the stakes of what she saw. 'It was', she wrote, 'a critical moment in the history of the Russian Revolution.' It seemed as if a democratic socialist coalition was about to be born.

But as the moment stretched out, the guns on the Neva sounded again. Their echoes shook the room – and the chasms between parties reappeared.

'A criminal political venture has been going on behind the back of the All-Russian Congress,' announced a Menshevik officer, Kharash. 'The Mensheviks and SRs repudiate all that is going on here, and stubbornly resist all attempts to seize the government.'

'He does not represent the Twelfth Army!' cried an angry soldier. 'The army demands all power to the soviets!'

A barrage of heckles. Right SRs and Mensheviks took turns now to shout denunciations of the Bolsheviks, and to warn that they would withdraw from proceedings, as the left howled them down.

The mood grew more bitter. Khinchuk of the Moscow Soviet took his turn to speak. 'The only possible peaceful solution to the present crisis', he insisted, 'continues to lie in negotiations with the Provisional Government.'

Bedlam. Khinchuk's intervention was either a catastrophic underestimate of the hatred for Kerensky, or a deliberate provocation. It drew fury from far more than just the incredulous Bolsheviks. At last, into the din Khinchuk yelled, 'We leave the present congress!'

But amid the stamping, booing and whistling that greeted that call, the Mensheviks and SRs hesitated. The threat to leave, after all, was a last card.

Across Petrograd, the Duma discussed Maslov's doom-laden phone call. 'Let our comrades know that we have not abandoned them; let them know we will die with them,' proclaimed the SR Naum Bykhovsky. Liberals and conservatives rose to vote yes, that they would join those bunkered in the Winter Palace under fire; that they, too, were ready to die for the regime. The Kadet Countess Sofia Panina declared she would 'stand in front of the cannon'.

Full of scorn, the Bolshevik representatives voted no. They would go too, they said, but not to the palace: to the Soviet.

The roll call done, the two competing pilgrimages set out in the darkness.

In Smolny, Erlich of the Jewish Bund interrupted proceedings with news of the city Duma deputies' decisions. It was time, he said, for those who 'did not wish a bloodbath' to join the march to the palace, in solidarity with the cabinet. Again the left shouted imprecations, as Mensheviks, Bund, SRs and a smattering of others rose and at last walked out. Leaving the Bolsheviks, the Left SRs, and the agitated Menshevik–Internationalists behind.

Trudging through cold night rain, the self-exiled moderates from Smolny reached Nevsky Prospect and the Duma. There they joined forces with its deputies, with the Menshevik and SR members of the Executive Committee of the Peasants' Soviets, and together they set out to show their solidarity with the cabinet. They walked four abreast behind Shreider, the mayor, and Sergei Prokopovich, the minister of supplies. Carrying bread and sausages for the ministers' sustenance, quavering the Marseillaise, the 300-strong group sallied forth to die for the Provisional Government.

They did not make it a block. At the corner of the canal, revolutionaries blocked their way.

'We demand to pass!' Shreider and Prokopovich shouted. 'We are going to the Winter Palace!'

A sailor, bemused, refused to let them through.

'Shoot us if you want to!' the marchers challenged. 'We are ready to die, if you have the heart to fire on Russians and comrades ... We bare our breasts to your guns!'

The peculiar standoff continued. The left refused to shoot, the right demanded their right to pass and/or be shot.

'What will you do?' yelled someone at the sailor who doggedly refused to murder him.

John Reed's eyewitness account of what happened next is famous. 'Another sailor came up, very much irritated. "We will spank you!" he cried energetically. "And if necessary we will shoot you too. Go home now, and leave us in peace."'

That would be no fit fate for champions of democracy. Standing on a box, waving his umbrella, Prokopovich anounced to his followers that they would save these sailors from themselves. 'We cannot have our innocent blood upon the hands of these ignorant men! ... It is beneath our dignity to be shot down' – let alone spanked – 'here in the street by switchmen. Let us return to the Duma, and discuss the best means of saving the country and the Revolution!'

With that, the self-declared *morituri* for liberal democracy turned and set out on their embarrassingly short return journey, taking their sausages with them.

Martov remained in the Assembly Hall with the mass meeting. He was still desperate for compromise. Now he tabled a motion criticising the Bolsheviks for pre-empting Congress's will, suggesting – again – that negotiations begin for a broad, inclusive socialist government. This was close to his proposal of two hours before – which, Lenin's desire to break with moderates notwithstanding, the Bolsheviks had not opposed.

But two hours was a long time.

As Martov sat, there was a commotion, and the Bolsheviks' Duma fraction pushed into the hall, to the delegates' delight and surprise. They had come, they said, 'to triumph or die with the All-Russian Congress'.

When the cheering subsided, Trotsky himself rose to respond to Martov.

'A rising of the masses of the people requires no justification,' he said. 'What has happened is an insurrection, and not a conspiracy. We hardened the revolutionary energy of the Petersburg workers and soldiers. We openly forged the will of the masses for an insurrection, and not a conspiracy. The masses of the people followed our banner and our insurrection was victorious. And now we are told: renounce your victory, make concessions, compromise. With whom? I ask: with whom ought we to compromise? With those wretched groups which have left us or who are making this proposal? But after all we've had a full view of them. No one in Russia is with them any longer. A compromise is supposed to be made, as between two equal sides, by the millions of workers and peasants represented in this congress, whom they are ready, not for the first time or the last, to barter away as the bourgeoisie sees fit. No, here no compromise is possible. To those who have left and to those who tell us to do this we must say: you are miserable bankrupts, your role is played out. Go where you ought to go: into the dustbin of history!'

The room erupted. Amid the loud sustained applause, Martov stood up. 'Then we'll leave!' he shouted.

As he turned, a delegate barred his way. The man stared at him with an expression between sorrow and accusation.

'And we had thought', he said, 'that Martov at least would remain with us.'

'One day you will understand', said Martov, his voice shaking, 'the crime in which you are taking part.'

He walked out.

Congress quickly passed a spiteful denunciation of the departed, including of Martov. Such barbs were unwelcome and unnecessary as far as the remaining Left SRs and Menshevik–Internationalists were concerned – as they were, too, to many Bolsheviks.

Boris Kamkov was warmly clapped when he announced that his group, the Left SRs, had stayed. He tried to revive Martov's proposal, gently criticising the Bolshevik majority. They had not carried the peasantry, or the bulk of the army, he reminded his listeners. Compromise was still necessary.

This time it was not Trotsky who responded, but the popular Lunacharsky – who had previously *agreed* to Martov's move. The tasks ahead were onerous, he concurred, but 'Kamkov's criticism of us is unfounded.'

'If starting this session we had initiated any steps whatever to reject or remove other elements, Kamkov would be right,' Lunacharsky continued. 'But all of us unanimously accepted Martov's proposal to discuss peaceful ways of solving the crisis. And we were deluged by a hail of declarations. A systematic attack was conducted against us ... Without hearing us out, not even bothering to discuss their own proposal, they [the Mensheviks and SRs] immediately sought to fence themselves off from us.'

In response, it could have been pointed out to Lunacharsky that Lenin had, for weeks, been insisting that his party must take power alone. And yet, all such cynicism notwithstanding, Lunacharsky was right.

Whether in joyful solidarity, truculently, in confusion, or whatever it might be, like everyone else of every other party, all the Bolsheviks in the hall *had* supported cooperation – a socialist unity government – when Martov first mooted it.

Bessie Beatty suggested that Trotsky failed to move as fast as he could in response to that first proposal, perhaps out of 'some bitter memory of insults he had suffered at the hands of these other leaders'. That was debatable, and even if true, the Mensheviks, the Right SRs and others had chosen to throw the vote back in the faces of the Bolsheviks. They had gone straight from it to opposition, denouncing those to their left.

Lunacharsky's question was reasonable: how do you cooperate with those who have rejected cooperation?

As if to underline the point, the departed moderates were, at that very moment, labelling the meeting only 'a private gathering of Bolshevik delegates'. 'The Central Executive Committee', they announced, 'considers the Second Congress as not having taken place.'

In the hall, the debate about conciliation dragged into the darkest hours. But by now the weight of opinion was with Lunacharsky, and with Trotsky.

It was endgame at the Winter Palace.

Wind intruded through smashed glass. The vast chambers were cold. Disconsolate soldiers, deprived of purpose, wandered past the double-headed eagles of the throne room. Invaders reached the emperor's personal chamber. It was empty. They took their time attacking images of the man himself, hacking with their bayonets at the stiff, sedate life-sized Nicholas II watching from the wall. They scored the painting like beasts with talons, left long scratches, from the ex-tsar's head to his booted feet.

Figures drifted in and out of sight, each unsure of who the other was. One Lieutenant Sinegub remained, committed to defending the government. He patrolled the besieged corridors for disjointed hours, awaiting attack, adrift in a kind of sedate panic, extreme, narcotic exhaustion, passing scenes like snips from some half-heard story: an old gentleman in the uniform of an admiral, sitting motionless in an armchair; an unlit, deserted switchboard; soldiers hunkered below the watching eyes of portraits in a gallery.

Men skirmished in stairwells. Any creak on the floorboards might be the revolution. Here came a junker heading somewhere, on some mission. He warned with a stilted calm that the person Sinegub had just passed – he had just walked past someone, yes – was probably one of the enemy. 'Good, excellent,' said Sinegub. 'Watch! I will make sure at once.' He turned and immobilised him – the other man, he saw, was indeed of the insurgency's party – by pulling his coat down, like a child in a playground fight, so he could not move his arms.

About 2 a.m., MRC forces pushed into the palace in sudden numbers. Frantic, Konovalov telephoned Shreider. 'All we have is a small force of cadets,' he said. 'Our arrest is imminent.' The connection broke.

From the hallways, the ministers heard futile shots. The last of their defence. Footsteps. A breathless cadet came running in for orders. 'Fight to the last man?' he asked.

'No bloodshed!' they shouted. 'We must surrender.'

They waited. A strange awkwardness. How best to be found? Not, surely, hovering embarrassedly, coats over their arm, like businessmen awaiting a train.

Kishkin the dictator took control. He issued the final two orders of his reign.

'Leave your overcoats,' he said. 'Let us sit down at the table.'

They obeyed. And thus they were, a frozen tableau of a cabinet meeting, when Antonov burst dramatically in, his eccentric artist's hat pushed back over his red hair. Behind him, soldiers, sailors, Red Guards.

'The Provisional Government is here,' said Konovalov with impressive decorum, as if in answer to a knock rather than an insurrection. 'What do you want?'

'I inform you, all of you,' said Antonov, 'members of the Provisional Government, that you are under arrest.'

Before the revolution, a political lifetime ago, one of those ministers present, Maliantovich, had sheltered Antonov in his house. The two men eyed each other, but did not mention it.

The Red Guards were furious to realise that Kerensky was long gone. Blood up, one shouted, 'Bayonet all the sons of bitches!'

'I will not allow any violence against them,' Antonov calmly replied.

With that he led the ministers away, leaving behind them their rough drafts of proclamations, crossed out, those criss-crosses meandering like the dreams of dictatorship into fanciful designs. A telephone began to ring.

Sinegub watched from the corridor. When it was over, his government gone, his duty done, he turned quietly and walked away, out into the blaze of searchlights.

Looters ferreted through the warren of rooms. They ignored the artworks and took clothes and knick-knacks. They trampled papers across the floors. As they left, revolutionary soldiers checked them and confiscated their souvenirs. 'This is the people's palace,' one Bolshevik lieutenant chided. 'This is our palace. Do not steal from the people.'

A broken sword handle, a wax candle. The pilferers surrendered their booty. A blanket, a sofa cushion.

Antonov led the ex-ministers outside, where a rough, fired-up and angry crowd met them. He stood protectively in front of his prisoners. 'Don't hit them,' he and other experienced – proud – Bolsheviks insisted. 'It is *uncultured*.'

But the growling anger of the streets would not be appeased so easily. After anxious moments, it was by luck, when the noise of nearby machine-gun fire sent people scattering in alarm, that Antonov took the opportunity to run across the bridge, shoving and dragging the detainees to incarceration in the Fortress of Peter and Paul.

As the door to his cell was about to close, the Menshevik internal affairs minster Nikitin found a telegram from the Ukrainian Rada in his pocket.

'I received this yesterday,' he said. He handed it to Antonov. 'Now it's your problem.'

In Smolny, it was that dogged naysayer Kamenev who gave the delegates the news: 'The leaders of the counterrevolution ensconced in the Winter Palace have been seized by the revolutionary garrison.' He unleashed joyful pandemonium.

It was past 3 a.m., but there was still business to be done. For two more hours Congress heard reports come in – of units coming over to their side, of generals accepting MRC authority. There was still dissent, too. Someone called for the release of those SR ministers in prison: Trotsky lambasted them as false comrades.

Around 4 a.m., in an undignified afterword to his exit, a delegation from Martov's group sheepishly re-entered, and tried to resubmit his call for a collaborative socialist government. Kamenev reminded the hall that those with whom Martov advocated compromise had turned their backs on his proposal. Still, ever the moderate, he moved to table Trotsky's condemnation of the SRs and Mensheviks, putting it discreetly into procedural limbo, to spare blushes should talks resume.

Lenin would not return to the meeting that night. He was making plans. But he had written a document, which it was for Lunacharsky to present.

Addressed 'To All Workers, Soldiers and Peasants', Lenin proclaimed Soviet power and undertook to propose a democratic peace immediately. Land would be transferred to the peasants. The cities would be supplied with bread, the nations of the empire offered self-determination. But Lenin also warned that the revolution remained in danger – from without and from within.

'The Kornilovites … are endeavouring to lead troops against Petrograd … Soldiers! Resist Kerensky, who is a Kornilovite! … Railwaymen! Stop all echelons sent by Kerensky against Petrograd! Soldiers, Workers, Employees! The fate of the revolution and democratic peace is in your hands!'

It took a long time to read the whole document aloud, interrupted as it was, so often, by such cheers of approval. One tiny verbal tweak ensured Left SR assent. A minuscule Menshevik faction abstained, preparing a path for reconciliation between left-Martovism and the Bolsheviks. No matter. At 5 a.m. on 26 October, Lenin's manifesto was overwhelmingly voted through.

A roar. The echo of it faded as the magnitude of the shouted resolution became slowly clear. Men and women looked around at each other. That was passed. That was done.

Revolutionary government was proclaimed.

Revolutionary government had been proclaimed, and that was enough for one night. It would more than do for a first meeting, surely.

Exhausted, drunk on history, nerves still taut as wires, the delegates to the Second Congress of Soviets stumbled out of Smolny. They stepped out of the finishing school into a new moment of history, a new kind of first day, that of a workers' government, morning in a new city, the capital of a workers' state. They walked into the winter under a dim but lightening sky.

Epilogue: After October

'Oh, my love, now I know all your freedom;
I know that it will come; but what will it be
like?'

Nikolai Chernyshevsky,
What Is to Be Done?

i

That strange book *What Is to Be Done?* casts a long shadow. In 1902, Lenin named his own seminal tract on leftist organisation after the novel of forty years previously.

Chernyshevsky's story is interspersed with dream sequences, of which the most celebrated is the fourth. Here, in eleven sections, the protagonist Vera Pavlovna journeys from the ancient past to a strange, affecting, utopian future. The hinge point of the book, the fulcrum from history to possibility, is the fourth dream's Section 7: that section, in its entirety, forms the epigraph to this book.

Two rows of dots. Something ostentatiously unspoken. The transition from injustice to emancipation. Informed readers would understand that behind the extended ellipsis lay revolution.

With such discretion the author evaded the censor. But there is something almost religious, too, in this unwriting, from this atheist son of a priest. A political *via negativa*, an apophatic revolutionism.

For those who cleave to it, a paradox of actually existing revolution is that in its potential for utter reconfiguration, it is, precisely, beyond words, a messianic interruption – one that emerges from the quotidian. Unsayable, yet the culmination of everyday exhortations. Beyond language and of it, beyond representation and not.

Chernyshevsky's dots, then, are one iteration of a strange story. This book has been an attempt at another.

And the urgent gasp, above, that Chernyshevsky has follow those dots? 'What will it be like?' That question, from the present vantage point in history, can only hurt.

ii

Late evening of 26 October 1917. Lenin stands before the Second Congress of Soviets. He grips the lectern. He has kept his audience waiting – it is nearly 9 p.m. – and now he waits himself, silent, as applause rolls over him. At last he bends forward and, in a hoarse voice, speaks his first, famous words to the gathering.

'We shall now proceed to construct the socialist order.'

That provokes new delight. A roar.

Lenin follows the Left SRs, proposing the abolition of private property in land. With respect to the war, Congress issues a 'proclamation to the peoples and governments of all the belligerent nations', for immediate negotiation towards democratic peace. Approval is unanimous.

'The war is ended!' comes a hushed exclamation. 'The war is ended!'

Delegates are sobbing. They break not into celebratory but funereal song, honouring those who have died in the struggle for this moment.

But the war is *not* yet ended, and the order that will be constructed is anything but socialist.

Instead, the months and years that follow will see the revolution embattled, assailed, isolated, ossified, broken. We know where this is going: purges, gulags, starvation, mass murder.

October is still ground zero for arguments about fundamental, radical social change. Its degradation was not a given, was not written in any stars.

The story of the hopes, struggles, strains and defeats that follow 1917 has been told before and will be again. That story, and above all the questions arising from it – the urgencies of change, of how change is possible, of the dangers that will beset it – stretch vastly beyond us. These last pages can only offer a fleeting glance.

Instantly after the uprising, Kerensky meets and plans resistance with the hard-right General Krasnov. Under his command, a thousand Cossacks move on the capital. Within Petrograd itself, motley forces around the Mensheviks and Right SRs in the city Duma form into a group, the Committee for Salvation, arrayed against the new Council of People's Commissars. The oppositionists' motivations run the gamut, from deep antipathy to democracy to the sincere anguish of socialists at what they see as a doomed undertaking. Strange and temporary bedfellows they may be, but a bed they decide they must share, including with the likes of Purishkevich: the committee plans an uprising in Petrograd to coincide with the arrival of Krasnov's troops.

But Milrevcom gets wind of the plans. October 29 sees a scrappy, short-lived 'Junker mutiny' in the capital, when military cadets attempt to take control. Again, shells rock the city and the resistance is crushed. Again, Antonov deploys his revolutionary honour, the cultivated culture of the militant, to protect captives from a vengeful crowd. His prisoners are spared: others are not so fortunate.

The next day, at Pulkovo Heights, twelve miles out of Petrograd, Krasnov's forces face a ragtag army of workers, sailors and soldiers, untrained and undisciplined but outnumbering them ten to one. The fight is ugly and bloody. Krasnov's forces fall back to the town of

Gatchina, where Kerensky is based. Two days later, in exchange for safe passage away, they agree to hand him over.

The erstwhile persuader has a last escapade in him. He makes a successful run for it, disguised in a sailor's uniform and unlikely goggles. He ends his days in exile, issuing tract after self-exculpating tract.

The pro-coalition All-Russian Executive Committee of the Union of Railway Workers demands a government of all socialist groups. Neither Lenin nor Trotsky, both hard-line on the question, attend the resulting conference: those Bolsheviks who do – Kamenev, Zinoviev and Milyutin – agree that a socialist coalition is the best chance for survival. But at that moment, when the new regime's survival is under most threat from Krasnov's approach, many SRs and Mensheviks are as much concerned with military resistance to the government as with negotiation. With Krasnov defeated, they convert to coalition – just as the Bolshevik CC adopts a harder line.

This line is not without controversy. On 3 November, five dissenters, including the Heavenly Twins Zinoviev and Kamenev, resign from the CC. But they will retract their opposition in December, when, with fanfare, the Left SRs join the government. For a brief moment, a coalition arises.

The consolidation of the revolution around the country is uneven. In Moscow, there is protracted, bitter fighting. Opponents of the new regime, though, are disoriented and divided, and the Bolsheviks extend their control.

At the start of January 1918, the government requires of the long-delayed, newly convened Constituent Assembly that it recognise the sovereignty of the soviets. When the CA representatives refuse, the Bolsheviks and Left SRs declare it undemocratic and unrepresentative in this new context: after all, its (Right

SR-dominated) membership was chosen before October. The radicals turn their back on it, leaving the assembly to wind down ignominiously. It is then suppressed.

Worse soon comes. On 3 March 1918, after weeks of strained, strange and strung-out negotiations, the treaty of Brest-Litovsk between the Soviet government and Germany and its allies brings Russia's role in the war to a close – but under shockingly punitive terms.

Lenin has fought a lonely battle insisting that the invidious demands be accepted, as for him the priority – at almost all costs – is to end the war, consolidate the new regime and await the international revolution. Many on the party's left demur, sure that the Central Powers are so pregnant with revolution that the war should continue until that very upheaval. But in the face of a devastating German advance, Lenin, threatening again to resign, finally wins the argument.

Russia gains peace but loses swathes of land and population, some of its most fertile regions, and vast industrial and financial resources. In these vacated territories, the Central Powers install counter-revolutionary puppet regimes.

In protest at the treaty, the Left SRs resign from government. Tensions escalate as the Bolsheviks respond to worsening famine with brutal measures of food procurement, antagonising the peasantry, as detailed in a scathing open letter from Maria Spiridonova.

In June, Left SR activists assassinate the German ambassador, hoping to provoke a return to now-'revolutionary' war. In July they stage an uprising against the Bolsheviks – and are suppressed. As peasant resistance to the requisitioning hardens, and Bolshevik activists are assassinated – Volodarsky, Uritsky – the government responds with repressive, often sanguinary measures. Thus the one-party state begins to entrench.

The days are punctuated with unlikely political moments. In October 1918, the Mensheviks, who in many cases remain opposed to it, recognise the October revolution as 'historically necessary'; the same year, as the government desperately shores up the collapsing economy, the left Bolshevik Shlyapnikov voices the strange indignation of many in the party that 'the capitalist class renounced the organising role in production assigned to it'.

For a while, Lenin remains bullish about the prospects for international revolution, long assumed to be the only context in which the Russian revolution might survive.

Even as Lenin recovers from a failed assassination attempt in August 1918, even after the dreadful murder of the Marxists Rosa Luxemburg and Karl Liebknecht in Germany and the collapse of their Spartacist rebellion, Bolshevik optimism is not, at first, much dampened. In the aftermath of the war, Germany is in the throes of a dramatic social polarisation, that will flare up repeatedly between 1918 and 1923. A soviet government arises in Hungary; class struggle erupts in Austria in 1918 and 1919; Italy sees the upheaval of the 'two red years' of 1919 and 1920. Even England is rocked by strikes.

But over the course of 1919 and beyond, instance by instance this wave is quelled, and reaction sets in. The Bolsheviks wake up to the extent of their isolation, as the situation within their borders, too, becomes desperate.

In May 1918, 50,000 soldiers of the Czechoslovakian Legion revolt. This, after the false start of Gatchina, kicks off the Civil War.

From 1918 to 1921, the Bolsheviks must fight several counter-revolutionary or 'White' forces, backed, assisted and armed by foreign powers. As the Whites encroach on the revolution's territories, animated by violent nostalgia, 'Green' peasant revolts – most famously that of the legendary anarchist Makhno in the Ukraine – stagger the Bolshevik regime. By 1919, Russian territory is occupied by American, French, British, Japanese, German, Serbian and Polish troops. Socialism, the red bacillus, is more irksome to the Americans, British and French than are their wartime foes. David Francis, the American ambassador to Russia, writes of his concern that 'if these damned Bolsheviks are permitted to remain in control of the country it will not only be lost to its devoted people but Bolshevik rule will undermine all governments and be a menace to society itself'.

Churchill is particularly obsessed with the 'nameless beast', the 'foul baboonery of Bolshevism', and perfectly explicit that it is his greatest enemy. 'Of all the tyrannies in history, the Bolshevist tyranny is the worst, the most destructive, and the most degrading,' he declares in 1919. 'It is sheer humbug to pretend that it is not far worse than German militarism.' As the war ends, he publicises his intention to 'Kill the Bolshie, Kiss the Hun'.

The Allies pour troops into Russia, screwing down an embargo, stopping food from reaching the starving population of Soviet Russia. And they funnel funds to the Whites, no matter how unsavoury – supporting a dictatorship under Alexander Kolchak, and regarding Grigory Semenov, whose Cossack forces unleash a reign of terror in Siberia, as, in the words of one American observer, 'tolerably severe'.

The fractious, squabbling Whites, however, for all their funding, for all the Allies' support, are unable to win militarily or to gain popular backing, due to their opposition to any concessions for the Russian peasantry or restive national minorities – and to their barbarism. Their troops engage in indiscriminate butchery, burning villages and killing some 150,000 Jews in enthusiastic pogroms, performing exemplary torture – mass flogging, burial alive, mutilation, dragging prisoners behind horses – and summary execution. Their instructions to take no prisoners are often graphically explicit.

Such terror is in the service of their dream of new authoritarianism. If Bolshevism falls to the Whites, the eyewitness Chamberlin writes, its replacement will be 'a military dictator ... riding into Moscow on a white horse'. Not the Italian language but the Russian would have given the world the word for fascism, as Trotsky later puts it.

Under such unrelenting pressures, these are months and years of unspeakable barbarity and suffering, starvation, mass death, the near-total collapse of industry and culture, of banditry, pogroms, torture and cannibalism. The beleaguered regime unleashes its own Red Terror.

And there is no doubt that its reach and depth expand beyond control; that some agents of the Cheka, the political police, seduced by personal power, sadism or the degradation of the moment, are thugs and murderers unconstrained by political conviction and wielding new authority. There are no shortage of testimonials as to their dreadful acts.

Other agents carry out their work with anguish. One may feel sceptical, even disgusted, at the notion of an attempt, under desperate necessity, at an 'ethical' terror, a terror as limited as possible, but the testimonials of agents tormented at what they believed they had no choice but to do are powerful. 'I have spilt so much blood I no longer have any right to live,' says a drunken and distraught Dzherzhinsky at the end of 1918. 'You must shoot me now,' he begs.

One unlikely source, Major General William Graves, who commanded US forces in Siberia, considers himself 'well on the side of safety when I say that the anti-Bolsheviks killed one hundred people in Eastern Siberia, to every one killed by the Bolsheviks'. Many of the Soviet regime's leaders struggle to restrain the degrading tendencies of their own Terror, of which they are horribly aware. In 1918, a Cheka newspaper notoriously calls for torture: the CC excoriates the editors and closes it down, and the Soviet renews its condemnation of any such practice. But without question a political and moral rot is setting in.

Faced with the wholesale collapse, and a continuing and devastating famine, in 1921 the regime rolls back the emergency measures of militarised requisitioning and control known as 'War Communism', replacing them with the New Economic Policy, or NEP. From 1921 to 1927, the regime encourages a degree of private initiative, allowing smaller-scale enterprises to make a profit. Wage policies are liberalised, foreign experts and technical advisors authorised. Though the government creates various large collective farms, much land is turned over to the wealthier peasants. The 'NEPmen', spivs and wheeler-dealers, start to make good on speculation and burgeoning black markets.

The country labours through a catastrophic aftermath, a rubble of industry, agriculture, and the working class itself. War Communism was a desperate exigency, and NEP is a necessary retreat, allowing a degree of stability, the boosting of production. An expression of weakness, it comes at a cost. The bureaucratic apparatus is suspended now above the broken remnants of the class for which it claims to speak.

Among the Bolsheviks are dissenting grouplets, official and unofficial. Kollontai and Shlyapnikov lead the 'Workers' Opposition', hankering to hand power to a working class that barely exists any more. Old-Bolshevik intellectuals, 'Democratic Centralists', oppose the centralisation. The Tenth Congress of 1921 prohibits factions. Advocates of the move, including Lenin, present it as a temporary exigency to unite the party. Those factions that, inevitably, come later – the Left Opposition, the United Opposition – will not be official.

Lenin's health is failing. He suffers strokes in 1922 and 1923, and struggles in what has been called his 'final fight', against the bureaucratic tendencies, the ossification and corruption he sees growing. He grows suspicious of Stalin's personality and his place within the machine. In his last writings, he insists Stalin be removed from his post as general secretary.

His advice is not followed.

Lenin dies in January 1924.

The regime swifty launches a grotesque death cult, the most ostentatious element of which remains in place today: his corpse. A gnarled and ghastly relic, receiving obeisance from its catafalque.

At the Fourteenth Party Congress, in 1924, against the protests of Trotsky and others, the party performs a giddying about-face.

Now it officially accepts Stalin's claim that 'in general the victory of socialism (not in the sense of final victory) is unconditionally possible in one country'.

The parenthetical caveat notwithstanding, the embrace of 'Socialism in One Country' is a dramatic reversal of a foundational thesis of the Bolsheviks – and others.

The shift is born of despair, as any prospects for international revolution recede. But if it is utopian to hope that international support is around the corner, how much more so is it to wager on the impossible – autarchic socialism? A hard-headed pessimism, no matter how difficult to metabolise, would be less damaging than this bad hope.

The effects of the new position are devastating. As any vestigial culture of debate and democracy withers, the bureaucrats become custodians of a top-down development towards a monstrosity they call 'socialism'. And Stalin, the 'grey blur' at the heart of the machine, builds up his power base, his own status as most equal of all.

Between 1924 and 1928 the atmosphere in Russia grows more and more toxic, infighting in the party more bitter, the shifting of allegiances and cliques more urgent and dangerous. Allies become opponents become allies again. The Heavenly Twins make their peace with the regime. Trotsky does not: he is squeezed out of the CC and the party; his supporters are harassed and abused, beaten up, driven to suicide. In 1928, his Left Opposition is smashed and scattered.

Threats against the regime multiply, and Stalin consolidates his rule. As crisis grips the world economy, he inaugurates the 'great change'. 'The tempo must not be reduced!' he announces in 1931. This is his first Five-Year Plan. 'We are fifty or 100 years behind the advanced countries. We must make good this distance in ten years. Either we do it or they crush us.'

Thus is justified brutal industrialisation and collectivisation, a ruthless centralised control and command economy and political culture. Party activists are hounded in great numbers, forced to betray others, to confess to preposterous crimes with stentorian declarations. They are executed by this counterrevolution against their tradition, in that tradition's name. Previous loyalty to Stalin is no defence: the long roll call of Bolsheviks put to death in the 1930s and after includes not only Trotsky and Bukharin, but Zinoviev, Kamenev, and countless others.

With this despotic degradation comes a revival of statism, anti-semitism and nationalism, and bleakly reactionary norms in culture, sexuality and family life. Stalinism: a police state of paranoia, cruelty, murder and kitsch.

After a protracted *sumerki*, a long spell of 'liberty's dim light', what might have been a sunrise becomes a sunset. This is not a new day. It is what the Left Oppositionist Victor Serge calls 'midnight in the century'.

iii

There have been a hundred years of crude, ahistorical, ignorant, bad-faith and opportunist attacks on October. Without echoing such sneers, we must nonetheless interrogate the revolution.

The old regime was vile and violent, while Russian liberalism was weak, and quick to make common cause with reaction. All the same, did October lead inexorably to Stalin? It is an old question, but one still very much alive. Is the gulag the telos of 1917?

That objective strains faced the new regime is clear. There are subjective factors, too, questions we must pose about decisions made.

The left Mensheviks, committed anti-war internationalists, have a case to answer, with their walkout in October 1917. Coming straight after the congress voted for coalition, this decision shocked and upset even some of those who went along with it. 'I was thunder-struck,' said Sukhanov, of an action he never ceased to regret. 'No one contested the legality of the congress ... [This action] meant a formal break with the masses and with the revolution.'

Nothing is given. But had the internationalists of other groups remained within the Second Congress, Lenin and Trotsky's intransigence and scepticism about coalition might have been undercut, given how many other Bolsheviks, at all levels of the party, were advocates of cooperation. A less monolithic and embattled government just might have been the outcome.

This is not to deny the constraints and impact of isolation – nor to exonerate the Bolsheviks for their own mistakes, or worse.

In his short piece 'Our Revolution', written in January 1923 in response to Sukhanov's memoir, Lenin rather startlingly allows as 'incontrovertible' that Russia had not been 'ready' for revolution. He wonders pugnaciously, however, whether a people 'influenced by the hopelessness of its situation' could be blamed for 'fling[ing] itself into a struggle that would offer it at least some chance of securing conditions for the further development of civilisation that were somewhat unusual'.

It is not absurd to argue that the ground-down of Russia had no real choice but to act, on the chance that in so doing they might alter the very parameters of the situation. That things might thereby improve. The party's shift after Lenin's death, from that plaintive, embattled sense that there had been little alternative but to strive in imperfect conditions, to the later bad hope of Socialism in One Country, is a baleful result of recasting necessity as virtue.

We see a similar curdling tendency in the depiction, at various times by various Bolsheviks, of the dreadful necessities of 'War Communism' as desiderata, communist principles, or of censorship, even after the Civil War, as an expression of anything other than weakness. We see it in the presentation of one-person management as part and parcel of socialist transformation. And in the traducing and misrepresentation of opponents; in what, for example, Serge calls the 'atrocious lie' according to which the 1921 uprising of Kronstadt sailors against the regime was a White attack, a slander justified (though not by him) as 'necessary for the benefit of the people'. Nor, considering the aftermath of that revolt, should we gloss over what Mike Haynes – a historian sympathetic to the Bolsheviks – chillingly calls their 'inability to resist executions'.

Those who count themselves on the side of the revolution must engage with these failures and crimes. To do otherwise is to fall into apologia, special pleading, hagiography – and to run the risk of repeating such mistakes.

It is not for nostalgia's sake that the strange story of the first socialist revolution in history deserves celebration. The standard of October declares that things changed once, and they might do so again.

October, for an instant, brings a new kind of power. Fleetingly, there is a shift towards workers' control of production and the rights of peasants to the land. Equal rights for men and women in work and in marriage, the right to divorce, maternity support. The decriminalisation of homosexuality, 100 years ago. Moves towards national self-determination. Free and universal education, the expansion of literacy. And with literacy comes a cultural explosion, a thirst to learn, the mushrooming of universities and lecture series and adult schools. A change in the soul, as Lunacharsky might put it, as much as in the factory. And though those moments are snuffed out, reversed, become bleak jokes and memories all too soon, it might have been otherwise.

It might have been different, for these were only the first, most faltering steps.

The revolutionaries want a new country in a new world, one they cannot see but believe they can build. And they believe that in so doing, the builders will also build themselves anew.

In 1924, even as the vice closes around the experiment, Trotsky writes that in the world he wants, in the communism of which he dreams – a pre-emptive rebuke to the ghastly regime of bones to come – 'the forms of life will become dynamically dramatic. The average human type will rise to the heights of an Aristotle, a Goethe, or a Marx. And above this ridge new peaks will rise'.

The specifics of Russia, 1917, are distinct and crucial. It would be absurd, a ridiculous myopia, to hold up October as a simple lens through which to view the struggles of today. But it has been a long century, a long dusk of spite and cruelty, the excrescence and essence of its time. Twilight, even remembered twilight, is better than no light at all. It would be equally absurd to say that there is nothing we can learn from the revolution. To deny that the *sumerki* of October can be ours, and that it need not always be followed by night.

John Reed interrupts his own narrative of Prokopovich's speech to the Duma deputies, prevented by exasperated sailors from martyring themselves. 'It is beneath our dignity to be shot down here in the street by switchmen,' he records him saying. Then: 'What he meant by "switchmen", I never discovered.' Louise Bryant, who was also present, likewise noted the odd word. 'Just exactly what he meant by that was too much for my simple American brain.'

There is a probable answer in an unlikely place.

In 1917, Chaim Grade was a young child in Vilna, Lithuania. Much later, when he had become one of the world's leading Yiddish writers, in the glossary to the English translation of his memoir *Der mames shabosim – My Mother's Sabbath Days –* he records the following:

> Forest Shack: Term for the switchmen's booths along the railway tracks in the vicinity of Vilna. Before the Revolution of 1917, the area around the Forest Shacks was the clandestine meeting place for the local revolutionaries …

A nickname from a meeting place. It seems likely that the word Prokopovich deployed as epithet was a disdainful term for 'revolutionaries'.

Prokopovich had been a Marxist. His move to liberalism paralleled that of many other heretics infected with so-called 'Economism', as well as that of the 'Legal Marxists'. There was a kind of bleak rigour to their stageist dogmas, in which the epochs must succeed one another perforce, like stations along a line.

Little wonder he would scorn the Bolsheviks as *switchmen*. What could be more inimical to any trace of teleology than those who take account of the sidings of history? Or who even take to them?

The revolution of 1917 is a revolution of trains. History proceeding in screams of cold metal. The tsar's wheeled palace, shunted into sidings forever; Lenin's sealed stateless carriage; Guchkov and Shulgin's meandering abdication express; the trains criss-crossing Russia heavy with desperate deserters; the engine stoked by 'Konstantin Ivanov', Lenin in his wig, eagerly shovelling coal. And more and more will come: Trotsky's armoured train, the Red Army's propaganda trains, the troop carriers of the Civil War. Looming trains, trains hurtling through trees, out of the dark.

Revolutions, Marx said, are the locomotives of history. 'Put the locomotive into top gear', Lenin exhorted himself in a private note, scant weeks after October, 'and keep it on the rails.'

But how could you keep it there if there really was only one true way, one line, and it is blocked?

'I have gone where you did not want me to go.'

In 1937, Bruno Schulz opens his story 'The Age of Genius' with a dizzying rumination on 'events that have no place of their own in time', the possibility that 'all the seats within time might have been sold'.

> Conductor, where are you?
>
> Don't let's get excited ...
>
> Have you ever heard of parallel streams of time within a two-track time? Yes, there are such branch lines of time, somewhat illegal and suspect, but when, like us, one is burdened with contraband of supernumerary events that cannot be registered, one cannot be too fussy. Let us try to find at some point of history such a branch line, a blind track onto which to shunt these illegal events. There is nothing to fear.

By the Forest Shacks are the points, the switches onto hidden tracks through wilder history.

The question for history is not only who should be driving the engine, but where. The Prokopoviches have something to fear, and they police these suspect, illegal branch lines, all the while insisting they do not exist.

Onto such tracks the revolutionaries divert their train, with its contraband cargo, unregisterable, supernumerary, powering for a horizon, an edge as far away as ever and yet careering closer.

Or so it looks from the liberated train, in liberty's dim light.

Glossary of Personal Names

Alexeev, Mikhail (1857–1918) General. Tsar's chief of staff until February 1917; commander-in-chief until May 1917. Died while fighting the Bolsheviks in the Civil War.

Antonov, Vladimir Alexandrovich (1883–1938) Bolshevik activist. Marxist since 1903, Bolshevik since 1914. Executed under Stalin.

Balabanoff, Angelica (1878–1965) Russian–Italian Marxist activist.

Bochkareva, Maria (1889–1920) Soldier. Founder of the Women's Battalion of Death. Executed by the Cheka, the Soviet state security organisation set up in December 1917.

Bonch–Bruevich, Vladimir (1873–1955) Bolshevik activist. An 'Old Bolshevik' and researcher on religious sects; Lenin's personal secretary.

Breshko–Breshkovskaya, Catherine (1844–1934) SR activist. Close to Kerensky, on the right of the SR party. Fled Russia after October.

Bubnov, Andrei (1883–1938) Bolshevik activist. Active in Moscow, and in the Military Revolutionary Committee. Executed under Stalin.

Chernov, Viktor (1873–1952) SR politician. Leader of the SR party, minister in Kerensky's government. Briefly chair of the Constituent Assembly in 1918, before fleeing Russia.

Chkheidze, Nikolai Semenovich (1864–1926) Menshevik politician. First chair of the Petrograd Soviet. After October moved to Georgia, then Europe.

Dan, Fyodor (1871–1947) Menshevik activist. Doctor and founding leader of the Mensheviks, on the presidium of the Soviet in 1917. Arrested and exiled in 1921.

Dyusimeter. L. P. (1883–?) Colonel. Head of the Republican Centre's Military Section; right-wing anti-Bolshevik conspirator in August 1917. In exile in Shanghai from 1920, where he died.

Fedorovna, Alexandra (1872–1918) Tsarina. Wife of the last tsar, Nicholas II. Arrested and sent with her family ultimately to Ekaterinburg; executed by the Bolsheviks on 16 July 1918.

Filonenko, Maximilian (1885–1960) Right SR, army commissar. Collaborator with Kerensky. After 1917, led an underground anti-Bolshevik group that assassinated Cheka chief Moisei Uritsky in 1918, provoking the Red Terror. Fled Russia in 1920.

Finisov, P. N. (?–?) Right-wing conspirator. Vice-president of the Republican Centre; conspirator against the Bolsheviks in August 1917.

Gapon, Georgy (1870–1906) Priest. Leader of the workers' march on Bloody Sunday in January 1905. A police contact, he was assassinated by SR activists.

Gorky, Maxim (1868–1936) Writer. Socialist activist, editor of *Novaya zhizn*, associate of leading leftists; grew increasingly disaffected with the Bolsheviks after 1917.

Gots, Avram (1882–1937) SR leader. Leading member of the Petrograd Soviet. In 1922, was arrested and tried with other Right SR leaders. Rearrested and shot in Kazakhstan.

Grand Duke Michael (1878–1918) The youngest brother of the last tsar Nicholas II. Declined the throne when Nicholas abdicated. Murdered by Bolshevik activists in 1918.

Guchkov, Alexander (1868–1936) Politician. Conservative Octobrist until February 1917. War minister in the Provisional Government until April. Supportor of Kornilov. Left Russia after the revolution.

Kamenev, Lev (1883–1936) Bolshevik activist and politician. An 'Old Bolshevik'; long-time collaborator with Lenin. Briefly in opposition to Stalin in the mid-1920s. Executed after a mass show trial under Stalin.

Kamkov, Boris (1885–1938) Left SR activist. A long-time internationalist, Zimmerwaldist Left SR. Increasingly opposed to the Bolsheviks after 1918; repeatedly arrested. Executed under Stalin.

Kerensky, Alexander (1881–1970) Trudovik/SR politician. Leading figure in the Provisional Government after February 1917; took several positions, becoming prime minister after July. Unsuccessfully attempted to retake Petrograd with loyalist troops after October 1917. Fled Russia and died in exile.

Kishkin, Nikolai Mikhailovich (1864–1930) Kadet politician. Spent time as minister of welfare in the Provisional Government in 1917. Granted 'special powers' by rump government in October;

arrested the same night. Later worked under the Soviet government's Commissariat of Health.

Kollontai, Alexandra (1872–1952) Bolshevik activist. Initially a Menshevik, joined the Bolsheviks in 1914. People's commissar for social welfare after October 1917. Later formed the 'Workers' Opposition' with Alexander Shlyapnikov.

Kornilov, Lavr (1870–1918) General. Hard-line authoritarian; briefly commander-in-chief in July 1917, before the 'Kornilov Affair' in August. Escaped confinement in November; fought against the Bolsheviks in the Civil War. Killed in battle.

Krupskaya, Nadezhda (1869–1939) Bolshevik activist. Long-time militant. Married to Lenin in 1898. Served as Soviet government's deputy minister of Education from 1929 until her death.

Latsis, Martin (1888–1938) Bolshevik activist and politician. An 'Old Bolshevik' active during 1905 and after, including throughout 1917; member of the Military Revolutionary Committee, then of the Cheka. Executed under Stalin.

Lenin, Vladimir Ilyich Ulyanov (1870–1924) Bolshevik activist and politician. Prolific writer and theorist. Inaugurator of the 1903 split between the Mensheviks and the Bolsheviks. Leader of the Bolsheviks during and after 1917, and of the Russian government after October. Died after a series of strokes.

Lunacharsky, Anatoly (1875–1933) Bolshevik activist and politician. Prolific writer, unorthodox Marxist theorist. Briefly a member of the Mezhraiontsy in 1917, then the Bolsheviks. First people's commissar for education in the Soviet government after October; lost influence under Stalin. Died of natural causes.

Lvov, Prince Georgy (1861–1925) Liberal politician. From a noble family, joined the Kadet party in 1905. First prime minister of Russia after February 1917, resigning in favour of Kerensky in July. Fled Russia after October.

Lvov, Vladimir Nikolaevich (1865–1940) Liberal politician. Ex-Duma member for the Progressive Party, in coalition with Kadets. Lay procurator for the Synod of the Orthodox Church between March and July 1917. Directly involved in the Kornilov Affair in August, then arrested. Supporter of the Whites 1918–20. Escaped Russia after October.

Martov, Julius (1873–1923) Menshevik activist. Popular leader of the Menshevik faction of the RSDWP after 1903. On the far left of the Mensheviks, opposed to the right Mensheviks in charge of the party after February 1917. Would not ally with the Bolsheviks, but supported them against the Whites in the Civil War. Left Russia for Germany in 1920. Died of natural causes.

Milyukov, Pavel (1859–1943) Kadet politician. Prominent historian and leading member of the Kadet party. Minister of foreign affairs in Provisional Government after February 1917; a staunch patriot committed to victory in the war; resigned after provoking a crisis in April. Left Rusia in 1918.

Nicholas II (1868–1918) Last tsar of Russia. Abdicated in March 1917, and lived under house arrest thereafter with his family. Executed along with them by the Bolsheviks on 16 July 1918.

Nogin, Viktor (1878–1924) Bolshevik activist. Initially a 'conciliator' who attempted to reunite Mensheviks and Bolsheviks in 1910. Active throughout 1917, including as chair of Moscow Soviet. Died of natural causes.

Plekhanov, Georgy (1856–1918) Marxist theorist. Founder of the Emancipation of Labour group in 1883. The pre-eminent Russian

Marxist theorist between the 1880s and 1900s. Initially sided with Lenin in the split with the Mensheviks in 1903, but moved to the right. An outspoken supporter of Russia's war effort in the First World War, very critical of the Bolsheviks. Left Russia after October 1917 and died of natural causes.

Radek, Karl (1885–1939) Marxist activist. Colourful Polish/German/Russian activist of long standing. Joined the Bolsheviks in 1917, then the Left Opposition of the party in 1923. Expelled from the Bolsheviks in 1927; capitulated to Stalin and re-entered in 1930. Imprisoned after a show trial in 1937. Died in a labour camp.

Rasputin, Grigori (1869–1916) A faith healer and priest of a peasant background, close to the last tsar and tsarina. Murdered by disaffected right-wingers.

Rodzianko, Michael (1859–1924) Conservative politician. A founder of the conservative Octobrist party in 1905, chair of the Fourth Duma from 1912 to October 1917. Supported the Whites in the Civil War. Died of natural causes.

Rovio, Kustaa (1887–1938) Marxist activist and police chief. Finnish Social Democrat and chief of the Helsingfors (Helsinki) police. Moved to Russia in 1918. Executed under Stalin.

Savinkov, Boris (1879–1925) SR politician. Member of the terrorist SR Fighting Organisation in 1904–5; joined the French army in the First World War; close to Kerensky in the Provisional Government in 1917. Organised counterrevolutionary anti-Bolshevik groups after October 1917, before fleeing Russia. Writer of sensationalist pulp political thrillers. Returned to Russia in 1921; died in prison in Moscow.

Semashko, A. I. (1889–1937) Bolshevik activist. Marxist militant, served in the First Machine Gun Regiment in Petrograd; active in the Bolshevik Military Organisation. Served in the government after October 1917. Grew disaffected and left for Brazil in 1924, to return in 1927, but was imprisoned. Executed under Stalin.

Shlyapnikov, Alexander (1885–1937) Bolshevik activist. 'Old Bolshevik', trade unionist, worker–intellectual. A leading Bolshevik in Petrograd in February 1917. Appointed commissar of labour after October. Leader of the Workers' Opposition with Kollontai in 1920. Executed under Stalin.

Shulgin, Vasily (1878–1976) Conservative politician. A hard-line anti-revolutionary; persuaded Nicholas II to abdicate when his position became untenable. Supported Kornilov in August 1917, then the White movement after October 1917, fleeing Russian in 1920.

Smilga, Ivar (1892–1938) Bolshevik activist. Elected to the Bolshevik CC in April 1917; chair of the Central Committee of the Baltic Fleet in 1917–18. Member of the Left Opposition within the Bolsheviks in the 1920s. Executed under Stalin.

Spiridonova, Maria (1884–1941) Left SR activist. Assassin of Luzhenovsky, notorious security chief of Borisoglebsk; spent eleven years in jail in Siberia. Returned to Petrograd in May 1917; marginalised by party moderates. After October, entered government with the Bolsheviks. Broke with them in 1918 and supported an uprising against them by Left SRs. Remained a left critic of the Bolsheviks, and was imprisoned in a psychiatric prison in 1919, released in 1921. Executed under Stalin.

Stahl, Ludmila (1872–1939) Bolshevik activist. Fled Russia for France in 1907, returning in February 1917, where she was active in the Petrograd organisation.

Sukhanov, Nikolai (1882–1940) Socialist writer. Originally a member of the SRs; took part in the 1905 revolution, and spent years as a non-aligned radical. Returned to St Petersburg in 1913, to edit socialist journals. Joined Martov's Menshevik–Internationalists that year, to leave in 1920. Wrote an engrossing diary of 1917. Executed under Stalin.

Trotsky, Leon (1879–1940) Marxist activist. Long-time leading socialist theorist and activist; originally close to the left Mensheviks; joined the Mezhraiontsy in 1917, then the Bolsheviks. Deeply involved in the revolution of 1917. First people's commissar for military and naval affairs after the revolution; head of Red Army in 1918. Leader of the Left Opposition within the Bolsheviks 1923–27. Exiled from the Soviet Union in 1929. Moved to Mexico in 1936, where he continued vigorous agitation against Stalin. Inaugurated the 4th International (of 'Trotskyist' anti-Stalinist socialist groups) in 1938. Murdered by a Stalinist agent.

Tsereteli, Irakli (1881–1959) Menshevik politician. Georgian Menshevik activist and Duma deputy; exiled to Siberia in 1913. Returned to Petrograd in March 1917; became a moderate socialist leader of the Soviet. Served in the Provisional Government in 1917, as minister of posts and telegraphs, then minister of the interior. Left Russia for Georgia after 1917, then moved to Paris in 1921.

Volodarsky, V. (1891–1918) Marxist activist. Initially a member of the Jewish Bund in 1905. Moved to the US in 1913, allying with the Menshevik–Internationalists during the First World War. Returned to Russia in May 1917, joined the Mezhraiontsy, and with them the Bolsheviks shortly afterwards. Assassinated by SR activists in 1918.

Woytinsky, Wladimir (1885–1960) Menshevik activist. From an intellectual background, joined the Bolsheviks in 1905; exiled to Siberia. Defected to the moderate Mensheviks during the First World War. Active in the Soviet in Petrograd in 1917. Fled to Georgia after 1917, then to Germany in 1921.

Zasulich, Vera (1849–1919) Marxist activist. Originally anarchist-influenced, attempted to assassinate the governor of St Petersburg, Trepov, in 1878; acquited by a sympathetic jury. Became a Marxist and co-founded the Emancipation of Labour group with Plekhanov in 1883. Joined the Mensheviks in 1903. Her political activism waned after 1905. Supported the Russian war effort in the First World War. Died of natural causes.

Zavoiko, Vasilii (1875–1947) Right-wing activist. A wealthy political intriguer, amanuensis and advisor to General Kornilov. Seems to have left Russia for the USA after the revolution.

Zinoviev, Grigory (1883–1936) Bolshevik activist and politician. An 'Old Bolshevik' and collaborator with Lenin from 1903. Closely involved in the revolutionary movement throughout 1917; involved in various power struggles within the regime thereafter. Capitulated to Stalin in 1928, but executed by Stalin.

Further Reading

The literature on the Russian Revolution, even for those of us only confident in English, is vast – there is far more than any one normal person can read. With the interested general reader in mind, what follows is a brief, curated list of selected titles that I have found particularly helpful and/or interesting in the long research for this book, accompanied by short and, of course, subjective glosses.

I have culled from the list very many fine works that I think likely to be of mostly specialist interest; I have excluded those that do not include a particular focus on the months between February and October themselves; and but for one irresistible indulgence, I have ruthlessly avoided the pleasure of falling down the rabbit hole of artistic and fictional works on, or from, the period. With a few exceptions, I have focused on books rather than scholarly essays. I have also refrained from listing those texts not only about but of the moment – for example, any of Lenin's many writings from these months, some mentioned in these pages. They, and much else relevant, are available at marxists.org.

Inevitably, there will be those who object to my inclusions or exclusions. My reasoning and my hope is simply that this list might provide some invaluable starting points for any reader eager to go deeper into these topics.

General Histories

E. H. Carr, *The Bolshevik Revolution, 1917–1923* **volumes 1–3 (1950–53).** This is only the first section of Carr's monumental work on Russia. Not a narrative but an analysis of the revolution's systems and structures and their evolution, it is long, dense and idiosyncratically though rigorously organised. It is no easy read: it is, however, a magisterial and brilliant one.

William Henry Chamberlin, *The Russian Revolution 1917–1921* **(1935).** Described sniffily as a 'sturdy workhorse' by Norman Stone, this remains a fine introduction.

Orlando Figes, *A People's Tragedy* **(1996).** Exhaustive in scope and research, written with élan and stuffed with anecdotes that make for compelling reading. This is not necessarily the easiest starting point for a new reader, however – its scale and detail can be overwhelming for someone unfamiliar with the material. It is also characterised by unconvincing tragedianism for some lost liberal alternative; jarring elitism ('when people learn as adults what children are normally taught in schools, they find it difficult to progress beyond the simplest abstract ideas making them resistant to the subsequent absorption of knowledge on a more sophisticated level'); preposterous offhand smears ('hatred and indifference to human suffering were to varying degrees ingrained in the minds of all the Bolshevik leaders'); and a strange disapproving obsession with the Bolsheviks' leather jackets – they are mentioned five times.

Sheila Fitzpatrick, *The Russian Revolution* **(2nd edition) (2008).** A useful short introduction, though unconvincingly wedded to an 'inevitabilist' Lenin-leads-to-Stalin perspective.

Tsuyoshi Hasegawa, *The February Revolution, Petrograd: 1917* **(1981).** Outstanding. *The* definitive telling of the early days of 1917.

David Mandel, *The Petrograd Workers and the Fall of the Old Regime* **(1983), and** *The Petrograd Workers and the Soviet Seizure of Power* **(1984).** Marxist, partisan, and impressive.

Richard Pipes, *The Russian Revolution* **(1990).** Like Figes's, Pipes's long book is often fascinating for its details and stories – and also fascinating, though perhaps not in the ways its author intends, for the sheer virulence of its animus against the left. Analytically, Pipes's Bolshevikophobia leads him to take various totally unconvincing positions, such as that both the April and the July Days were attempted Bolshevik putsches.

Alexander Rabinowitch, *Prelude to Revolution: The Petrograd Bolsheviks and the July 1917 Uprising* **(1991), and** *The Bolsheviks Come to Power* **(2004).** Superb, meticulous, detailed, exciting, indispensable.

Victor Serge, *Year One of the Russian Revolution* **(1930).** Unlike (too) many observers, the anarchist-, libertarian-inclined Bolshevik Serge never allows his commitment to the revolution to dim his critical analysis of its trajectory – hence the melancholy behind this remarkable clear-eyed narrative, written not long after the heady year itself. His perspective can be ascertained from a letter he published in the US journal *New International* in 1939: 'It is often said that "the germ of all Stalinism was in Bolshevism at its beginning". Well, I have no objection. Only, Bolshevism also contained many other germs, a mass of other germs, and those who lived through the enthusiasm of the first years of the first victorious socialist revolution ought not to forget it. To judge the living man by the death germs which the autopsy reveals in the corpse – and which he may have carried in him since his birth – is that very sensible?' This wonderful riposte to the canard has deservedly become celebrated – so much so that it is now something of an anti-Stalinist socialist cliché. What too often seems to escape the notice of, especially Trotskyist, admirers is that as well as defending the Bolshevik tradition, the passage allows that it contained authoritarian tendencies – which Serge did not hesitate to criticise.

Leon Trotsky, *History of the Russian Revolution* **(1930).** Justly celebrated as a towering, vivid, historically vital work.

Theoretical Discussions and Collected Volumes

Edward Acton, Vladimir Cherniaev and William G. Rosenberg (eds), *Critical Companion to the Russian Revolution* **(1997).** An absolutely invaluable collection of essays on the people, organisations, issues and events of the revolution, by an impressive array of writers. Very many of the essays within its pages could deservedly be listed separately within this list. In particular these include Alexander Rabinowitch on Maria Spiridonova; Ziva Balili and Albert Nenarokov on Tsereteli, and on the Mensheviks; Michael Melancon on the SRs and Left SRs; as well as several articles on regions.

Edith Rogovin Frankel, Jonathan Frankel, Baruch Knei-Paz (eds), *Revolution in Russia: Reassessments of 1917* **(1992).** Includes valuable work on various regions, the peasantry and the workers, and the Red Guards.

Mike Haynes, *Russia: Class and Power 1917–2000* **(2002).** A short, provocative general history. Haynes's sympathetic approach to the revolution is at the heart of his analysis of Russia's later trajectory.

Steve Smith, *Red Petrograd* **(1983).** Not the easiest book for the general reader, but a key examination of Petrograd's working class, including factory committees, trade unions, and the specifics of early 'workers' control'.

Various (eds), *Russia's Great War and Revolution Series,* **five volumes so far (2014–).** Slavica publishers is involved in this ongoing multi-volume project. Each book comprises a collection of essays around a shared theme by experts in the field: at the time of writing there are five volumes, all outstandingly useful. They are listed separately in the relevant sections that follow.

Rex A. Wade (ed.), *Revolutionary Russia: New Approaches* (2004). This book contains some very useful pieces of, particularly, social and cultural history, including on the particular nuance of the term 'democracy', by Boris Kolonitskii, a fascinating look at crime and policing in Petrograd by Tsuyoshi Hasegawa, and more by Michael Melancon on the SRs.

Anarchists, Bolsheviks, Mensheviks, SRs

Barbara Allen, *Alexander Shlyapnikov, 1885–1937: Life of an Old Bolshevik* (2015). This biography of a Bolshevik worker–intellectual provides a vivid alternative to the common focus on the party's best-known leaders, and insight into Bolshevik political culture, internal debates and all.

Abraham Ascher (ed.), *The Mensheviks in the Russian Revolution* (1976). Collected Menshevik documents, illustrating the range of and changes in Menshevik analyses before, during and after the revolution.

Paul Avrich, *The Anarchists in the Russian Revolution* (1973), and *The Russian Anarchists* (2005). Pioneering, sympathetic and involving.

Tony Cliff, *Lenin*, four volumes (1975–79). Volume 2 of this quartet is the most pertinent for this book. A valuable political biography, and an articulation of a particular 'Leninism'. Though not hagiographical, Cliff's enthusiasm sometimes leads him to retrospectively 'en-wisen' Lenin and/or 'Leninify' wisdom, as for example when he describes the Bolsheviks during the Kornilov Affair as 'following the line put so clearly by Lenin', when it was in fact reached before any – latterly approving – word from Lenin arrived.

Isaac Deutscher, *The Prophet: The Life of Leon Trotsky* **(2015).** This is the collected edition of Deutscher's magisterial three-volume biography written in the 1950s and 1960s.

Israel Getzler, *Martov: A Political Biography of a Russian Social Democrat* **(1967).** A seminal, sympathetic, not uncritical portrait of the man consigned by Trotsky to 'the dustbin of history', by a writer melancholically committed to the 'losers' of the revolution – his term. His later book, *Kronstadt 1917–21: The Fate of a Soviet Democracy* (1983) is also of great interest.

Lars T. Lih, *Lenin* **(2011).** This very short book is chosen here as an introduction to Lih's pioneering work. Over many years, in books and articles, Lih has been assiduously revolutionising and demythologising our understandings of the political positions of the Russian revolutionaries, most famously in *Lenin Rediscovered: 'What Is to Be Done?' in Context* (2006). The discussion above of the Bolshevik responses to Lenin's 'Letters from Afar' is indebted to Lih's archival work, in 'Letters from Afar, Corrections from Up Close' (2015), in *Kritika: Explorations in Russian and Eurasian History*, volume 16, number 4.

Jane McDermid and Anna Hillyar, *Midwives of the Revolution: Female Bolsheviks and Women Workers in 1917* **(1999).** A key text bringing to the fore the central role of women in the revolution, focusing on Bolshevik activists and masses, as well as the better-known cadre.

Oliver Radkey, *The Agrarian Foes of Bolshevism: Promise and Default of the Russian Socialist Revolutionaries February–October 1917* **(1958).** A wonderful and vivid overview of this strange, fractured party.

Liliana Riga, *The Bolsheviks and the Russian Empire* **(2012).** Fascinating on the sheer cosmopolitanism of the revolutionary movement.

Beyond Petrograd

Sarah Badcock, *Politics and the People in Revolutionary Russia* **(2007).** The revolution as experienced from a variety of perspectives in two Volga provinces, with an enlightening focus on the dynamics between political leaders and the grassroots.

Sarah Badcock, Liudmila G. Novikova and Aaron B. Retish (eds), *Russia's Home Front in War and Revolution, 1914–22. Book 1. Russia's Revolution in Regional Perspective* **(2015).** One of the excellent volumes in Slavica's ongoing series, containing essays by a large number of scholars on various issues and regions.

Andrew Ezergailis, *The 1917 Revolution in Latvia* **(1974).** A detailed examination of one of the most intriguing and exciting revolutionary regions of the empire in 1917.

Orlando Figes, *Peasant Russia, Civil War: The Volga Countryside in Revolution, 1917–1921* **(1989).** More specialist and focused than the book for which he is most famous, and a clear and useful exposition of the trajectories of rural insurgency.

Diane Koenker, *Moscow Workers and the 1917 Revolution* **(1981).** A classic work, focusing on the second city, and on the politics and agency of its working class.

Eric Lohr, Vera Tolz, Alexander Semyonov and Mark von Hagen (eds), *The Empire and Nationalism at War* **(2014).** One of Slavica's multi-volume series, on the war, the empire and the revolution around Russia and its territories.

Kevin Murphy, *Revolution and Counterrevolution: Class Struggle in a Moscow Metal Factory* (2005). An excellent close examination of the revolution from below, this deservedly won the Deutscher Memorial Prize.

Ronald Suny, *The Baku Commune, 1917–1918: Class and Nationality in the Russian Revolution* (1972). An indispensable examination of the complexities of class and intersecting national politics.

Eyewitnesses, Memoirs and Primary Voices

W. Astrov, A. Slepkov and J. Thomas, *An Illustrated History of the Russian Revolution*, two volumes (1928). Dated and rather obscure, but full of wonderful photographs and reportage – including the full captivating tale of Lieutenant Sinegub's wanderings in the Winter Palace, of which only a snatch could be retold above.

Bessie Beatty, *The Red Heart of Russia* (1918). Sometimes florid to the point of comedy (within the book's first two short paragraphs Petrograd is a forest in the silver twilight and is also strange, mysterious, inscrutable, compelling, and a candle – drawing moths, of course) but, or as a result, oddly engaging.

Louise Bryant, *Six Red Months in Russia* (1918). A vivid and exciting telling by a radical journalist.

Jonathan Daly and Leonid Trofimov (eds), *Russia in War and Revolution, 1914–22: A Documentary History* (2009). A wonderful compendium of primary texts, ranging from various official and semi-official declarations to anonymous letters and recollections.

Eduard Dune, *Notes of a Red Guard* (1993). The reminiscences of Dune's days as a teenager, a politically developing activist with the Bolsheviks, and an armed militia member. The book includes vivid memories of the urban fighting in Moscow in October.

Sheila Fitzpatrick (ed.), *In the Shadow of Revolution: Life Stories of Russian Women from 1917 to the Second World War* **(2000).** Life stories from a wide range of women bringing powerfully up close the lived realities of these days.

Michael Hickey (ed.), *Competing Voices from the Russian Revolution: Fighting Words* **(2010).** A large and extraordinarily useful collection of primary texts, arranged by theme.

A. F. Ilyin-Genevsky, *From the February Revolution to the October Revolution 1917* **(1931).** A charming and moving memoir from a man later as well- or better-known as a chess master as he was as a Bolshevik revolutionary.

Mark Jones (ed.), *Storming the Heavens: Voices of October* **(1987).** More focused and shorter than the Hickey, Pitcher or Steinberg, but no less invaluable in the pieces it contains.

Dimitri Von Mohrenschildt (ed.), *The Russian Revolution of 1917: Contemporary Accounts* **(1971).** Valuable memoirs and first-hand accounts edited by the remarkable later spy and anti-Soviet Cold War warrior, who died aged 100 in 2002.

Harvey Pitcher (ed.), *Witnesses of the Russian Revolution* **(2nd edition, 2001).** The testimonials collected here, unlike those in most collections, are not by Russians, but by visitors to the country during the revolutionary year: Americans and Britons. They include among others Arthur Ransome and Morgan Philips Price, both of whose invaluable writing on the subject is collected in dedicated volumes.

F. F. Raskolnikov, *Kronstadt and Petrograd in 1917* **(1925).** The vivid recollections of one of the key figures among the Kronstadt revolutionaries.

John Reed, *Ten Days That Shook the World* (1919). A justly celebrated committed journalist's account.

Mark D. Steinberg (ed.), *Voices of Revolution, 1917* (2001). A compendium of powerful primary texts separated into three chronological sections, each introduced with a useful essay. It is from this book that soldier Kuchlavok's letter is excerpted. It is an extraordinary piece of writing that deserves to be read in full – as do many of the achingly powerful soldiers' letters.

Nikolai Sukhanov, *The Russian Revolution of 1917: A Personal Record* (1984). It is impossible not to be caught up with the vivid, thoughtful, honest and meticulously observed reminiscences of one of history's very great observers, Sukhanov.

Other

Boris Dralyuk (ed.), *1917* (2016). A captivating collection of poetry and prose from the revolutionary year.

Orlando Figes and Boris Kolonitskii (eds), *Interpreting the Russian Revolution* (1999). This collection includes many excellent essays on the revolution's political culture.

Murray Frame, Boris Kolonitskii, Steven G. Marks and Melissa K. Stockdale (eds), *Russian Culture in War and Revolution, 1914–22. Book 1: Popular Culture, the Arts, and Insitutions* (2014), and *Book 2: Political Culture, Identities, Mentalities, and Memory* (2014). Two from Slavica's multi-volume series, containing essays by a large number of scholars on political representation, memory and heritage, among an enormous range of cultural issues.

Mary Hamilton-Dann, *Vladimir and Nadya: The Lenin Story* (1998). A curious but intriguing telling of the lives of the revolutionary couple, which fills out various details most others mention only in passing. As does the same author's obscure but engrossing *Lenin in the Recollection of Finns* (1979).

Marianne Kamp, 'Debating Sharia: The 1917 Muslim Women's Congress in Russia' (2015), in *Journal of Women's History*, **volume 27, number 4.** A rare resource on this fascinating and important event.

David C. King, *Red Star over Russia: A Visual History* **(2009).** The aged monochrome of most contemporary photographs notwithstanding, the visuals of the revolution are absolutely compelling, both in deliberate iconography and in chance conjunctions – as the images here illustrate.

Adele Lindenmeyr, Christopher Read and Peter Waldron (eds), *Russia's Home Front in War and Revolution, 1914–22. Book 2: The Experience of War and Revolution* **(2016).** This book in Slavica's series contains essays on an extraordinary variety of topics from the Russian revolution, including philanthropy, drunkenness, drugs, gardening, monasticism, and the representation of Jews.

Anatoly Lunacharsky, *Revolutionary Silhouettes* **(1923).** A captivating series of reminiscences by Lunacharsky, of various revolutionaries of his acquaintance.

Richard Stites, *Revolutionary Dreams: Utopian Vision and Experimental Life in the Russian Revolution* **(1989).** For the most part Stites's classic text focuses on the early years of the revolutionary regime itself, but it is included here via the excuse of the precursor utopianism it outlines because it is such a thoroughly transfixing, moving, sometimes hilarious exposition of the avant-garde in everyday life.

Ian D. Thatcher, 'The St Petersburg/Petrograd Mezhraionka, 1913–1917: The Rise and Fall of a Russian Social Democratic

Workers' Party Unity Faction' (2009), in *Slavonic and East European Review,* **volume 87, number 2.** One of the very few sources on the small, intellectually and politically scintillating group, associated in particular with Trotsky. Of all the various not-yet-written books on the Russian Revolution, a volume on and selected translations from this 'Interdistrict group' clamour most loudly for existence.

Acknowledgements

This book, more than anything else I have written, has not merely benefitted from, but relied on, the engagement and insights of readers and interlocutors. I am more grateful than I can say for their patience and generosity, and for their trenchant and thought-provoking help, feedback, suggestions and criticisms.

I owe an immense debt to all the enormous number of writers from whose work I have learned during my research. I have also been privileged to have received thoughtful and detailed responses to drafts of this manuscript from leading researchers on the topics it touches, who in many cases even shared as-yet-unpublished work. I extend my deepest gratitude to Gleb Albert, Barbara Allen, Clayton Black, Eric Blanc, Lars Lih, Kevin Murphy and Ronald Suny. *October* is immeasurably better for their generous help.

I am profoundly grateful, too, to many other readers. Their detailed thoughts and responses have been quite invaluable. My thanks to Mic Cheetham, Maria Headley, Frank Hemmes, Susan Powell, Jord Rosenberg and Rosie Warren.

In Russia, I was very fortunate to benefit from the hospitality of and conversations with Boris Kolonitskii, Artemy Magun, Yoel Regev, Alexander Reznik, Alexander Skidan and Elizaveta Zhdankova.

I am deeply grateful to the Rockefeller Bellagio Center, Italy, for granting me a residency fellowship for the writing of this book. I am also thankful for their invaluable support and help, in various ways, to David Broder, Valeria Costa-Kostritsky, José – Gurru – Corominas, Cassia Corominas-Miéville, Indigo Corominas-Miéville, Boris Dralyuk, Brian Evenson, Tsuyoshi Hasegawa, Stuart Kelly, Jemima Miéville and Paul Robbins.

For their solidarity and friendship, and for being constant sources of political and intellectual inspiration, I thank my fellow founding editors of *Salvage*: Jamie Allinson, Richard Seymour and Rosie Warren.

My thanks also to all at Verso, especially Mark Martin, Anne Rumberger, Sarah Shin and Lorna Scott-Fox, for copy-editing above and beyond the call of any duty. Finally, in particular, I am grateful to Sebastian Budgen, my editor and friend. This book came about from his suggestion, and I owe him an immense intellectual and political debt.

Index